New Approaches in Sociology
Studies in Social Inequality, Social Change, and Social Justice

Edited by
Nancy A. Naples
University of Connecticut

A Routledge Series

New Approaches in Sociology
Studies in Social Inequality, Social Change, and Social Justice
Nancy A. Naples, *General Editor*

The Social Organization of Policy
An Institutional Ethnography of UN Forest Deliberations
Lauren E. Eastwood

The Struggle over Gay, Lesbian, and Bisexual Rights
Facing Off in Cincinnati
Kimberly B. Dugan

Parenting for the State
An Ethnographic Analysis of Non-Profit Foster Care
Teresa Toguchi Swartz

Talking Back to Psychiatry
The Psychiatric Consumer/Survivor/Ex-Patient Movement
Linda J. Morrison

Contextualizing Homelessness
Critical Theory, Homelessness, and Federal Policy Addressing the Homeless
Ken Kyle

Linking Activism
Ecology, Social Justice, and Education for Social Change
Morgan Gardner

The Everyday Lives of Sex Workers in the Netherlands
Katherine Gregory

Striving and Surviving
A Daily Life Analysis of Honduran Transnational Families
Leah Schmalzbauer

Unequal Partnerships
Beyond the Rhetoric of Philanthropic Collaboration
Ira Silver

Domestic Democracy
At Home in South Africa
Jennifer Natalie Fish

Praxis and Politics
Knowledge Production in Social Movements
Janet M. Conway

The Suppression of Dissent
How the State and Mass Media Squelch USAmerican Social Movements
Jules Boykoff

Are We Thinking Straight?
The Politics of Straightness in a Lesbian and Gay Social Movement Organization
Daniel K. Cortese

"Rice Plus"
Widows and Economic Survival in Rural Cambodia
Susan Hagood Lee

"Between Worlds"
Deaf Women, Work, and Intersections of Gender and Ability
Cheryl G. Najarian

If I Only Had a Brain
Deconstructing Brain Injury
Mark Sherry

Minority within a Minority
Black Francophone Immigrants and the Dynamics of Power and Resistance
Amal I. Madibbo

Gender Trouble Makers
Education and Empowerment in Nepal
Jennifer Rothchild

GENDER TROUBLE MAKERS
Education and Empowerment in Nepal

Jennifer Rothchild

Routledge
Taylor & Francis Group
LONDON AND NEW YORK

Routledge
Taylor & Francis Group
711 Third Avenue
New York, NY 10017

Routledge
Taylor & Francis Group
2 Park Square
Milton Park, Abingdon
Oxon OX14 4RN

© 2006 by Taylor & Francis Group, LLC
Routledge is an imprint of Taylor & Francis Group, an Informa business
First published in paperback 2012

International Standard Book Number-13: 978-0-415-98015-9 (Hardcover)
International Standard Book Number-13: 978-0-415-65494-4 (Paperback)

No part of this book may be reprinted, reproduced, transmitted, or utilized in any form by any electronic, mechanical, or other means, now known or hereafter invented, including photocopying, microfilming, and recording, or in any information storage or retrieval system, without written permission from the publishers.

Trademark Notice: Product or corporate names may be trademarks or registered trademarks, and are used only for identification and explanation without intent to infringe.

Library of Congress Cataloging-in-Publication Data

Rothchild, Jennifer.
   Gender trouble makers : education and empowerment in Nepal / Jennifer Rothchild.
     p. cm. -- (New approaches in sociology)
   Includes bibliographical references and index.
   ISBN 0-415-98015-1 (alk. paper)
   1. Sex role--Nepal. 2. Sex discrimination in education--Nepal. 3. Girls--Education--Nepal. 4. Girls--Nepal--Social conditions. 5. Socialization--Nepal. 6. Nepal--Social conditions. I. Title. II. Series.

HQ1075.5.N35R67 2006
371.822095496--dc22
                                                                                             2006017489

Visit the Taylor & Francis Web site at
http://www.taylorandfrancis.com

and the Routledge Web site at
http://www.routledge-ny.com

Endorsements

"The World Bank and other donors are spending billions to widen girls' access to schooling, to deliver basic literacy. Jennifer Rothchild details how these well-intentioned efforts will fail until we understand how homes—even so-called modern schooling—can reinforce, not lessen, gender disparities. Rothchild takes us into the daily lives of Nepal's mothers and daughters—foraging for firewood, arguing with brothers, competing for scarce school opportunities—to reveal the telling mechanisms that reproduce and adjust new forms of gender inequality. She also shows how determined public policies, from hiring female teachers to encouraging young women to become medical doctors, does open new horizons for Nepalese girls. Drawing on feminist theories and her keen understanding of rural Nepal, Rothchild confronts the paradox of moving girls from lives of grinding poverty without having aid agencies subvert the underlying social fabric."

—Bruce Fuller, Professor of Education & Public Policy at the University of California, Berkeley and author of *Standardized Childhood: The Political and Cultural Struggle over Early Education*

"*Gender Trouble Makers* offers a fascinating look into the ongoing reproduction of inequalities between girls and boys, and women and men, in a small, impoverished village in Nepal. School and family are sites of interlocking gendered practices that maintain old patterns, as well as the sites of challenges to these practices. This book is a hopeful account of beginning change, and a first-rate example of ethnographic research that takes the experiences of ordinary people as its starting point. Jennifer Rothchild's reflections on her own, often contradictory, experiences of fieldwork provide a model for doing it honestly and well."

—Joan Acker, Professor Emerita at the University of Oregon and author of *Class Questions: Feminist Answers*

"Through poignant observations of the entrenched expectations of tradition and culture, Rothchild attempts to give a deeper understanding of the gender barriers that impede the dreams and potential of Nepalese girls. The stories Rothchild collects and the accompanying analysis remind us that we live in many worlds, yet each of us rarely has the perspective to see beyond one. Rothchild's self-reflection and compassion provide a unique narrative that gives affecting significance to the struggles Nepalese girls face in the school and in the home."

> —David Sadker, Professor of Education at American University and co-author of *Failing at Fairness: How America's Schools Cheat Girls* and *Teachers, Schools, and Society*

"This book is an illuminating insight into the educational realities of an indigenous community in Eastern Nepal. I urge any individual who is interested in conducting fieldwork in a developing society to read this book before pursuing such research. This book is a major contribution in the sociology of education."

> —Janardan Subedi, Professor of Sociology at Miami University and Director of Miami University Center of Nepal Studies

*In dedication to the memory of
Violet Swenson Sammelson (1911–2005)
and Sam Rothchild (1910-2001)*

Contents

List of Figures and Tables	xi
Acknowledgments	xiii
Chapter One Introduction: Gender and Education	1
Chapter Two Setting the Context: Nepal, Jiri, and Education	21
Chapter Three Telling the Story: An Overview of the Research Design	51
Chapter Four Social Construction of Gender in the Family and Community	75
Chapter Five Reinforcing Gender in Schools	99
Chapter Six Gender Trouble Makers: Individuals Resisting Gender Constraints	127
Chapter Seven Conclusions: Gender, Education, and Empowerment	141
Chapter Eight Epilogue: Reflections on the Process	147

Notes	169
Bibliography	181
Index	193

List of Tables and Figures

TABLES

2.1	Number of Allocated and Vacant Staff Positions Occupied During the *Panchayat* and Multiparty System at the Jiri Hospital, 1975–2000	25
2.2	Number of Schools by Region, District, and VDC (1997)	27
2.3	Summary of Government Schools in Jiri VDC	28
2.4	Numerical and Percentage Distribution of Population by Ethnic Group in Nepal, 1991	32
2.5	Composition of Population in Nepal by Mother Tongue, 1991	33
2.6	Sources of Financing for Education in Nepal	36
2.7	Trends in Public Expenditure on Education at Current Prices	37
2.8	Budget Estimates by Sub-sectors	37
2.9	Nepal's Formal Education System in Comparison to U.S. System	42
2.10	Net Enrollment Rates by Gender and School Level (1997)	44
2.11	Enrollment Numbers by Gender in Ten Jiri VDC Government Schools, 1999–2000	45

2.12	Promotion, Repetition and Dropout Rates for Classes 1–10 (1996)	47
2.13	Trained and Untrained Teachers in Nepal (1997)	49
2.14	Trained and Untrained Teachers in Jiri (1999–2000)	49
3.1	Interviewees	63
4.1	Educational Attainment of Community Members Interviewed	76
4.2	Educational Attainment of Class 5 Student Home Visit Parents/Guardians	77
4.3	Educational Attainment of Class 9 Student Home Visit Parents/Guardians	77
4.4	Composite of Typical Time Allocations for Students by Gender	90

FIGURES

2.1	Map of Nepal	22
2.2	Population Distribution by Sex for Years 1981, 1991, and 2001 (Estimated)	30
3.1	Social Mapping Exercise	61
4.1	Women Working	85
4.2	Children Working	90
4.3	Typical Jiri Home	93
5.1	Younger Students in Jiri Classroom	106
5.2	Older Students in Jiri Classroom	107

Acknowledgments

This body of work would not have been possible without the assistance, input and inspiration of many people. I am indebted to the following individuals in Nepal: Sworneem Tamang, Mala Rai, Robin Singh, the entire Jiri Helminth Staff, Ali Pook, Naike Jirel, Sumon Tuladhar, the K.C. family, the Joshi family, and the Basnet family. I thank them for their help with this project as well as their hospitality and friendship. A very special thanks goes to the people of Jiri VDC. I will always be grateful to them for sharing their lived experiences with me. In Pokhara, I thank Dinesh and Rekha Rajbhandari for cultural orientation and language training, but most of all, I thank them for their friendship spanning many years. Two young Nepali women in particular, Munu Kharki and Rama K.C., inspired this book and continue to motivate me to work for social change.

In the States, I would like to acknowledge my mentors along the way. Gay Young, Bette Dickerson, David Sadker, and Jean Davison were far more than a dissertation committee—they are role models for scholar activism. I wish to thank Charles Kurzman, Claire Sterk, and Kirk Elifson for their support and encouragement at the very beginning of this project. And I will always be indebted to Janardan Subedi for introducing me and many other undergraduate students to his home country of Nepal. He also deserves credit for leading me to Jiri VDC.

I wish to acknowledge the generous funding provided by the Oxley Foundation of Tulsa, Oklahoma, the Association for Women in Science (AWIS) Educational Foundation in Washington, D.C., and an American Dissertation Fellowship from the American Association of University Women (AAUW) in Washington, D.C. This project would not have been brought to fruition without the support of these organizations.

I am grateful to those who read several drafts of this book: Christopher Butler, Jonathan Rothchild, Jennifer Fish, Dinesh Rajbhandari, Ann

Ridley, and Jagat Basnet. I thank Debbie Kuehn for her wonderful copy-editing work. At Routledge, I wish to thank Benjamin Holtzman—it was a distinct pleasure working with him. I am indebted to Nancy Naples, not only for her inclusion of my work in her series, but also the model she provides as a feminist methodologist, activist and sociologist. I must also acknowledge the work of Judith Lorber and Judith Butler. They both have argued that gender is and can be "troubled." Their work has influenced me tremendously, and the title of my book is an homage to their inspiring scholarship.

I deeply appreciate those who have shared Nepal with me both in-country and from afar: my dear friends Bevin Gumm, Jeff Dickson, Christi Heidt, Kelly Senay, Christina Block, and Kate Lenehan. I also thank Margaret Arrowsmith for listening. I am so grateful to Jennifer Fish for her collaboration, reflections and mentoring. At every stage of this project, I drew strength from her example and our friendship. Katie Hyde encouraged me to take our first trip to Nepal together in 1992. Our shared experiences and many years of friendship enriched this project in countless ways.

I wish to offer my sincerest thanks to my immediate and extended families, but particularly, I want to recognize my parents, Ruth and Irwin Rothchild, and Carole and John Butler, and my siblings (Jon Rothchild and Charlotte Radler, Susan and Karl Lowe, John Butler and Jennifer Forshey, and Julie and Tom Lundin). I thank each of them for their unconditional love and ongoing support. I am most grateful for my best friend and husband, Chris Butler. His presence in my life inspired the realization of this book and my work today. I find words inadequate to express my gratitude, admiration and love.

I dedicate this book not only to the gender trouble makers of the world but also to my maternal grandmother Violet Sammelson and my paternal grandfather Sam Rothchild. Both valued education but, much like many of the girls and boys in this book, they were constrained by their gender and class. Neither one had the opportunity to study past the eighth grade. They always encouraged me to go far with my education, and this book is dedicated to them.

Chapter One
Introduction: Gender and Education

> I am always struck by how dark this classroom seems when I first walk in. Even with the new plastic roof donated by the Japanese government, very little light comes through. Walls made from stones and packed mud, windows without glass, and packed mud floors make the classroom perpetually cold. During the winter, the girls cover themselves with their shawls, if they have them.
> —Fieldnotes, December 13, 1999

Around the world, government agencies, local non-government organizations, researchers, and international organizations continue to concentrate efforts on increasing the enrollment of girls in schools. Third World countries[1], usually working with well-funded international non-governmental organizations (INGOs), have made significant attempts to promote girls' access to and participation in formal education systems. In Nepal, researchers, funding agencies, and various governmental offices have noted the substantially low enrollment of girls in its schools, and donor agencies such as USAID and the World Bank have spent millions of dollars on education initiatives aimed at girls.[2]

This funding has been supported by a substantial body of literature that promotes educating girls and women for social and economic benefits.[3] In an effort to increase the number of girls enrolled in school, many national and international initiatives focus on the *obstacles* to girls' schooling. Researchers have generated a long list of factors that determine girls' enrollment and participation in school, including parents' socioeconomic status, religion, distance to schools, cultural attitudes, poverty, and parents' non-literacy.[4] Yet, these analyses only tell part of the story.

Most research on girls in schools in Third World countries has been insightful. However, the modes of analysis typically employed fail to apprehend the complexities of gender in the cultures and societies where these educational inequalities exist. Reports of unequal distribution of girls' and boys' participation in schools are important, but a critical analysis must move beyond enrollment numbers and participation charts. To integrate a gender perspective in education, researchers must investigate not only who has the opportunity to attend school, but also the ways students and teachers interact, what is taught, and how that knowledge is conveyed in the classroom and in textbooks (Davison & Kanyuka 1990; 1992; Staudt 1998; Hurst & Gartrell 1991).

I argue that we need to implement an additional level of analysis by examining how gender, as a process, is constructed and maintained in both homes and schools. By looking at gender as a *process* rather than a demographic factor, we can begin to understand the obstacles *and* opportunities for girls and boys in school. Gender has long been used to legitimize inequality between girls and boys in school. Consequently, gender negatively impacts both girls' and boys' potential to succeed in school and impedes their ability to improve standards of living through education, and, ultimately, opportunities gained through education.

Educational funding initiatives aimed at girls tend to assume girls and boys enter schools that are gender neutral. I view the family and school as social institutions where established gender patterns are embedded within the organizational dynamics of those institutions. In other words, the very institutions of family and school as historically determined put girls at a severe disadvantage when it comes to maximizing opportunities for education and future opportunity. Furthermore, the processes within schools and homes serve to maintain that social inequality. By failing to recognize this beforehand, research and initiatives to help girls in school risk missing the centrality of gender as a social construction—through which deeply embedded asymmetrical power relations are mutually reinforced in the family and school institutions. This embeddedness of gender roles perpetuates inequalities, particularly in the context of Nepal's schools.

Analyzing gender inequality in schools should be problematized with a careful exploration of how gender is socially constructed and maintained in *both* the school and the home. Then we can begin to understand and devise more effective ways to increase all students' enrollment, participation and success in school. By doing this, INGOs, other donor agencies, and government programs will be able to formulate educational initiatives that anticipate and address attitudes and behaviors in regard to gender. These initiatives, in the long run, will help girls enjoy longer, more meaningful and more productive school experiences.

The future of successful development processes (particularly those concerned with educational equity) will require a careful examination and

Introduction

nuanced understanding of the social construction of gender. This book presents an analysis of social constructions of gender and the ways in which gender was reinforced and maintained in rural Jiri, Nepal in 1999–2000.[5] Three objectives served as touchstones for the field research: (1) To examine the socially constructed processes of gender within the institutions of family and school through interviews eliciting attitudes and behavior of community members, parents and guardians, head teachers (school principals), and teachers in the village of Jiri, Nepal; (2) To investigate behavior and interaction in classroom and school settings through direct observations and interviews; and (3) To examine the consequences of socially constructed gender constraints through observations and interviews in school and home settings.

This study established an in-depth multi-dimensional case study to address these objectives. Research techniques to collect data included direct classroom observations; field observations of the daily lives of school-age children; structured interviews with community members, parents and guardians, teachers, head teachers, and students; and collection of life narratives from older girls and boys, as well as adult women and men. Using several data collection methods concurrently enabled me to validate data by means of triangulation and ensure integrity in the findings presented throughout this book.

Nepal offered a particularly illuminating set of social circumstances for examining the construction of gender as it relates to education and opportunities for learning.[6] At the time of this study, the context for education in Nepal was marked by gender inequality as reflected in the country's legal, political, economic, and family institutions. These institutions were founded upon cultural and religious beliefs that maintained similar attitudes about gender (Bennett 1981; Acharya 1981; Acharya & Bennett 1981; Ashby 1985; Subedi 1993; Shtrii Shakti 1995; Singh 1995). To isolate and analyze the strains of thought that supported gender inequality in Nepali schools, I will discuss the ways in which gender was socially constructed, reinforced, and maintained within the rural village of Jiri VDC. Specifically, my research (conducted in 1999–2000) examines families, the local education system, and the processes of gender (e.g., socialization patterns beginning at an early age, attitudes towards gender and education, and interactions with and control of youth) as exhibited in this particular village.[7]

This chapter will review some of the past and current literature on the benefits of girls' education, but, more to the point, will reveal how a social constructionist perspective can add to the writing extant on this subject. A social constructionist perspective will also be employed to discuss the shortcomings of research and development efforts regarding girls' education. Briefly put, current work in developing nations fails to consider access to schools and participation in schools as part of gender processes taking place within gendered institutions. This oversight has resulted in initiatives that endorse girls' education and increase initial enrollment numbers. Over a longer period of time, however, girls' attrition rates remain high and the benefits of an education go underutilized. I suggest that these conditions are explained through the intersection of institutional processes and socially embedded norms that continue to reinforce gender inequality. This research merges gender constructionism with an applied case study that delves into the complexities of girls' education as it manifests in daily practices that are reinforced at the institutional level of society.

GENDER AS A SOCIAL CONSTRUCTION

Gender has been conceived as a system in which biological females and biological males are classified, separated, and socialized into specific sex roles. Gender construction theorists (e.g., O'Brien 1983; Mies 1986; Connell 1987; Acker 1990; Lorber 1994; Risman 1998; Kimmel 2004) assert that gender, as a social system, is not natural and that differences between women and men—aside from purely anatomical and reproductive ones—are *socially constructed* and maintained. Much effort goes into marking gender differences (Connell 1987), dividing people into contrasting social categories, "girls" and "boys," "women" and "men," and "feminine" and "masculine."[8]

My work draws heavily from this conceptualization of gender—that is, gender as a socially constructed identity and role, reinforced by processes and institutions that maintain similar attitudes and distinctions about gender. This results in a gendered social order that reflects those beliefs, even if they may be untrue (Lorber 2000). Gender, then, is a *process*, rather than an attribute, and gender differences become ideas that are taught and reinforced by individuals through socialization rather than tangible distinctions as determined by biology. In this light, gender is not what we are, but instead, something we *do* (West and Zimmerman 1987), and each social interaction serves to create and reinforce these ideas.

At the macro level, it is often assumed that social institutions are gender neutral, but this assumption ignores that most social institutions were contrived under circumstances of gender inequality. Jean Potuchek explains that social institutions formed within a context of unequal power and opportunity for women and men serve to institutionalize that inequality, to give it greater strength (1997). Assumptions of male dominance render the inequality maintained by these institutions invisible and underscore the idea that everyone has equal potential to succeed in these institutions (Kimmel 2004). Joan Acker states that the concept of gender neutrality "covers up, [and] obscures the underlying gender structure, allowing practices that perpetuate it to continue even as efforts to reduce gender equality are underway" (1990:146). So, instead of gender-neutral institutions, I argue that social institutions such as the family and school are *gendered institutions* in that they establish patterns of expectations for individuals according to their gender. These gendered institutions create normative standards and express an institutional logic that produces and promotes the differences many assume to be the inherent qualities of individuals. Thus, these gendered institutions determine the power, privileges, and economic resources available to a person based on her or his gender (Davison & Kanyuka 1990; Lorber 2000).

However, as gender is socially constructed, it is also dynamic: It can be reshaped and resisted by individuals through social interactions that flaunt existing assumptions about differences between women and men, girls and boys (Lorber 2000; Butler 1990). Therefore, the potential exists for people to make choices and have agency over their lives (Risman 1998). Several participants in this study, particularly students, illustrate this point.

Groups seeking to foster change in school systems of developing nations must apprehend the false grounds that support gender differences within a society's institutions. This understanding at once invalidates old assumptions about the abilities of girls and boys, and identifies the potential to change these assumptions. However, it is also important to have a solid understanding of gender at the next level, as practiced and emphasized within the family and school.

This study draws heavily from gender construction feminism, a theoretical framework put forward by gender scholars from the West. As a Western researcher myself, I must acknowledge that I am applying a predominately Western feminist perspective to a non-Western context, and some may argue that this may lead to incomplete or inadequate findings.[9] Chandra Talpade Mohanty and others have raised concern that women in the "Third World" are often non-differentially depicted as poor, illiterate victims in need of saving by educated, liberated Western feminists. Emphasizing Third World women's experiences of social, political, economic and religious oppressions leads to conceiving of all Third World women as the monolithic "other." This essentializing of all Third World women negates the diversity of their lives and their agency in resisting oppression (Naples 2003). Mohanty argues that these "assumptions of privilege and ethnocentric universality, on the one hand, and inadequate self-consciousness about the effect of Western scholarship on the Third World in the context of a world system dominated by the West, on the other, characterize a sizeable extent of Western feminist work on women in the Third World" (1991:53). How do Western feminists avoid this?

Mohanty calls for *local analyses* to counter this trend in feminist scholarship and stresses linking the local with the "universal:" She emphasizes the "importance of the particular in relation to the universal—a belief in the local as specifying and illuminating the universal" (Mohanty 2004:224). This involves not only understanding the "local in relation to larger cross-national processes," but also grounding "analyses in the particular local feminist praxis" (Alexander & Mohanty 1997:xix). Important to this process is the valuing of individuals' standpoint—grounding one's research in individuals' own perspectives and everyday experiences.[10] Because women's and men's (as well as girls' and boys') gendered experiences vary individually and by socio-historical context, an examination of the social construction of gender inequality needs to be rooted in individual standpoints and understood in the context of different experiences. Furthermore, Mohanty argues, "the particular standpoint of poor indigenous and Third World/South World women provides the most inclusive viewing of systemic power" (2004:232). She explains that

> If we pay attention to and think from the space of some of the most disenfranchised communities of women in the world, we are most likely to envision a just and democratic society capable of treating all its citizens fairly. Conversely, if we begin our analysis from, and limit it to, the space of privileged communities, our visions of justice are more likely to be exclusionary because privilege nurtures blindness to those without the same privileges. Beginning from the lives and interests of marginalized communities of women, I am able to access and make the workings of power visible—to read up the ladder of privilege . . . . This particular marginalized location makes the politics of knowledge and the power investments that go along with it visible so that we can then engage in work to transform the use and abuse of power (2004:231).

Therefore, I attempt to link the "particular" with the "universal"—with a "broad and inclusive focus on justice" (Mohanty 2004:234) by grounding my analysis in individuals' standpoints and continually reflecting on my inherent privileges in the research process. My goal in this book is to link my "grounded particularized analyses" of gender constructs and their effects on educational equity in a rural village of Nepal with larger cross-national

Introduction

processes. I begin by taking a critical look at the existing literature on gender, families and educational access.

GENDER IN THE HOME

A large portion of the literature dedicated to girls and education in developing countries has focused on identifying the *barriers* to their education and advancement. This important work enabled more recent research to focus on processes within girls' lives and methods to overcome these impediments. A study sponsored by the United States Agency for International Development (USAID) determined that obstacles to girls' education in Nepal fall into five categories: economic barriers, labor issues, cultural attitudes, physical barriers, and national commitments (ABEL 1996).

Both Ashby (1985) and Jamison and Lockheed (1987) identify three factors that tend to lower incentives for investment in the education of daughters relative to sons: (1) daughters are expected to leave their natal households through marriage in their mid-teen years, while sons are expected to contribute to the welfare of parents in their old age; (2) non-agricultural employment is perceived as more appropriate and realistic for males than for females; and (3) the accepted gender-based division of agricultural work requires more routine work from females than from males. In a survey of rural farm households, Jamison and Lockheed (1987) showed that girls are discouraged from attending school in order to care for small children. Studies like these indicate that processes of gender outside school influence girls' participation in school and the extent of that participation.

Household-Related Factors

Parental attitudes toward gender differences in intelligence, academic potential, and current and future responsibilities often influence both academic participation and achievement for children by gender. In order to identify the deep-seated roots of gender inequality in terms of access to and participation in education, we must first look at the processes of gendering in the gendered institution of the household: the gendered division of labor, control over domestic decision-making, marriage, and gendered access to resources and opportunities.

Parents often perceive daughters as responsible for household chores and childcare. This division of labor, most often guided by patriarchal ideology, is based on the notion that women are "naturally" and distinctively endowed to nurture and raise children as well as take care of their husbands and families (Stromquist 1990; Lorber 2000). The assumption of women's "natural" ability to serve as mothers, wives, and housekeepers forms the cornerstone of the household division of labor which manifests itself in a wider variety of expectations for women (Lorber 1998). The often-cited rationale for the gendered social order is to be found in the stability it offers social arrangements. The assignment of women to predominately domestic, familial roles assures that women will be available to fill them.

Many Nepali families prioritize sons (Reinhold 1993), and parents typically define girls in terms of being good wives and housekeepers (ABEL 1996). Sons often marry and live with their parents, whereas daughters go to "others' house," meaning they go to live with their husband's families once their marriages are arranged. Because daughters eventually "leave," their economic value to their natal families is greatest during the middle childhood and teen years (which happens to coincide with schooling-age years), when, as my observations and interviews demonstrate, they contribute significant amounts of labor. Sons, on the other hand, are expected to be of greatest economic values to their parents later—by providing security for them in their old age. In this sense, the way parents and guardians conceive of their children and education is rational, although inequitable.

During a preliminary study conducted in Jiri in 1996, I interviewed head teachers and parents. Though some parents emphasized the importance of educating sons and daughters, almost every parent gave priority to the education of their sons. In general, parents spoke of girls' education in terms of their presumed current and future roles as daughters, wives, mothers, and daughters-in-law, rather than as a source of individual opportunity and empowerment; in other words, parents perceived girls' education as utilitarian rather than emancipatory. Daughters were educated to fit into a pre-existing gender structure, not to change it or move beyond it. By these restrictions and pre-ordained destinies, the gendered social order, and its inherent gender inequality, was upheld: A girl's education, or lack thereof, was rationalized by the stability it offered social arrangements.[11]

Some parents cite Hindu caste or purity of caste to justify decisions made for their daughters (Mathema 1998).[12] Especially common among high-caste Hindus in Nepal, maintaining purity requires restricting women's sexuality and reproductive powers so that the paternity of a child, especially of a son, is not in question. Hindus have argued that only through such control can purity of lineage be maintained, a purity that is considered vital to maintain the caste system. Hindus are often so concerned with the purity of women that they require a bride to be a virgin and forbid widows to re-marry, as widows are regarded as polluted (Mathema 1998). To ensure virginity, marriages are often arranged before the onset of puberty, a practice commonly known as *kanyadan* (gift of a virgin daughter).[13] Though Nepalese law forbids child marriage, many families in rural Nepal arrange

Introduction

their daughters' marriages when they are as young as 10 years of age (Subedi 1993) and on average, at the age of 14 (ABEL 1996). This socio-cultural construction of gender has forced girls into a pre-chosen role and has limited their opportunities to further their education.

Many Hindu parents, as well as non-Hindu parents, fear their grown-up, unmarried daughters might go astray and bring shame to the family (Mathema 1998). Even though women and girls who belong to Tibeto-Burmese ethnic groups and who practice Buddhism generally lead a less restricted life than their Hindu counterparts, many parents of all castes and ethnicities do not allow their unmarried, grown-up daughters to frequent the marketplace for fear their daughters may develop a relationship with men whose caste or ethnicity is unknown (Mathema 1998). Although the household division of labor and the control of women's sexuality operate across societies and societal classes, women in low social classes are affected more severely by these constraints (Stromquist 1990).

Women and men in Nepal tend to have gendered access to resources and opportunities. In rural households, women spend more hours doing productive and reproductive work than do men (Cameron 1995). Women constitute an estimated 40.5% of the labor force, predominately in agriculture (Singh 1995), yet much of this work, often unpaid, is not considered work *per se*, and is subsequently devalued (Subedi 1993). Furthermore, the labor market in Nepal has offered limited opportunities for girls who complete school, thus reducing the incentive for parents to invest in their daughters' education. Opportunity costs or indirect costs to education are often cited as a major obstacle to girls' participation in and completion of education.[14] It has been argued that opportunity costs of schooling for girls are greater than those for boys. Many, but not all, parents believe they would lose labor by sending daughters to school. They feel it is in their best interest to keep daughters at home to work.

In 1996 I interviewed 18 school-aged children (14 girls and four boys), ages nine to 18, who were not enrolled in school. They reported that household chores, familial responsibilities, and a parent's decision prevented them from continuing their education. In parents' minds, the opportunity costs were too great. For example, a 10-year-old girl named Mingma[15] explained,

> In the beginning, I used to go [to school] and had attended Class 1, but now I don't go because my parents said not to go. Now I look after cattle.

With severely limited resources, many Nepali parents opt to send boys to school rather than girls (Ashby 1985; Shrestha, *et al*. 1986).[16]

Nelly Stromquist, in her survey of research on girls' education, found that most studies demonstrated that opportunity costs of schooling for girls are greater than for boys (1990). However, she asserts that what the literature fails to clarify is that these opportunity costs are greater by social definition, largely determined and defined by the way societies construct gender roles and expectations, and not because of innate abilities of girls.

Gender in the Community: Political and School-Related Factors

Also significant are socially constructed obstacles at the community and school level. Stromquist's (1989a) study indicates that family and school-related factors in determining girls' participation and achievement in education are interrelated. The United Nations Children's Fund (UNICEF) blames the gender gap in education on such factors as poverty, non-availability of gender-segregated schools, absence of women teachers, inflexible school schedules, as well as irrelevant and gender-insensitive curriculum (UNICEF 1992). The United Nations Educational, Scientific and Cultural Organization (UNESCO) cites poverty, unemployment, sex discrimination, inadequate infrastructure, and lack of schools as major problems related to the education of girls (UNESCO 1992). In addition to school costs, perceived threats to girls' security pose an obstacle to girls' education (O'Gara, et al. 1999).[17]

Among the institutional obstacles, ABEL (1996) cites national commitment barriers in Nepal. These barriers include lack of government initiative to provide facilities for all those eligible for education and limited support for girls' education initiatives (e.g., limited monetary incentives to encourage girls' education, slow response to girls' education campaigns). The ABEL study also identifies physical barriers that discourage girls' attendance, such as remote rural areas having limited access to schools, overcrowding of schools offering limited spaces for new girls, and the poor condition of schools, with unclean, marginal facilities, as well as inadequate toilet facilities. Similar to the household-related factors, these political and school-related factors that hinder girls' access to and participation in school are also gendered. The schools, as gendered institutions, have been structured unequally with men heading most schools, few women teachers, and a continuing lack of attention to gender bias in the classroom and in instructional materials.

To summarize, while identifying the obstacles to girls' education (e.g., parents' socioeconomic status, religion, distance to school, cultural attitudes, poverty, availability of schools, parents' education, and unsuitable curriculum) is important, analyzing these obstacles in a disconnected fashion without examining the significance of gender as a social construction

Introduction

"confuses immediate with ultimate causes and fails to understand gender as an institutionalized expression of power in society" (Stromquist 1990:108). In other words, perceived differences between the abilities for girls and boys form the basis for the aforementioned obstacles within a family context. Analyzing the obstacles without accounting for assumptions about gender may negate the potential for change at this level and within family institutions worldwide.

BENEFITS OF EDUCATING GIRLS AND WOMEN

To overcome "obstacles" to girls' education, many international donor agencies, government programs, and researchers have presented the case for educating girls. There exists a substantial body of literature that supports educating girls and women for social and economic benefits (e.g., Cochrane, O'Hara, & Leslie 1980; Kelly & Elliott 1982; Pitt & Rosenzweig 1989; Schultz 1989; Floro & Wolf 1990; Beenstock & Sturdy 1990; King 1990; Behrman 1991; King & Hill 1993; Subbarao & Raney 1993; Brock & Cammish 1997). Many studies argue specifically that educating girls yields outcomes such as increased female productivity; lowered infant, child and maternal mortality rates; reduction in population growth; healthier children; as well as better reared children (Cochrane 1979; Wolfe & Behrman 1984; King 1990; Herz, *et al*. 1991; Prather 1991; UNICEF 1992; Rugh 2000). UNESCO documents argue that an educated woman is much more likely to educate her daughter as well as her son, ensuring that the next generation will be healthy and educated (UNESCO 1990).

The dominant discourse emphasizes that the education of girls results in a return on investment (Heward 1999). For example, a document sponsored by UNICEF explains that, "Major efforts now under way to increase the education of girls are considered good investments because they yield high economic returns" (Kurz & Prather 1995:5). In March of 1995, at the UN Conference on Poverty convened in Copenhagen, First Lady Hillary Rodham Clinton made a widely publicized speech in support of the USA's investment of $100 million over 10 years in girls' education as a mean of reducing poverty by lowering fertility, improving child health, and raising women's income earnings (Heward 1999). Other studies have attempted to demonstrate the link between a mother's education and lowered fertility rates and family health (e.g., Mehotra & Jolly 1997; Cleland & Kaufman 1998).

While positive in many respects, the literature of the dominant discourse presents a limited categorization of girls, and essentializes girls and women by lumping them all into one amorphous group. Gendering processes and gendered institutions vary by race, class, caste, culture, religion, and context. For this reason, we need to disaggregate our studies of girls to include national, socio-cultural, class, race, and religious differences to better meet the needs of specific populations. Furthermore, the literature of the dominant discourse overlooks the argument that education enhances social equality for girls and women *by their own person*.

Studies have tended to use men and boys as a yardstick for measuring the benefits of girls' and women's education, creating an underlying assumption that education befits men, whereas education for women needs to be justified in terms of benefiting others in society. Those "others" are typically boys and men. For example, in their book *Women's Education in Developing Countries: Barriers, Benefits, and Policies*, Elizabeth M. King and M. Anne Hill write, "Failing to invest adequately in educating women can reduce the potential benefits of educating men" (1993:1). Likewise, O'Gara, *et al.* (1999), in their evaluation of programs that work for the education of girls in several countries, including Nepal, conclude that boys clearly and consistently benefit from initiatives aimed at girls' schooling needs. There is little attention given to how the girls themselves benefit—through enhanced self-esteem, greater social status and power, and broadened choices.[18]

In my preliminary study of Jiri, Nepal, conducted in 1996, parent and head teacher interviewees often associated girls' education with an enhancement of their potential, not as individuals, but as future wives, mothers, and daughters-in-law. Several head teachers recited the rhetoric: "If you educate a man, you educate a person; if you educate a woman, you educate the entire family," thereby justifying a girl's education in terms of benefiting her future family.[19] It would seem that international agencies and national programs promote educating girls for instrumental reasons, anticipating efficient payoffs to society, but ignore other factors that may eventually shake apart the existing gendered order, such as an improved and new sense of empowerment, leading to new choices.

EFFORTS TO PROMOTE GIRLS' ACCESS TO AND PARTICIPATION IN SCHOOL IN NEPAL

Since 1971, the Nepalese government has tried to implement several different educational initiatives to increase girls' enrollment at the primary and secondary levels as well as to ensure that girls stay in school. As an effort to improve female literacy, for example, the government of Nepal, with special assistance from UNESCO, UNDP, and USAID, implemented the "Equal Access to Education Project" (1971–1992). This project sought to

Introduction

train and place women primary school teachers in rural schools as a way to encourage rural parents to send their daughters to school.

The Nepalese government has also pushed for the recruitment of at least one woman teacher in all of the primary schools in the country. Despite these government efforts, the proportion of women teachers to men teachers has remained low. In 1987, women teachers were 10.5% and 9.5% of the primary and secondary teachers, respectively. By 1996, nine years later, the percentage had increased to 20.6% at the primary level, but only 11.7% at the secondary level (Tuladhar & Thapa 1998). At that rate, attaining gender parity in teaching, even at the primary level, appeared to be decades away.

Regional circumstances also influence the participation of women teachers. They are found more often in urban than in very rural areas. The lowest proportion of women teachers is found in the Far-Western Region, while the highest proportion of women is in the Central Development Region, where the Kathmandu Valley is located (Tuladhar & Thapa 1998). The government awards annual scholarships to 400 girls studying education in higher secondary or campus levels in remote districts to encourage more women teachers in those areas (Tuladhar & Thapa 1998). There are also programs that offer hostels and free textbooks.

Additionally, the Nepalese government has established several initiatives to encourage more girls in rural areas to continue their schooling. One such program is the "Local School Scholarships" program, which awards a monthly stipend to selected girls in Classes 6, 7, 8, 9, and 10 (The amount of that stipend depends on their class level). Past government projects included a "School Award Program," coordinated by the Ministry of Education and Culture, which awarded cash prizes to schools in 18 districts that enrolled the highest number of girls. Financial incentives were also given to schools in 10 of the districts of the Western Development regions for enrolling a total of 32,000 girls at the primary level. Additionally, the government provided snacks for the girls in these districts.

To address girls' non-literacy in one pilot zone, the government introduced the Chelibeti program in 1981 under the Seti Education for Rural Development Project launched in the Seti Zone, in Western Nepal. This program provided an equivalent to Class 3 literacy and numeracy skills for girls unable to attend school full time. In its first phase, the program benefited 2,000 girls in the project districts. In 1991, it was absorbed into the non-formal education division of the Ministry of Education and Culture's Basic Primary Education Program (BPEP). Other non-formal education programs established by the government include flexible schedules, shortened instructional days and modified curricula (CERID 1996). These programs and others like them, developed at the central or national level, have not been effectively implemented at the community and school levels. Tuladhar & Thapa (1998) suggest two factors limiting program effectiveness: lack of efficiency in administration and unclear scholarship policies. Additionally, the absence of gender sensitivity or awareness in the educational administrative structure—from the top to the local level—creates a gap between planning and implementation of these programs (Tuladhar & Thapa 1998).

Projects for girls are also popular with donors supporting education in Nepal. For example, between the years 1994 and 1997, USAID funded a massive program through Private Agencies Collaborating Together, Inc. (PACT) and World Education/Nepal (two international non-government organizations) to increase the number of literate women and girls in Nepal. The program goal of PACT was to make 270,000 women and girls literate during the three years of the project. World Education worked with the District Education Offices to help build their capacity for non-formal education activities. During 1997–1998, USAID sponsored several evaluations of their literacy programs (e.g., Burchfield 1997; El-Sanabary 1997; Benoliel, et al. 1998), which concluded that although USAID-funded programs provided basic literacy to thousands of women during the three years of the project,[20] the project proved to be too large and finite. El-Sanabary's (1997) report concluded that future programs will be necessarily smaller than in the past and recommended revising the literacy programs, with the objective of providing a minimum of 100,000 women with a package of integrated interventions—basic literacy, economic participation, and legal literacy and advocacy.

Another program, "the Female Education Scholarship Program" (1991–1995), which was also funded by USAID and implemented by a Nepali NGO (the Women's Development Center), provided scholarships of 80 Rupees[21] per month to all girls residing in one project area (the Banke District in the Western Terai), who graduated from Class 5 and continued their public education through Class 10. An evaluation, sponsored by USAID, determined that this program contributed to improved enrollment of girls at the secondary level. However, the evaluation determined that it was "too early to measure the program's effects on secondary school completion, achievement, fertility rates, or age of marriage" at the time of the evaluation (ABEL 1996:49). By 2000, five years after the program ended, neither the Nepalese government nor USAID had provided a follow-up assessment. This is an example of yet another program with inadequate means of assessing impact.

Though certainly full of good intentions, national programs, international donor-funded projects, and others like them fail to challenge the existing social order in any substantial way by concentrating exclusively on "females." In a review of current policies, the Institute for Integrated Development Studies (IIDS) in Kathmandu persuasively argued that,

> Female education . . . cannot be dealt with merely by ad hoc measures such as distribution of free textbooks or by providing a number of scholarships. The real issue is how to change the legal system which disinherits married women from parental property and . . . which mandatorily forces the married female out of her parental household. The core questions also concern correcting society's perceptions of girls as "liabilities" and glorification of women as "mothers." Similarly, they are also related to changing a religious belief system that compels females to be married at an early age and couples to breed sons for their after-life salvation (IIDS 1994:137).

The IIDS argument raises an important point: What must be addressed, first and foremost, is the gendered nature of existing social structures in Nepal. Government programs that try to remedy the inequality girls encounter, rather than transform the underlying gendered structures, have only limited effect. Each initiative, at best, intends to improve upon existing systems, while leaving the underlying gendered structures intact and unchanged. Donors and directors of programs are seemingly unwilling to confront the male-dominated power structure within the education system. Consequently, the gendered institution of education remains minimally affected by "projects for girls."

GENDERED EDUCATION

Literature on the benefits of educating girls and on programs working to promote girls' education largely focuses on increasing enrollment numbers and participation rates of girls. It presumes that girls' access to school will lead to equality between girls and boys, and that girls' passing through an educational system will guarantee their actual participation in schools and equal participation in society. A girl enrolling in school enrolls in a gendered institution, not a gender-neutral one. Though promoting access to and participation in existing formal education programs is clearly necessary, it is not sufficient to transform gender power relations in the broader society.

I argue that school is the most appropriate place to start transforming and empowering the lives of girls in developing countries. Not only can education equip girls with the necessary intellectual development, but it can also foment a liberating and enabling view of the world. As Kathleen Staudt asserts,

> Education should do much more than reinforce a gender-constructed social order. It should provide an atmosphere for intellectual development. Comprehensive education has great potential to facilitate awareness of structures of domination and subordination . . . . Education in and outside the classroom provides the space in which to develop solidarity relations for active involvement in community and social change (1998:84).

While schools can be a source of social change, they can also act to maintain the existing system of norms. In countries such as Nepal, with a history of rigid social and political control, educational systems have been used to maintain existing gender constructions by transmitting representations and beliefs about a "natural" and "appropriate" gendered social order (Stromquist 1992). School experiences often provide girls and boys with messages that reinforce rather than challenge the prevailing gendered division of labor (Stromquist 1989a). As social institutions, schools most often reflect current gender norms rather than challenge them. However, when viewed as a tool for empowerment, education can threaten the existing gendered order. Stromquist explains,

> While there is evidence that educated women do become better mothers and wives, it is also clear that education may develop in women the ability to think more analytically and thus, introduce an element of risk in their subsequent behaviors. Specifically, the assertiveness, self-esteem, and egalitarian beliefs that women may develop through education threaten those who benefit from women's unpaid work and docile attitude (1990:99).

In Dorothy Smith's (2000) review of the literature on gender and schooling, she concludes that the research confirms a continuous reinforcement of existing gender relations through text materials and student-teacher interactions. Male voices and male activities are privileged in the classroom, on the playground and sports field, and in the hallways, even in highly industrialized, democratic countries such as the United States (Best 1983; Thorne 1993; Orenstein 1994) and Australia (e.g., Lee 1996). Myra Sadker and David Sadker (1994) found that teachers in the United States are more likely to use their expertise to praise, probe, question, and correct boys, which, in turn, helps boys to sharpen their ideas, refine their thinking, gain confidence, and obtain higher achievement. When a girl is passed over by a teacher in order to elicit the ideas and opinions of boys, she is conditioned to be silent and to defer to boys and men. Girls receive a "gendered education" in schools. The gendering they experience at home is reinforced in schools, as girls are encouraged to be docile, passive and dependent (Staudt 1998).

Gender bias in teaching compounded with a gender-biased curriculum only perpetuates the reproduction of gender inequality. Textbooks frequently impose stereotypical images of women and girls. Further, despite the vast diversity of race, ethnicity, language, and culture represented by students in schools, educational curricula and textbooks tend to offer homogenous images and expectations of women and girls (Staudt 1998). Stromquist (1989b) cites several studies conducted in developing countries that demonstrate gender stereotypes in textbooks, including Harber (1988) for Kenya; Tembo (1984) for Zambia; Anderson and Herencia (1983) for Peru; Pinto (1982) for Brazil; and Silva (1979) for Columbia. Most studies cited reveal that women in textbooks were portrayed as passive, uncreative, and self-satisfied. Often they were represented as functioning only within the home and, if employed, then only in sub-professional positions.

At times, development projects have advocated removing gender stereotypes from school textbooks, but there was little reporting if and how curricula and textbooks had been changed to equalize gender.[22] For example, in 1990, the World Bank proposed a curriculum model for Nepal that would generate a broad base of human resource development, provide relevant education, and consider the needs of specific groups, which included girls. However, Joshi & Anderson (1994) concluded that this report did not elaborate on the specific needs of girls. Nor did it adequately consider the types of materials schools used at the time, or offer suggestions for the ways materials and curriculum could be transformed and implemented. Stromquist (1995) points out that although governments often draft proposals to offer non-sexist education, new policies generally do not go so far as to institute anti-sexist education to make school staff and administrators aware of their own gendered biases and behaviors in order to correct them in concordance with curriculum reform.[23] It is not sufficient to change textbooks and other instructional materials unless the gendered behaviors and attitudes of educators—teachers and administrators—also change.

GOALS OF THIS BOOK

In this book, I argue that development efforts in education that fail to consider gender as a socially constructed process subsequently fail to see how these processes legitimize gender inequality among students, thus limiting the effects of education development work. Specifically, assumptions about gender (by parents, students, and teachers) not only affect who goes to school, but also students' perceptions of their own abilities, their educational achievement, particular areas of study, and career aspirations. I argue that socially constructed gender processes are institutionalized expressions of power, and these processes—enacted by community members, parents, guardians, teachers, and head teachers and reproduced in Nepali homes and schools—constrained some students and enabled others. Furthermore, students, acting under the weight of these constraints, consequently "did gender" (West and Zimmerman 1987) within these socially constructed parameters.

Derived from interviews and observations, my findings indicate that many students (both girls and boys), when talking about education, had come to accept and embrace the *different* socially assigned roles and aspirations for women and men as adults in Nepali society. Thus, I argue that gender not only constrained girls' educational opportunities, but it also operated to benefit men and boys in Nepal's male-dominated society. However, as pervasive as gender has been and continues to be in social institutions like the state, schools and the family, gender constraints can be resisted and reshaped by "gender trouble makers" (Lorber 2000; Butler 1990). This study examines not only the constraints placed upon students, especially girl students, but also students' agency in resisting and negotiating those constraints.

CONTRIBUTIONS OF THIS RESEARCH

It should be noted that this study was limited to a rural village community in the Himalayan foothills of Eastern Nepal. One cannot make broad generalizations about other populations from this research. However, documenting the processes of social interaction as they occur among different groups of people has a broad range of applications. Such an approach can be applied to observing processes of gender construction in diverse settings. For example, do gendered attitudes and behavior of adults towards girls at school carry over to other community settings?

The various meanings and interpretations individuals construct, value and claim regarding gender and education have profound implications for educational systems, research and reform. In contributing to the body of studies that document the way gender constructions affect girls' and women's educational opportunities and, subsequently, their life chances, I anticipate that this research will advance the design and implementation of educational programs, especially for women and girls in rural Nepal. This research might also assist education policy planners, non-governmental organizations (NGOs), communities, and individuals in developing strategies to restructure social institutions and to transform social relations in Nepal to maximize all children's access, participation, and achievement in schools.

I also hope this study contributes to a variety of research arenas. This book offers an examination of a group relatively unstudied. This research is one of the most comprehensive studies of Jiri VDC. This study is also unique in that it is one of the first analyses of structured interaction in Nepali classrooms.

ORGANIZATION OF THE BOOK

This book is divided into eight chapters. Chapter Two gives an overview of the research setting, including specific details regarding the educational systems at the national and local levels. The research design and methodology for this study are presented in Chapter Three. Chapters Four through Six are the analytical chapters of this book. Chapter Four examines how gender was socially constructed in the home and how students' access to and participation in school were subsequently affected. This chapter investigates various gendering processes that led to existing gender social constructions and constraints, especially for girls. Chapter Five delves into similar issues with an examination of social constructions of gender in schools. It analyzes how gender, first constructed and taught in the home, was maintained and reinforced in the education system. It also analyzes how students subsequently "did gender" as a consequence of socially constructed gender constraints. Specifically, I examine how family/community gendering practices, as well as gendering processes in schools, constrained or bolstered students' access to and participation and achievement in school. Chapter Six examines students' resistance—"gender trouble makers"—and other agents of social change, and Chapter Seven presents conclusions and implications, as well as suggestions for future research. Chapter Eight (the Epilogue) reflects on the research process as a whole with particular emphasis on the application of feminist methodologies.

Chapter Two
Setting the Context: Nepal, Jiri, and Education

The intention of this chapter is to provide a context for this study of gender and education. First, I present an overview of the geographical, social, cultural, economic, and political realms of both Nepal and the research site, Jiri Village Development Committee (VDC) at the time of this study.[1] As discussed in Chapter One, all social institutions are gendered. Therefore, a summary of the existing various Nepalese institutions and their intricate connections to education are critical to the context of this study. Second, I outline national educational system policies and structures at the particular time of this research project. Third, I discuss educational access and participation in Nepal and Jiri with a focus on the role of gender. Finally, educational quality and its relationship to gendered education are discussed.

NEPAL AND THE RESEARCH SITE: JIRI VILLAGE DEVELOPMENT COMMITTEE (VDC)

Landlocked between India and Tibet, the Kingdom of Nepal (54,362 square miles) is an independent nation with a constitutional monarchy. Known for its Himalayan mountain range, which includes such peaks as *Sagarmatha* (Mt. Everest), Nepal consists of three distinct geographical zones, each with its own ecological features. All three parallel each other, from east to west, occasionally bisected by the country's river systems. As part of their regional development planning, the government divided these ecological regions into development sectors (Savada 1993).

The southern part of Nepal, known as *Terai,* is a lowland tropical and subtropical belt of fertile plains that stretch along the Nepal-India border and run parallel to the Hill region. Several rivers nourish the forests and the

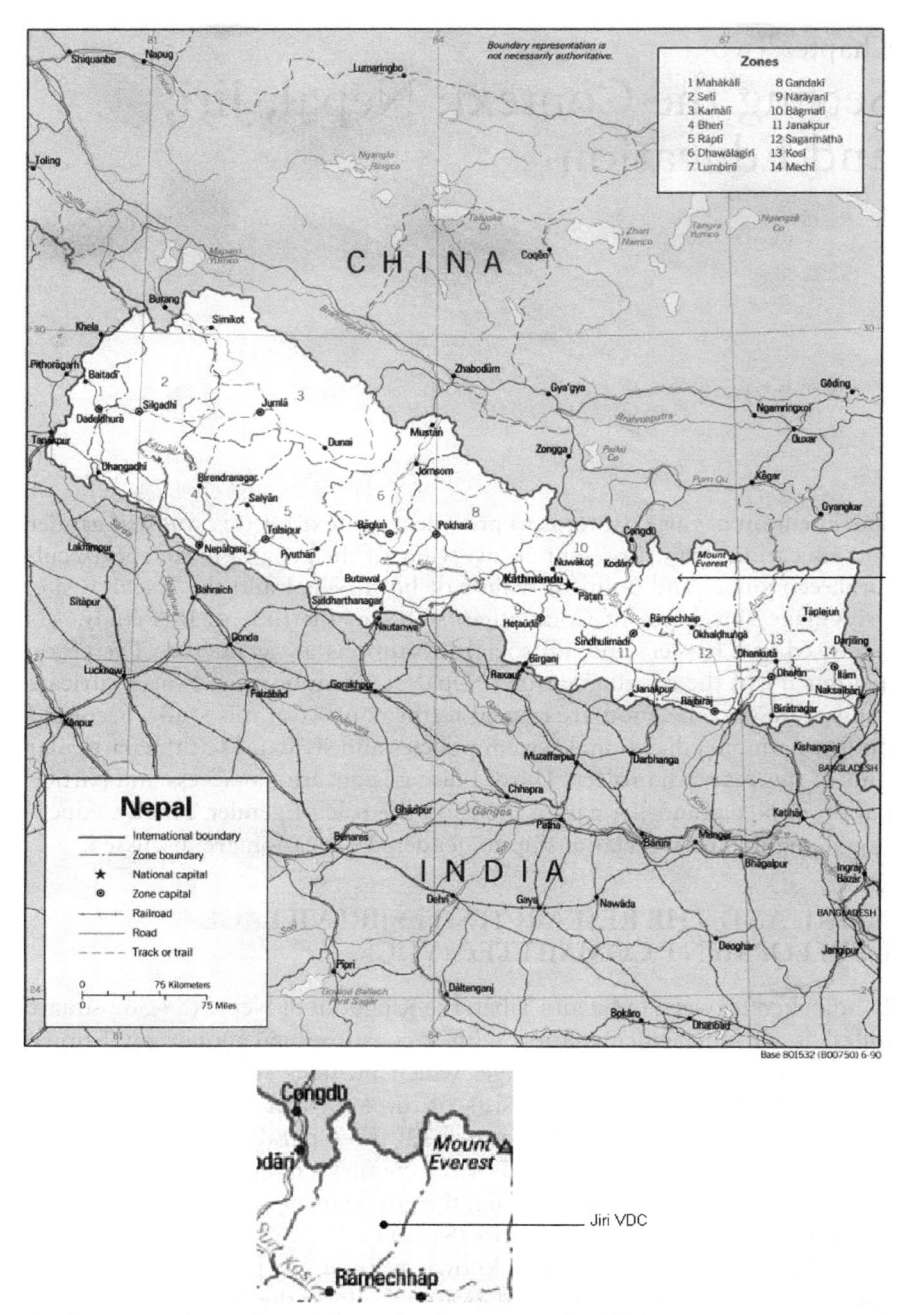

Fig. 2.1. Map of Nepal, with Area of Enlargement of Dolakha District. Courtesy of the University of Texas Libraries, The University of Texas at Austin.

farmlands. The Hill or Central region ranges between 1,000 and 4,000 meters in altitude. It features many foothills, rivers, and valleys, including the Kathmandu Valley—the country's most fertile and urbanized area. This region is the political and cultural center of Nepal, with decision-making power centralized in Kathmandu, the nation's capital and largest city. The lower hills and valleys of this region are densely populated. The *Himalayas* ("high mountains") dominate the Mountain or Northern region, situated at 4,000 meters above sea level and higher. The region is characterized by inclement climatic and rugged topographic conditions. Therefore, human habitation and economic activities are extremely limited and difficult. The region is sparsely populated, and farming activity is limited to the low-lying valleys and river basins (Savada 1993).

Jiri VDC is located in eastern Nepal—in Dolakha District, in the Janakpur Zone and Central Mountain Region—and is situated 190 kilometers east of Kathmandu. With an average elevation of 2,000 plus meters, the Jiri area is comprised of several small independent valleys. Two major rivers, the Khimati Khola and the Tama Koshi, form its borders to the east and west, respectively. Fifty-three percent of Jiri VDC is forest, but the Nepalese government took direct control of the forestland and pastures in 1957, placing firm restrictions on the use of timber.

SOCIAL AND CULTURAL CONTEXT

Human Development Status in Nepal

Nepal has one of the lowest-ranked levels of human development by UNDP (United Nations Development Program) standards: At the time of this study, the UNDP ranked Nepal 129th of 162 countries (UNDP 2001); in 2005, Nepal ranked 136th of 177 countries (UNDP 2005).[2] For 1999 reports, the life expectancy at birth was 58, infant mortality rate was 75 per 1,000 births, and the under-five (child) mortality rate was 104 per 1,000 births (UNICEF 2001).[3] Female life expectancy was 98% of that for the male population in 1999, giving Nepal the distinction as one of three countries in the world with a lower life expectancy for women than men. The maternal mortality ratio reported for 1980–1999 was estimated as 540 per 100,000 live births (UNICEF 2001).[4]

Access to health care has traditionally been an enormous obstacle for the people of Nepal. Raj Panday (1999) estimated 12,000 doctors in the country, with an average of one doctor per 16,000 people. Health services are often ill distributed, as most doctors live and work in Kathmandu and a limited number in other urban areas (Raj Panday 1999). It is estimated that 45 out of the 75 districts in Nepal suffer from chronic food deficits (UN World Food Programme 2001). Nutritional problems are widespread, with approximately half the children under five years of age suffering from moderate to severe malnutrition and two-thirds of all the deaths of children under five involving malnutrition (UN World Food Programme 2001). An estimated 15% of the population has access to safe drinking water, out of the 61% who reported having a regular supply (Raj Panday 1999).

In terms of education, the adult literacy rate was estimated as 45% of the total population for 1995–1999, with an estimated 63% of males literate as opposed to 28% of females (UNICEF 2001).[5] Between the 1970s and the 1990s, the male literacy rate increased faster than the female literacy rate (Shtrii Shakti 1995), indicating a widening gender gap. Furthermore, only about 14% of adult women in Nepal have ever attended school (LeVine, LeVine, & Schnell 2001). The net primary enrollment ratio estimated for the years 1995–1999 was 79% for boys and 60% for girls (UNICEF 2001).

The low educational status of the majority of the adults and the scarcity of medical and social services, compounded by persistent poverty, pose significant obstacles to social development. The mountainous terrain affects the provision of social services such as clinics, hospitals, and schools. While mountain areas have the least access to social services, western and far-western regions also suffer due to their remoteness and government neglect (Khaniya & Kiernan 1995) as well as the political conflicts that have intensified in the western part of the country since 1996.

Regional disparities in education standards have stemmed from diverse factors including distances children live from school, depressed economic conditions, and social factors such as religion, caste, ethnicity, and language. Schools have been unevenly distributed due to both topography and political influence (Khaniya & Kiernan 1995). Educational investment in teachers' training and salaries, school infrastructure, and teaching materials have been substantially more in the capital, where money and political power have also been more prevalent. The Central region, where Kathmandu is located, has had the highest number of students obtaining the School Leaving Certificate (SLC)[6] at the end of secondary school and continuing on to higher education (Singh 1995).

Human Development Status in Jiri VDC

Jiri is unique in comparison to most places in the mountains of Nepal. The once isolated Jiri Valley was changed dramatically with the introduction of the Swiss Association for Technical Assistance (SATA) multipurpose development project in 1957 (Bista 1980). At that time, the Swiss government, along with His Majesty's Government of Nepal (HGM), attempted to develop the area with such enterprises as the building of the Lamosangu-Jiri Road (which connected Jiri to Kathmandu), agricultural development, and education. The project was based on the assumption that the creation

Setting the Context

of a new infrastructure and improved agricultural productivity would foster the development process by raising income levels, which in turn would bolster demand for non-agricultural products in the region (Hamill, et al. 2000a). SATA started with agricultural projects, building construction, and local workforce recruitment (Bista 1980). To improve health care, the Swiss built a hospital, and to improve education, they started a technical school. Finally, they established the Jiri cheese factory to increase dairy production.

The Lamosangu-Jiri Road has had a significant impact on Jiri VDC and the Dolakha District. It has affected the flow of information as well as consumer goods, and has stimulated immigration, contributing to an influx of new values and ideologies. Further, this road has made the area more accessible for military purposes (Hamill, et al. 2000a). Other than the Lamosangu-Jiri Road, transportation infrastructure, as well as developed communication systems, have been sparse in Jiri. At the time of this study, electricity and running water were accessible to some wards, but electricity poles generally did not reach those living in the more isolated, elevated wards. A few houses had radios and television sets.

The road linking Jiri to Kathmandu also assisted in the development of Jiri's health care. Within three years of its inception as a health clinic in 1957, the Jiri Hospital expanded into a full-fledge regional healthcare facility with

Table 2.1. Number of Allocated and Vacant Staff Positions Occupied During the *Panchayat*[7] and Multiparty System at the Jiri Hospital, 1975–2000

Type of Health Staff Positions	Number of Health Positions in the Jiri Hospital			
	Panchayat System (1975–1989)		Multiparty System (1990–2000)	
	Allocated	Occupied	Allocated	Occupied
Physicians	3	3	2	1
Health Assistants	0	0	1	1
Nurses	13	13	5	2
Lab Technicians	2	2	2	0
X-Ray Technicians	2	2	1	0
Auxiliary Health Workers	3	3	2	1
Administration	4	4	2	2
Support Staff	21	21	9	9
Total	48	48	24	16

Source: Subedi, et al. 2000a.

a 25-bed capacity. Facilities expanded, and, as a result, people from rural communities around Jiri and beyond sought treatment at the Jiri Hospital. In the late 1980s, when the government switched to a multi-party system, regional hospitals were placed under the supervision of the district health authorities. Soon thereafter, the daily operations of the Jiri Hospital went largely ignored. The Jiri Hospital was no longer able to adequately provide for the health care needs of the local people, and by 2000, most physicians and health workers assigned to provide medical services at the Jiri Hospital had abandoned their posts and left for Kathmandu (Table 2.1). Subsequently, many people of Jiri have turned or returned to the indigenous folk healers.

In 1995, a team of US biomedical researchers, along with two Nepali physicians from Kathmandu, established the Jiri Health Clinic to provide a variety of preventive and curative services free of charge. According to clinic reports, as of December 1999, 35,000 patients have been treated in the Jiri Health Clinic. However, the Clinic is only a temporary measure, with plans to close once the US-based research is complete (Subedi, *et al.* 2000a). Furthermore, health posts, hospitals, and health centers in the Janakpur Zone (where Jiri is located) decreased in number from 1988–89 to 1997–98 (CBS 1999). With decreasing health care facilities, many people in Nepal consider heath care a luxury. Because of the importance of health care to overall human development, it is critical to understand the availability of basic needs in relation to education.

Educational Development in Jiri

Jiri has not suffered from geo-isolation as much as other VDCs in the eastern and mountainous areas of Nepal. The Lamosangu-Jiri Road connected Jiri not only to Kathmandu, but also to Charikot, the district headquarters. At the time of this study, the Chief District Officer for Education, based in Charikot, made frequent trips to Jiri. Furthermore, it was probably not a coincidence that the largest schools in Jiri VDC—the higher secondary school and the lower secondary school—were located next to the Lamosangu-Jiri Road. At the very end of the Lamosangu-Jiri Road, the lower secondary school, the D School,[8] sat perched on a slight hill, just above the stalls and shops of the Dhunge Bazaar that line the road and the path up to the school.

In 1999–2000, Jiri VDC had a total of 15 schools (Table 2.2).[9] Of the 12 primary schools in Jiri VDC, nine were government (public) schools, and three were private (boarding) schools. One of the primary boarding schools was not registered with the VDC government office. Of the two

Setting the Context

Table 2.2. Number of Schools by Region, District, and VDC (1997)

SCHOOLS	National Total	Central Mountain Region	Dolakha District	Jiri VDC
No. of Primary Schools	23,284	865	317	12
No. of Lower Secondary Schools	6,082	167	60	1
No. of Secondary Schools	3,322	79	29	2

Sources: Statistics Section, Ministry of Education (MOE) 1997; Jiri VDC office records 2000.

secondary schools, one was a government school, and the other was a private school.[10]

All of the schools in Dolakha District were integrated by gender, including the 15 schools in Jiri VDC.

During the *Panchayat* Period in Nepal (1961–1988/89), when Jiri was known as Jiri *Panchayat*, there was limited formal education as well as literacy in Jiri. There were very few schools, and those in existence were primary schools. As the Jiri VDC Chair (government head of the VDC) explained,

> At that time of Jiri *Panchayat*, very few people knew about it [education]. At that time, nobody knew about the education except very few people who used the bamboo leaf to write down [their thoughts] on their thigh.

The VDC Chair also offered an overview of the history of the first school in Jiri:

> During the *Panchayat* time, there was a [Buddhist] monastery of Jirel people in Ward 9 where some teachers who came from Burma used to teach some people. At that time, what is now called *vidhyalaya* ["school"] was called *pathsala* [old word for "school"]. Later, the Swiss started a primary school in the same place where today the J School is located. The school building was like a cowshed, made up of bamboo. This way, Classes 1, 2, and 3 were conducted. The first teacher studied [up to] Class 8 in Burma. He started teaching from the Kot [village in Jiri]. This is what I heard. The name of the school was Jiri Multi-purpose School. People from the very far [away] places

such as Okhaldunga, Solu, Ramechhap, Suri, [and] Jhyapu of Dolakha District used to come here to study. The education standard was very good at that time because the Swiss were always there to help.

When Nepal ushered in a democracy in 1988–89, Jiri was redefined, from a *Panchayat* to a VDC (Village Development Committee). During a nine-month Communist rule shortly thereafter, the Communist government conducted a program known as *Aafno Gaaun Aafai Banau*,[11] which allocated funding to Jiri VDC for school buildings and materials. Jiri villagers provided the labor for the construction of the eleven government schools now in use.

Government Schools in Jiri

In 1999–2000, each of the nine wards in Jiri VDC contained at least one school. All 11 of the government schools in Jiri VDC (Table 2.3) had men head teachers except for two schools (the H School and the Sh School).

Table 2.3. Summary of Government Schools in Jiri VDC[12]

Alias	Location (Ward)	Year Opened (A.D.)	Type of School/ Classes (Grades) Offered	No. of Students Enrolled (1999)	No. of Class-rooms	Predominant Ethnic Group of the Student Body	No. of Teachers (Total)	No. of Women Teachers
H	1	1985	Primary (1–5)	124	4	Sherpa, Chhetri	4	1
SP	5	1989	Primary (1–5)	137	5	Chhetri/ Brahmin	3	0*
MS	2	1993	Primary (1–4)	138	4	Jirel	4	1
B	3	1989	Primary (1–5)	74	6	Jirel**	3	1
JW	6	1983	Primary (1–5)	85	5	Jirel	4	1
Ch	8	1993–94	Primary (Nursery–3)	57	4	Jirel	3	1
Sh	2	1973	Primary (Nursery/1–5)	95	5	Jirel	4	2
ST	4	1990–91	Primary (1–5)	129	5	Jirel	3	0

(continued)

Setting the Context

Table 2.3. Summary of Government Schools in Jiri VDC[12] (continued)

Alias	Location (Ward)	Year Opened (A.D.)	Type of School/ Classes (Grades) Offered	No. of Students Enrolled (1999)	No. of Class- rooms	Predominant Ethnic Group of the Student Body	No. of Teachers (Total)	No. of Women Teachers
D	7	1983	Lower Secondary (Nursery–8)	446	11	Jirel, Chhetri, Sherpa, Tamang	14	5
J	9	1959***	Higher Secondary (1–12)	816****	14	Jirel, Chhetri, Sherpa	19	2
C	5	?	?	?	?	?	?	?

Sources: Interviews with Jiri VDC Government School Head Teachers 2000; Jiri VDC office records 2000.

Notes:

* This school previously had a woman teacher, who was transferred to the D School by the district office, for reasons unbeknownst to the SP School. The head teacher told us that the girl students were "devastated" when the woman teacher left.

** This was the only school in the VDC where all the students (as well as all of the teachers) were Jirel.

*** The J School was first a primary school (1959) and then a high school (1967). It became a higher secondary school in 1994.

**** Enrollment number for Classes 1–10 only.

In 1999–2000, the proportion of women teachers to men teachers was significantly small: Less than a quarter (21.3%) of the total number of teachers was women, and two schools had no women teachers at all. The dearth of women teachers left girls, as well as boys, with a scarcity of role models and may have discouraged girls from attending and participating in school.

Population Changes and Demography

In 2001, the population in Nepal was estimated at 24 million people (World Bank 2006), with over 85% living in rural areas (LeVine, LeVine, & Schnell 2001). In the mountainous region, only nine of the 39 districts had towns, and nearly 90% of Nepali homes were scattered among approximately 28,000 villages that were isolated from each other both socially and

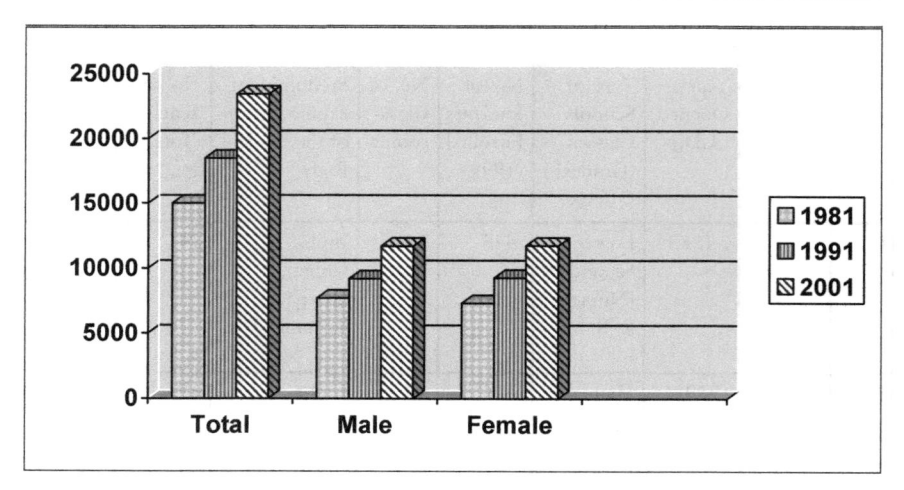

Figure 2.2. Population Distribution by Sex for Years 1981, 1991, and 2001 (Estimated)
Source: Central Bureau of Statistics (CBS) 1999.

physically (Sharma 1989). UNICEF (2001) estimated the average annual urban growth rate for Nepal to be 5.3% from 1990–1999. In 1961, the total population was only 9.34 million, but by 1991, the population had doubled (Figure 2.2). Demographers project the population will continue to rise.

A precipitously growing population puts added pressure on already fragile educational infrastructure and opportunities. This could affect processes of gendering and the gendered social order: The larger the population, the greater the demand on resources, particularly educational resources, and the greater likelihood for gender bias in the distribution of those resources.

Like the rest of the country, the population of Jiri VDC has grown: The Nepali Census of 1991 estimated the total population of Jiri VDC to be 7,138. In 1999, the total population was estimated at 9,000, and the predominant ethnic group—the Jirels—were estimated at 3,500 to 4,000 individuals or 41.7% of the total Jiri VDC population (Subedi, *et al.* 2000b). At the time of this study, the population of Jiri VDC was scattered in villages or *gaauns* within the nine wards; some villages were more isolated than others.[13]

In 1999–2000, most households in Jiri VDC were composed of parents, unmarried sons and daughters, married sons, their wives, and their children. There were nuclear families and extended families that changed

URGENT :

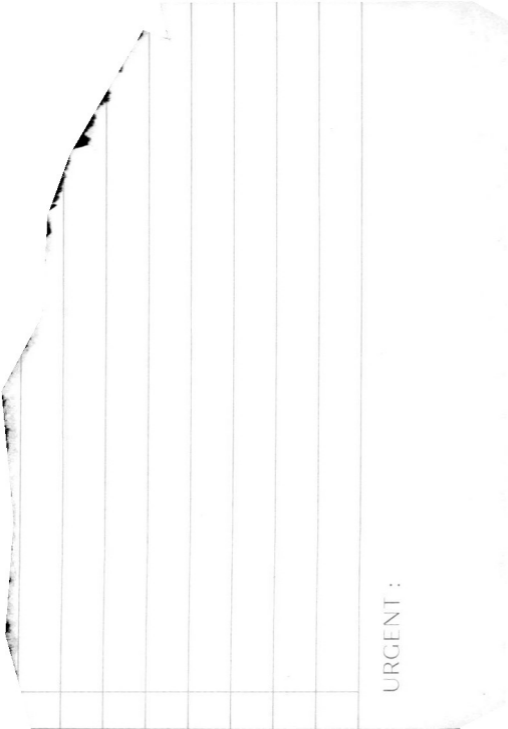

Setting the Context 31

over time with deaths, daughters moving out upon marriage, brides being brought in by sons, and the birth of grandchildren. Within the largest ethnic group, the Jirels, there were 12 major "clans" and 11 "sub-clans" in Jiri VDC. These clans and sub-clans were made up of patrilineally extended, patrilocal families. Typically, when a Jirel family's first son married, the new couple would reside with the groom's father's family. When a second son in the family was married, the eldest son and his wife and children would move out and establish their own household. Only the youngest son would continue to live with his parents. Upon the death of the father, each of the sons would inherit a share of the land and livestock. The youngest son, however, would receive his share as well as the house and the contents of the house. Daughters usually did not receive land but might have received jewelry and other items at the discretion of their fathers at the time of marriage (Sidky, *et al.* 2000).

ETHNICITY AND CASTE

Nepal has been highly complex in its ethnic, religious and language composition. In general, the people of Northern Nepal are of Tibeto-Burmese descent, while those residing further south tend to be Indo-Aryan (CBS 1993). The 1991 census identified 60 different ethnic groups and listed 35 different languages, but it has been estimated that approximately 100 distinct ethnic groups reside in Nepal, with 28 such groups representing 90% of the population (Dahal 1995). To be noted, Dilli Dahal (1995) identifies these groups as "ethnic/caste groups," but I want to distinguish ethnicity from caste based on the following distinction: *Ethnicity* refers one's cultural/racial affiliation while *caste* refers specifically to the system of social classification as defined in the Hindu religion. Interestingly, the Nepali term *jat* connotes both "caste" and "ethnic group," and it is quite common in Nepal not to distinguish between these two categories and to treat various ethnic groups as castes (Karan & Ishii 1996; Gellner 1997).

ETHNICITY

The most prevalent and widespread ethnic groups in Nepal have been the Chhetri and Brahmin of the Hindu castes. Other major ethnic groups include Magar, Tharu, Newar, Tamang, and Kami (Table 2.4).

In addition to Jirels, other ethnic groups in Jiri VDC have included Sherpas, Tamangs, and Sunwars, along with the Brahmin, Chhetri, Newar, and Dalit peoples of the Hindu castes. Jirel culture closely resembles that

Table 2.4. Numerical and Percentage Distribution of Population by Ethnic Group in Nepal, 1991

Ethnic Groups	Population	
	Number	Percentage
Chhetri	2968	16.1
Brahmin	2388	12.9
Magar	1339	7.2
Tharu	1194	6.5
Newar	1041	5.6
Tamang	1018	5.5
Kami	964	5.2
Yadav/Adhir	765	4.1
Muslim	653	3.5
Rai	526	2.8
Others*	5635	30.5
Total	18491	100.0

Source: Central Bureau of Statistics (CBS) 1991.

Note: Grand totals may not tally with the sum of corresponding figures because of rounding off.

* Includes 55 ethnic groups, including Sherpas and Jirels.

of the Sunwars (Bista 1980). Most Sunwars and Jirels are farmers who have cultivated the hill slopes and river valleys. At the time of this study, a relatively small group of the Sunwars lived throughout the Jiri area. While they were once major landholders in the Jiri Valley, they have slowly lost their traditional tribal lands to other groups (Hamill, *et al.* 2000b). The Tamangs are one of the largest ethnic groups in Nepal and are probably of Tibetan origin (Bista 1980). They inhabited the western portion of the Jiri area (Hamill, *et al.* 2000b). The Sherpas trace their roots to Tibet, the area to the north of Nepal, from which they emigrated approximately 500 years ago (Fürer Haimendorf 1964). The Hindu castes of Brahmins and Chhetris first arrived in the Jiri area during the military expansion of King Prithvi Narayana Shah in the 18th century (Fournier 1974). In 1999–2000, they were the wealthiest ethnic groups in Jiri VDC. Chhetris, in particular, were large in number, comprising approximately 37% of the population of the Dolakha District, in which the Jiri Valley is situated (Hamill, *et al.* 2000b).

LANGUAGES

There are six major languages in Nepal—Nepali, Maithili, Bhojpuri, Tharu, Tamang, and Newari (Table 2.5), which together constitute more than 80% of the population (United Nations 1996). The official language of Nepal is Nepali, which is classified as an Indo-European language (Hamill, *et al.* 2000b). However, it has been estimated that there are more than 50 different languages and dialects, varying most notably by region and ethnicity (United Nations 1996).

Table 2.5. Composition of Population in Nepal by Mother Tongue, 1991

	Number (in '000)	Percent
Language Groups		
Nepali	9303	50.3
Maithili	2192	11.8
Bhojpuri	1380	7.5
Newari	690	3.7
Gurung	228	1.2
Tamang	904	4.9
Abadhi	375	2.0
Tharu	993	5.4
Magar	430	2.3
Limbu	254	1.4
Rai/Kirati	439	2.4
Bhote/Sherpa	122	0.7
Rajbansi	86	0.5
Urdu	202	1.1
Hindi	171	0.9
Other*	722	3.9
Total	18491	100.0

Source: Central Bureau of Statistics (CBS) 1991.
Note:
* The category "Other" includes languages spoken in the Dolakha District such as Jirel.

Many languages are named for the ethnic groups who speak them; for example, the Jirels speak Jirel, and the Sherpas speak Sherpa. The most common languages spoken in the Dolakha District are Tamang, Nepali, Sherpa, and Jirel (CBS 1999). The languages of the Jirels, Sunwars, Sherpas, and Tamang are classified as Tibeto-Burmese languages (Hamill, *et al.* 2000b).

Nepali is the language of instruction at all levels of the national education system. In the 1970s, the Nepalese government prepared all lower and secondary grade textbooks in the Nepali language and made education in Nepali compulsory, regardless of students' cultural background and first language (Karan & Ishii 1996). Although the government of that time period prohibited use of other languages, people demanded the use of other mother tongues for education and mass communications during and after the democratic movement of 1990. The democratic constitution of 1990 guarantees the civil rights of ethnic minorities, including the right to use one's own language. At the time of this study, students in Jiri VDC schools were required to speak Nepali (and English, especially in English courses), but their families spoke their own language (e.g., Jirel) at home. Progress in the use of minority languages in teaching and in skills has been limited due to the absence of a writing system in many languages, the lack of administrative efficiency, and a conflict of interests (Karan & Ishii 1996).

RELIGION AND CASTE

As the world's only Hindu Kingdom, a large majority of the Nepalese population (86.5% in 1998–1999) is Hindu. For that same year, Buddhists were 7.8% of the population, and 5.7 % were other religions, including Islam and Christianity (CBS 1999). In Nepal, Hindus and Buddhists have traditionally lived together and worshipped each other's deities and celebrated each other's festivals. Muslims (3.5% of the population in 1998–99) form the third largest religious group (CBS 1999).

In the Dolakha District, the majority of people at the time of this study were Hindu, followed by Buddhists, Christians, Jains, and Muslims—in that order (CBS 1999). Although Jirels are predominately Buddhists, they have been influenced by Hindu beliefs and practices for centuries. For example, Jirels have celebrated all the major Hindu rituals and festivals, such as *Maghe Sankranti, Saune Sankranti, Chaite Dashain, Dasami Tika* (also known as *Dashain*), and *Bhai Tika* (also known as *Tihar*). When asked to give their religion, many Jirels in Jiri replied that they were "Buddhist and Hindu." Sunwars has also been heavily influenced by Hinduism, increasingly reliant on Brahmins, rather than their own traditional priests, to conduct many of their religious ceremonies (Fournier 1974; Hamill, *et al.* 2000b). Sherpas reflected their Tibetan heritage in their practice of Buddhism.

Based on the Hindu *Varna* system, the Hindu caste structure is divided into four major castes: *Brahmin* (priest), *Chhetri* (warrior), *Vaishya* (trader), and *Shudra* (untouchable). A significant proportion of the Brahmins and Chhetris have been wealthy and influential members of Nepalese society, but these castes have not necessarily dictated class or an economic status. The *Muluki Ain* (National Code) of 1963 outlawed discrimination on the basis of caste (United Nations 1996). Although illegal as a basis for discrimination and ideologically condemned by many, the caste system has been heavily entrenched in Hinduism, and, practically speaking, it has had a wide impact on the low caste people's access to positions of privilege and power and to social capital (including access to education) outside of their castes.

Women's and men's lives have often been drastically different based on religion and caste. For example, an interweaving of religion, caste, economics, and socio-cultural influences has determined marital arrangements for women and men. Buddhist communities, particularly those in the mountains that include matriarchal societies, have practiced polyandry in the past,[14] while in Hindu communities, especially those in the Terai plains, patriarchal and polygynous[15] households have been relatively common (Shtrii Shakti 1995; Sibbons 1998). Most Hindus in Nepal and in Jiri have followed the practices and rites of Hinduism, which includes restrictions on caste interactions and women's privileges versus men's. Women from Dalit (untouchable) castes have suffered from both sexism and casteism in Nepalese society; their access to resources and opportunities has often been compounded by their poverty-stricken status. As far as access to schooling is concerned, the geographical as well as the economic and socio-cultural aspects of a community has influenced school attendance.

ECONOMIC CONTEXT

Nepal and the Economy

With an estimated gross national income per capita of US $190 for 2001 (World Bank 2006), Nepal ranks among the world's poorest countries. Agriculture dominates the economy, but with such mountainous and forested terrain, less than one-fifth of the land is actually under cultivation. The pressure of the rapidly expanding population on the limited arable land is intense, causing considerable migration (Sibbons 1999). As a landlocked country, Nepal is dependent on its routes into India for all exports and imports, including all of the important fuel oils (Karan and Ishii 1996). Extensive foreign aid from both Eastern and Western countries has been

Table 2.6. Sources of Financing for Education in Nepal

Sources of Financing	Percentage in 1991–92	Percentage in 1995–96
Internal Sources	92.8	78.1
Foreign Assistance	7.2	21.9
Grants	2.0	7.7
Loans	5.2	14.2
Total education expenditure	100.0	100.0

Source: Raj Lohani 1998.

used to support construction projects such as roads and hydro-electricity. In his 1999 book *Nepal's Failed Development*, Devendra Raj Panday reported that among five countries in South Asia—Nepal, Bangladesh, India, Pakistan, and Sri Lanka—Nepal was the only country where official development assistance as a percentage of the total GNP increased between 1980 and 1996. While there has been a drastic decline in development assistance for those other countries, Raj Panday laments, "there is no sign of any reduction in the government's dependence on foreign aid for financing public expenditure" (1999:62).

Donor contributions to the education sector also increased (Table 2.6). The funds received from external assistance in 1991 accounted for 7.2% of the total education expenditure in Nepal, but jumped to 25% in 1994–95 and 21.9% in 1995–96. Of the total development expenditure, foreign aid accounted for 78% (Raj Lohani 1998).

Between 1991–92 and 1995–96, the percentage of loans more than doubled as a means of financing education. Nepal's continued indebtedness to bilateral and multi-lateral donors such as USAID and the World Bank has consequences that could ultimately shape educational reform in Nepal, particularly the direction of gender in educational reform, as these major creditors are gendered institutions themselves.[16]

Nepal's Gross National Product in 1998 was estimated at $4.9 billion in US dollars (World Bank 2000). The Nepalese Ministry of Education (MOE) reported that in 1996–1997, the public current expenditure on education as a percentage of the GDP was 2.9% (MOE 1997), up from 2.5% in 1995–96. The share of education in the total government expenditure increased from 8.8% in 1990–91 to almost 14% in 1996–97 (Table 2.7).[17]

Setting the Context

Table 2.7. Trends in Public Expenditure on Education at Current Prices

Year	Share of education in GDP percentage	Share of education in government budget percentage
1975–76	1.3	12.0
1980–81	1.4	9.4
1990–91	1.8	8.8
1991–92	2.0	10.9
1992–93	2.5	13.4
1993–94	2.2	12.8
1994–95	2.5	13.3
1995–96	2.5	12.9
1996–97	2.9	13.9
1997–98	*	13.1

Sources: Raj Lohani 1998; MOE 1997.
Note: * Data not available.

A number of important observations can be made from the analysis of the education expenditure by sub-sectors (Table 2.8). The share allocated to primary education shows continual expansion from 48.6% in 1991–92 to receiving more than half the education budget (51.2%) in 1997–98. There was also a substantial increase in the allocation to secondary education. Meanwhile, teacher education and pre-primary education were largely ignored in budget allocations, which had serious implications for the quality of education (Raj Lohani 1998).

Table 2.8. Budget Estimates by Sub-sectors

Sub-Sectors	Percentage in 1991–92	Percentage in 1997–98
Primary education	48.6	51.2
Secondary education	13.0	21.0
Higher secondary education	0.0	0.2
Technical and vocational education	1.7	1.6
Higher education	27.6	21.0
Non-formal education	0.6	1.5
Other	8.5	3.5
Total	100.0	100.0

Source: Raj Lohani 1998.

Jiri and Economics

At the time of this study, the economy of Jiri VDC was largely subsistence, based on the cultivation of millet, maize, wheat, barley, and potatoes on upland terraces, and a small amount of rice at lower elevations. Some villagers had started to grow leafy vegetables for the village markets. Others cultivated spices for local consumption. Many raised goats, cattle, pigs, and buffaloes, and almost every household had a few chickens.

Given the limited amounts of arable land available in Jiri VDC (only 47% was cultivable land), few families were able to produce enough food to last them the entire year. Providing for subsistence needs depended on an individual's or household's livelihood, the amount of land owned, and the number of adult laborers in the family. Many families either supplemented their income or derived their entire livelihood by maintaining a booth at the local bazaar, doing wage labor (from construction to carpentry to carrying loads), or working in the local clinic and hospital, schools, forestry office, or other governmental posts. Many Sunwars were recruited into the Gurkha regiments of the British and Indian armies, as well as into the Royal Nepal Army. These military activities lent support to their low incomes. It seemed Jirels were generally not accepted into or not attracted to the military service, leaving them at an economic and social disadvantage compared to the Sunwars (Bista 1980).

As of 1999–2000, the cheese factory started by the SATA project was still in operation, but belonging then to the Nepalese government. The Sherpas maintained herds of yak at high altitudes in Jiri and subsequently provided the milk for the cheese factory and controlled milk production. Not keeping yaks, Jirels did not profit from the cheese factory, and few could afford to buy the dairy goods produced there. Most of the cheese was exported to Kathmandu, and very little of what was produced was consumed locally (Hamill, *et al.* 2000a).

With the Lamosangu-Jiri Road, a cash market economy emerged. Two local bazaars subsequently developed, and at the time of this study, the Brahmins, Chhetris, Newars, and Sherpas controlled the Jiri economy as the main business proprietors in the bazaars. Once the road was built, it replaced the old trail to Everest Base Camp that went south of the Jiri Valley. The flow of trekkers and tourists was thus diverted through the Jiri Valley; all the small shop owners and people who operated businesses from Lamosangu onwards subsequently migrated to Jiri with their businesses and shops. In 1999–2000, Jirels owned only three of approximately 20 lodges in the main bazaar and just one store in the smaller bazaar. To earn money, some Jirel subsistence farmers distilled *raksi* (an alcoholic drink made from fermented millet or corn) for these markets, acting as suppliers

Setting the Context 39

to the Sunwar, Sherpa, and Hindu caste merchants. Jirels also sold chickens and goats to supplement their incomes.

After its construction, the Lamosangu-Jiri Road brought trekking and tourist industry to Jiri, which, in turn, brought business to the Sunwar, Sherpa, Brahmin, Chhetri, and Newari-owned shops, lodges, and teashops. Jirels were less able to capitalize on the tourist trade. Jirels were once employed as porters, carrying merchandise and equipment to the connecting districts and the Everest Base Camp area, but Jirels later found these jobs replaced with daily helicopter flights to transport goods (Hamill, *et al.* 2000a).

The Lamosangu-Jiri Road not only introduced a cash economy to Jiri, but it also brought the type of development Skinner and Holland (1996) describe as common to roadside bazaars: merchandise from foreign markets, teashops, electricity, a cinema hall, Coca Cola, "English boarding schools," buses, cars and news stalls. The road has increased the flow of western ideas, tastes and preferences, while fueling consumerism. Many families have competed with one another for higher status, buying televisions, and sending their children to boarding (private) schools (Hamill, *et al.* 2000a).

Jiri and the Economics of Education

Households incurred direct costs when a student goes to school: They were responsible for payment of fees, students' subsistence, and the purchase of textbooks, school supplies, and school uniforms. Many households in Jiri found these expenditures difficult. The Jiri VDC Chair explained that,

> When we surveyed all the schools of Jiri VDC, we found that around 200 students were in a very poor, economic condition. They even can't buy stationeries [school supplies], uniform. Some of these children don't have their mother or father. Some of their parents have to do the labor work [wage-labor such as working as a porter or coolie].

On the national level, textbooks and admission/registration fees account for a large share of household expenditures on education (Raj Lohani 1998).

POLITICAL CONTEXT

Since 1990, tumult and tragedy have defined the political atmosphere of Nepal. After the *Panchayat* system changed to the multiparty system in April 1990, a constitution was drafted in September of 1990, and a democratically elected government was formed in May of 1991. As part of the multiparty system, the Jiri Valley followed a local level political unit—the Village Development Council. The Council contained within it a committee known as the Village Development Committee (VDC). The Committee included the chair and vice-chair of the Council, the chair of each of Jiri's nine wards, and two community members. The Council nominated these two members, and notably, one of them had to be a woman. All eligible members of the Council (men and women, 21 years and older) elected the chair and vice chair of the Council (Maharjan 1998). The VDC Chair in 1999–2000 was affiliated with the Communist Party.

As a constitutional monarchy, individuals have traditionally run for office under their respective party banners. For many years, the major parties have included the Nepali Congress Party, the Communist Party, and the National Democratic Party. The Office of the Election Commission during the 1991 elections, however, officially recognized 43 parties. In the Jiri Valley, the Communist Party and the Nepali Congress Party were the most visible and active at the time of this research. Therefore, in 1996–2000, most Jiri residents identified themselves with either the Communist or the Nepali Congress Party (Subedi, *et al.* 2000b).

Most existing political parties in Nepal have been plagued by intra- and inter-party quarrels over the distribution of appointments and business contracts, with the lion's share going to relatives, friends and political supporters of key party leaders (Bhattachan 1994). For example, over time, the Nepal Communist Party has split, merged, split and re-merged on several occasions. The Maoist Party was one such split, evolving through several phases including its most recent incarnation as a violent rebellion against King Gyanendra. Maoist groups have attacked police outposts in rural areas and pressured villagers to give one child to the Maoist cause. Maoists have demanded an end to the monarchy and call for the initiation of a Communist republic. In turn, King Gyanendra's army has led violent attacks against both Maoists and Maoist sympathizers and has imprisoned countless suspected "terrorists." The result of this and the conflict between and within political parties has been constant flux and turmoil with dispiriting factionalism and conspiracy.[18]

With the intensifying conflict between the Maoists and the King's Army, the local economy of Jiri VDC has suffered. As noted earlier, Jiri marks the head of the trekking trail to Mt. Everest, and Jiri has been dependent on tourism to support local people. The fighting between Maoists and the military has largely frightened away this valuable source of income. Since 1996, the conflict in certain parts of the Jiri Valley has also affected students' and teachers' ability to attend school. Schools have closed if there was a rumored strike or attack by Maoists guerillas, and some Jiri residents have not traveled through certain areas of Jiri at particular times of the day for fear of being kidnapped and forced to join the

Setting the Context

Maoist forces or for fear of the army associating them with the Maoists and retaliating.

Much further back in Nepal's history, the Rana regime in Nepal (1846–1951) felt it easier to control its subjects by keeping them uneducated and therefore refused to provide public schools. Conversely, the Shah kings (1951-present) wanted educated subjects who would "develop" Nepal (Skinner & Holland 1996:273). Many young Nepali students absorb the development rhetoric found in their textbooks and lectures, and passionately identify with the needs of their country. Yet, at the same time, schools in Nepal have always been considered the centers of political thought and action. By the mid-1980s, teachers and students struggled to convert the school from a site of state control to a site of critical discourse, looking critically at not only the state but also at systems of caste, class, and gender privilege embedded in Nepalese society (Skinner & Holland 1996). Students are given partial credit for the ushering in of the multiparty system and the demise of the *Panchayat* system in 1990.

OVERVIEW OF EDUCATIONAL SYSTEM POLICIES AND STRUCTURES

Educational Policy

Nepal has made enormous strides since it took its first steps toward developing a national education policy and establishing a Ministry of Education in 1951, the year that marked the end of a century of Rana feudal rule. Starting in 1956, the government established a system of Five-Year National Development Plans, which included the education sector. With only a two percent literacy rate in 1951, the first nine Development Plans set ever-increasing targets for primary enrollment and national literacy. Some progress was made: In 1975, girls comprised only 18.3% of the primary school enrollment, whereas by 1994, the percentage had risen to 39.4 (UNESCO 1991; CBS 1996). Nepal's official goal was to provide universal primary education by the year 2000 (UNESCO 1991). Yet with one of the 12 poorest economies in the world, an estimated 2.05% growth rate for primary through secondary school-age children (CBS 1996), a drop-out rate of 23.1% in Class 1 (MOE 1997), and a host of other factors, Nepal was not able to meet its universal primary enrollment goal in 2000.

Structure of the Nepalese Educational System

In 1999–2000, the structural system in Nepal included five years of primary education, three years of lower secondary school education, and two years of secondary school (Table 2.9).

Table 2.9. Nepal's Formal Education System in Comparison to U.S. System

Nepal System	Year/Class/Grade	U.S. System
Primary School	1	Elementary School
	2	
	3	
	4	
	5	
Lower Secondary School	6	Middle School
	7	
	8	
Secondary School	9	High School
(High School)		
	10*	
"10+2"/Intermediate/Campus	11	
	12**	
Bachelor's/Diploma***	13	Bachelor's
	14	
Master's/Degree	15	
	16	
	17	Master's

Notes:

* This has been typically the year a student takes the Student Leaving Certificate (SLC) exam and finishes secondary school in Nepal.

** This has been typically the year a student graduates from high school in the United States.

*** A Bachelor's in Nepal generally takes 2–3 years to complete, and Master's in Nepal usually takes 2–3 years to complete.

Higher education was broken down into three 2-year stages: 10+2, (also know as intermediate or campus); diploma (Bachelor's); and then degree (Master's). Although the government provided these timetables, it was estimated that in 1998–99 only about 37% of the primary school-age children actually completed their primary education within a period of five to 13 years, and only 37% of girls, compared with 38% of boys, completed the primary level within the five-to-13-year timeframe (UNDP 1999). Further, many parents consider it normal for students to drop out of primary grades

Setting the Context

for a year or two and then rejoin the school later (UNDP 1999). This lag creates a clog in the system, resulting in overcrowded classrooms and inefficient use of teachers' time and materials. Khaniya & Kiernan (1995) estimate that typically only 15% of the secondary entry cohort completes secondary education.

Dropout and repetition rates have been high at all levels, but especially at the primary level. In 1996, the Ministry of Education (MOE) reported less than half of the students (47.5%) at the secondary level passing the SLC exam (MOE 1997). That year's SLC results indicated that the pass percentage among boy students (27.5%) was slightly higher than that among girl students (25.8%). However, the means of the total scores for girls in all of the five regions as well as in all of the three geographical belts were lower than those of boys. In 1996, the percentage of girls who passed the SLC was highest in the hills,[19] and lowest in the mountains (Tuladhar and Thapa 1998), indicating a marked regional disparity in achievement among girls.

A contributing factor to these issues has been students' lack of preparedness at the entry level, especially in Class 1. Many parents choose to send an under-aged child to school, particularly if she or he was in the company of older sisters and brothers.[20] Another student-related factor has been language ability. In most ethnic groups, especially in the rural areas, students have traditionally spoken a language other than Nepali at home. Subsequently, when they first enroll in school, they have not been prepared to respond to the teacher in Nepali, the language of instruction, because they do not understand the language. In such a situation, students have been more likely to drop out or repeat a grade. UNESCO (1987) also cites poor health and malnutrition as factors contributing to high rates of students dropping out or having to repeat a grade.

EDUCATIONAL ACCESS AND PARTICIPATION

Access to Schooling

In the years following 1951, school access and participation in Nepal steadily increased, but by 1999, the levels were still inadequate compared with the world's averages.[21] For that year, children under 15 years of age constituted about 43% of the total population, and approximately 20% were under 6 years of age (UNDP 1999). A little more than 2.9 million (13.1%) belonged to the primary school-age cohort (six to 10 years), and only about three-fourths of these children (72%) were enrolled in schools. Therefore, approximately 928,000 children, ages six to 10, did not have access to primary education. Of the 928,000 children not enrolled in schools in 1998–99, approximately two-thirds were girls (UNDP 1999).

Table 2.10. Net Enrollment Rates by Gender and School Level (1997)

	Primary (1–5)	Lower Secondary (6–8)	Secondary (9–10)	Total (1–10)
Net Enrollment Rate (percentage)				
Boys	78.9	34.0	24.1	56.3
Girls	59.9	22.3	14.3	40.7
Total	69.6	28.2	19.1	48.6

Source: Statistics Section, Ministry of Education (MOE) 1997.

The primary school net enrollment ratio for 1997 was estimated at 78%, with a 93% boys' net enrollment ratio and a 63% girls' net enrollment ratio (World Bank 2000). However, the actual numbers frequently drop during the course of a school year (MOEC/USAID 1988). Also, enrollment figures tend to be consistently inflated due to the high rate of over- and under-age repeaters and the schools' incentive to report high enrollment figures in order to receive grants-in-aid in the form of free textbooks and teacher salaries (Khaniya & Kiernan 1995). Furthermore, national statistics tend to mask the vast differences among the regions, and within regions among the different climatic zones (Sibbons 1999).

Lower secondary school enrollment has steadily increased, with 305,409 students enrolled in 1987–1988 and nearly 10 years later, an estimated 828,767 students enrolled in 1996–1997, which was more than double (CBS 1999). Secondary school enrollment increased ten-fold, from 4,899 students in 1951 to 496,821 students in 1985 (Khaniya & Kiernan 1995). While some progress has been made, girls' enrollment rates still lag behind those of boys. The total net enrollment rate for boys for 1997 was over half (56.3%); in contrast, the total net enrollment rate was less than half (40.7%) for girls. The net enrollment rates for girls decreased more dramatically than those for boys with each additional level (Table 2.10).

Access and Enrollment in Jiri

Generally, boys and girls in remote communities located in the mountains have very poor access to schools, and enrollment in the mountain area schools tends to be low (Sibbons 1999). For example, in 1997, girls made up only 37.1%, 32.1%, and 29.0% of the total enrollment for primary, lower secondary, and secondary levels, respectively, in the Central Mountain Region. For that same year, girls were only 34.3%, 31.6%, and 29.4% of the total enrollment for

Setting the Context

the same levels, respectively, in Dolakha District (MOE 1997).[22] Distance to schools has been a critical issue in Jiri VDC. For example, in the remote area of Ward 1, there was only one primary school (the H School) at the time of this study, and it was an hour's walk from the Lamosangu-Jiri Road. Furthermore, the nearest lower secondary school and higher secondary school were both over two hours away by foot. The head teacher of a school in Ward 2 reported that the lower secondary school was "just too far away."

Those students who were enrolled often found themselves in very crowded classrooms. In the country as a whole, where facilities are insufficient, classes are often held outdoors (Upadhyay 1990). At the H School in Jiri, for instance, the Class 1 teacher regularly elected to conduct class outside, due to the large number of students enrolled in Class 1 at that school.[23] In terms of gender, the boys outnumbered the girls in nine out of 10 Jiri VDC schools in 1999–2000 (Table 2.11).

Table 2.11. Enrollment Numbers by Gender in Ten Jiri VDC Government Schools, 1999–2000

Alias	Type of School/ Classes (grades) Offered	No. of Students Enrolled	No. of Girls Enrolled	No. of Boys Enrolled
H	Primary (1–5)	124	44	80
SP	Primary (1–5)	137 *	49	88
MS	Primary (1–4)	138	58	80
B	Primary (1–5)	74	29	45
JW	Primary (1–5)	85	39	46
Ch	Primary (Nursery-3)	57	22	35
Sh	Primary (Nursery/1–5)	95	33	62
ST	Primary (1–5)	129	58	71
D	Lower Secondary (nursery-8)	446	242	204
J	Higher Secondary School (1–12)	816 **	343	473

Source: Interviews with Jiri VDC Government School Head Teachers, 1999–2000.
Notes:
* The head teacher explained that they often "fix" the registration books for the government in terms of enrollment numbers because they only get one teacher per 45 students.
** Enrollment number for Classes 1–10 only.

The D School, where in 1999–2000, 242 girls were enrolled compared with 204 boys, had received local and district-wide praise for its high numbers of girls enrolled. However, interviews and observations revealed that many of the boys living in the market area of the D School (sons of the bazaar merchants and shopkeepers) attended private schools in Jiri VDC, which might have accounted for lower numbers of boys in that particular government school.

Private Schools

The Nepalese government encouraged privatization of education in the Seventh Development Plan (1985–1990), and the 1990s and early 2000s saw an expansion in the number of independent primary schools as well as private higher education institutions. These private schools have tended to cater to the wealthy Nepalese, who can afford the private school tuition. Elite, affluent families who live in Kathmandu and in towns have sent their children to private schools, intensifying the poor/rich, rural/urban dichotomy.

Sibbons (1998) explains that boys are more likely to be offered the opportunity to study at a private school than are girls, stemming from a variety of reasons which include perceptions of personal security, attitudes toward the value of education, and preferences for the use of marginal household cash incomes. While many residents in Jiri could not afford to send their children or child to a private school, most residents believed the government schools were poor in quality; for them, sending their child, particularly their son, to a private school was an ideal.

Persistence through the Educational System

An equally formidable challenge is persistence in the schooling process once students are enrolled. In regard to gender, the number of girls in Nepal who drop out, as well as those who repeat, has been notable. In 1996, only 34.8% of girls in Class 1 were promoted to Class 2, while 41.2% repeated, and 24% dropped out (Table 2.12). For some class levels (e.g., Classes 3, 4, 6, and 9) in 1996, girls were promoted at a slightly higher rate than the boys, and girls had a lower percentage of dropouts than did boys in Classes 3, 4, 6, 8, and 9 for the same academic year.

It should be noted that for 1996 dropout rates, girls and boys were nearly even for Class 2 but in Classes 3 and 4, almost twice as many boys dropped out. This might have been due to boys leaving government schools to attend private schools or dropping out to herd livestock. For Class 5 in the same year, more girls dropped out of school than did boys. This may be explained as a factor of parents deciding to arrange daughters' marriages at that time. The UNDP offers the following explanations for the low

Setting the Context 47

participation rates in Nepal: housework burden of children, irregularity of school operation, income poverty, physical distance to schools, low perceived relevance of education, caste and ethnic discrimination, and neglect of mother-tongue in school (UNDP 1999). As stressed in Chapter One, an examination of school participation and persistence, however, is incomplete without considering the existing gender constraints within the gendered institutions of home and school. These socially constructed gender constraints might have not only discouraged girls from participating in school but also impeded girls' persistence in schooling once they were enrolled.

Table 2.12. Promotion, Repetition and Dropout Rates for Classes 1–10 (1996)

	Promotion			Repetition			Dropout		
	Girls (%)	Boys (%)	Total (%)	Girls (%)	Boys (%)	Total (%)	Girls (%)	Boys (%)	Total (%)
Class (Grade)									
1	34.8	35.5	35.2	41.2	42.0	41.7	24.0	22.5	23.1
2	68.8	72.1	70.8	26.4	23.4	24.6	4.8	4.4	4.6
3	73.6	71.1	72.1	21.1	18.8	19.7	5.3	10.1	8.2
4	71.4	69.6	70.4	21.6	20.0	20.6	6.9	10.4	9.0
5	60.9	65.4	63.6	22.3	20.7	21.3	16.8	13.9	15.1
6	72.3	71.8	72.0	20.6	18.2	19.1	7.1	10.0	8.9
7	76.1	80.5	78.8	17.7	16.2	16.8	6.2	3.4	4.4
8	71.1	72.7	72.1	25.8	21.7	23.3	3.1	5.6	4.7
9	72.9	70.0	71.0	21.1	17.6	18.9	6.1	12.4	10.1
10	**	**	**	22.8	17.7	19.6	**	**	**

Source: Statistics Section, Ministry of Education (MOE) 1997.

EDUCATIONAL QUALITY IN JIRI

Quality of education has a significant impact on parents' commitment to education and on children's participation in schooling. When asked about the current issues in Jiri's educational system, the Jiri VDC Chair replied, "There are so many physical discomforts [that] exist in the school." The Chair mentioned lack of toilets, water, and furniture at the schools. Like many schools in the rural areas of Nepal (Shrestha 1990), classrooms in Jiri were most often small and dark with earthen floors and few windows. From my perspective, the classrooms seemed sparse. Because there was no electricity in any of the schools studied, windows, without glass, provided the only source of light, and cold wind blew through them during the winter months, much to the discomfort of students and teachers. Children sat in cramped rows of wooden benches. At every school observed in Jiri, there was a dearth of instructional materials.

Poor physical facilities may also adversely affect the instructional quality in schools at all levels, which in turn, affects student achievement. Further, inadequate instructional facilities, as well as insufficient materials, may negatively affect the morale of both the teachers and the students. These environmental factors, combined with the substantial distance often required to access education, present enormous barriers to the quality of education.

The national curriculum has set standards and defined the scope and sequence of teaching-learning activities. Teachers have rarely been involved in the formation of the various level curricula. Missing in the process of curriculum development has been a component for field-testing the curriculum, which involves teachers, head teachers, other specialists, and students themselves. Lack of clarity and specificity in curriculum affects the quality of textbooks. Both curricula and textbooks in Nepal have typically been found to be outdated; textbooks have tended to portray men and women in stereotypical roles. A lack of pre-testing of textbooks has adversely affected the quality and usefulness of textbooks at all levels.

Another constraint affecting the quality of Jiri VDC education identified by the VDC Chair included lack of regular attendance of the teachers and insufficient teacher preparedness. A majority of teachers in Nepal were untrained with the greatest problem being at the lower secondary level. Less than a third of the lower secondary teachers had been trained (Table 2.13).

Overall, less than half of the teachers in Nepal had had training. Further, those who were trained often implemented the lecture or "telling" method of imparting knowledge and skills, which limited student involvement and

Setting the Context 49

Table 2.13. Trained and Untrained Teachers in Nepal (1997)

	Primary (1–5)	Lower Secondary (6–8)	Secondary (9–10)	Total (1–10)
Total Teachers	91464	20641	16494	128599
Total Trained	42039	6411	7743	56193
Percentage of Total Trained	46.0	31.1	46.9	43.7

Source: Statistics Section, Ministry of Education (MOE) 1997.

Table 2.14. Trained and Untrained Teachers in Jiri (1999–2000)

	Primary (1–5)	Lower Secondary (6–8)	Secondary (9–10)	Total (1–10)
Total Teachers	28	14	19	61
Total Trained	13	5	12	30
Percentage of Total Trained	46.4	35.7	63.2	49.2

Source: Head Teacher Interview and School Observations, Jiri, 1999–2000.

participation and diminished opportunity to develop analytical skills and independent learning. Chanting and rote memorization predominated.

In 1999–2000, less than half of the total teachers in Jiri VDC government schools had had some training (Table 2.14). Yet compared with the 1997 percentages at the national levels (Table 2.13), Jiri VDC was ahead, particularly at the lower secondary and secondary levels.

Though professional support to teachers for improving classroom instruction has been a rarity in Nepal, Jiri VDC's government, especially the Council and Chair of 1999–2000, made concerted efforts to reach out to teachers in Jiri. For example, in 1999, the VDC enlisted a British volunteer and a local (Jirel) counterpart to conduct primary teacher training. After meeting with me on several occasions to plan and discuss how gender sensitivity or awareness might be incorporated into the training, the two trainers incorporated gender awareness, behavior, and use of materials into subsequent training workshops.

CONCLUSIONS

Important to the research findings and analyses is an understanding of the context in which the research took place. General information about

Nepal and its educational system, as well as the geographical, social and economic profiles of the research site, provide a context for analyzing gender constructions at home and school in Jiri. At the macro level, Nepal, as one of the most impoverished nations in the world, has had very few resources for improving its educational system. Financially and program-wise, Nepal has been heavily dependent on foreigner donors and loans in order to address issues of quality and gender. At the time of this study, the quality of education and the extent of gender inequality were affected by a matrix of interacting factors: region (including the urban/rural divide); socio-cultural aspects such as ethnicity, religion, language, and caste; economics; and politics. The inequitable distribution of resources in the provision of schools, teacher training, and educational materials were mirrored in the situation of Jiri's educational system. Further, the extent to which individual students were able to access and persist in the existing educational system depended on the gendered nature of all other social institutions in Nepal.

Chapter Three
Telling the Story: An Overview of the Research Design

This research project implemented a qualitative research design and methodology in order to reach an in-depth understanding of the social phenomena of gender inequality. Three objectives guided this research:

- To examine the social construction of gender within the gendered institutions of family and school, through interviews eliciting attitudes and behavior of community members, parents/guardians, teachers, and head teachers in Jiri.
- To investigate gendered behavior and interaction in classroom and school settings through direct observations and interviews.
- To examine the consequences of gender constraints through observations and interviews in school and home settings.

This chapter begins with a discussion of the theoretical assumptions underlying the research and the relevance of the case study method for understanding the particular context of this study. I next present the research questions that guided the inquiry. Then, I explain my means of entry into the community and field orientation, including the hiring and training of research assistants and selecting focus schools and interviewees. In a discussion of methodology, I explain how a triangulation of data collection methods enhanced the research objectives. Finally, I discuss the methods of data analysis employed.

THEORETICAL ASSUMPTIONS AND THE QUALITATIVE CASE STUDY METHOD

If gender is socially constructed, as feminist theories suggest, then investigating and collecting data on the attitudes and experiences of the people of Jiri offers excellent insight into their behavior and institutions beyond enrollment numbers alone. Christine Williams insists that a researcher must ask herself or himself: "What can the insights and experiences of this particular group tell us about the general theoretical problem before us?" (1991:239). How and to what effect was gender inequality maintained in the social institutions of the family and education in Jiri? Going back to real people in concrete situations and to their descriptions of their experiences brings light to the social organization and processes that underlie everyday life (Smith 1979).

Using feminist theories as a guide, this project drew on case study research. Sharan Merriam explains that "case study research, and in particular qualitative case study, is an ideal design for understanding and interpreting observations of educational phenomena" (1988:2). An in-depth study of a specific group can illuminate social phenomena that theories suggest are experienced in the wider society (Williams 1991). According to Feagin, Orum, & Sjoberg (1991), fundamental lessons are conveyed by the case study. First, it permits the grounding of observations and concepts about social action and social structures in natural settings studied at close hand. This project grounds an understanding of the social process of gender inequality in a very real and specific setting. Second, the case study method provides information from a number of sources and through multiple research techniques over a period of time. It permits a more holistic study of complex social networks, social action, and social meanings. This study reveals not only the complexities of Jiri society's construction of roles of women and men, girls and boys, and beliefs about them, but also gives an understanding of the real life impacts of such beliefs and constructions. Studying the complexities of social meanings offers a sense of people's motives that lead to specific decisions and outcomes regarding education. This awareness enables the development of claims as to how personal as well as collective lives have been defined and created in the Nepalese context.

Throughout this project, I remained committed to implementing feminist methodologies, grounding my research in the lives of study participants, particularly women and girl participants. While my interpretation and application of feminist methods is informed by postcolonial feminists' and Third World feminists' critiques of Western liberal feminist research in Third World contexts,[1] the meanings associated with feminist methods are vast and shaped by broadly shared perceptions about their worth and application in particular fields. Feminist researchers typically identify gender as the key point of analysis for effecting social change with scholarship and applied research.

For me, "feminist research methods" implies taking a critical look at existing patriarchal norms and addressing social inequalities by linking activism, scholarship, and valuing "everyday knowledge" (Collins 1991).

Telling the Story 53

This means resisting the elitist power structures traditionally associated with research, which typically maintain divisions between those *leading* studies and those *being* studied. In other words, instead of asking, "What do I see these women doing?" feminist methodologists would ask, "What do these women see themselves doing?" Feminist methodologies are grounded in a notion of struggle and solidarity with women around the world, and individuals' standpoints and lived experiences drive feminist research projects. I once saw a poster that read: "If you came to help me, you can go home again. But if you see my struggle as part of your own survival, then perhaps, we can work together–Australian Aborigine artist and activist Lilla Watson." My intention in this research project was to link my own struggles with those of my study participants.

Feminist methods most commonly embrace triangulated qualitative approaches, using in-depth interviews, participant observation, and other components of ethnographic work. By prioritizing these methods over quantitative approaches, I valued the depth of data and relationships over the number of responses gathered, and relied on induction analysis rather than deductive processes. This emphasis on qualitative methods is evident throughout feminist research. *But what makes a particular method or methods feminist?* A *feminist* methodology distinguishes itself from related fields through the intended outcomes of its research; that is, the redress of power imbalances and the facilitation of enhanced quality of life, especially for women and girls, through the bridging of scholarship, activism, and everyday knowledge. Thus, my plan was to put "feminist ideology into practice" (Fish 2006). Through my studies of feminist scholarship and applied research practices, I designed this research project with the following goal in mind: to work with community members and contribute to the improvement of individuals' lives in this particular community.

RESEARCH QUESTIONS

Research questions fell into two categories: those related to family and community, and those related to school and classrooms. The questions concerned four groups of respondents: (1) community members; (2) parents/guardians; (3) head teachers and teachers; and (4) students. The following questions guided the inquiry on gender construction related to education:

Family/Community

(1) How was gender constructed in the family and community, and what processes of gender led to such social constructions?

(2) How did family/community practices of gender constrain or bolster girl students in comparison to boy students in terms of access, participation, and achievement in school?

A more specific set of sub-questions focused on attitudes, values, and behavior reflecting gender constructions among parents/guardians and community members:

1. What were parents'/guardians' attitudes and behavior towards their daughters' and sons' attendance, participation, and success in schools?
2. What were community member's attitudes and behavior towards girls' and boys' attendance, participation, and success?

Schools: Head Teachers

(1) How was gender constructed in the school? In what ways were schools gendered institutions and what processes led to gendered institutions?
(2) How did these processes of gender constrain or bolster girl versus boy students' access, participation, and achievement in school?

A set of specific sub-questions was designed in regard to attitudes, values, and behavior that reflected specific gender constructions among head teachers:

1. What were head teachers' attitudes and behavior towards boy students' and girl students' attendance, participation, and success in schools?
2. Did the school facilities affect student attendance, participation, and success in school by gender?
3. What curriculum was implemented in the schools and how were girls and women and boys and men portrayed in the curriculum, instructional materials, and textbooks?
4. What kinds of programs, if any, were in existence to increase girls' enrollment, participation, and success in schools? To what extent did these strategies to increase girls' enrollment in schools meet their objectives?

Schools: Teachers

(1) How was gender constructed in the classrooms and what processes of gender led to such social constructions?

Telling the Story

(2) Did existing processes of gender in the classroom constrain or bolster girl students in comparison to boy students in terms of participation and achievement in school?
(3) What were the gender dynamics between teachers and students in classroom settings?
(4) What were teachers' attitudes and behavior towards boy students' and girl students' attendance, participation, and success in the classrooms?

Students

(1) Did students perceive gender being constructed at home, in the community, and at school? How did this vary between girl students and boy students?
(2) Did girl students, in comparison to boy students, perceive processes of gender as either constraining or bolstering their access, participation, and achievement in school?
(3) In what ways did students resist socially constructed gender constraints? How did this vary by gender?

METHODOLOGY

This section provides an overview of the methodology implemented for this research project. Issues such as power differentials in the field, entry into the community and getting oriented in the field, working with the research assistants, selecting the study schools and interviewees, as well as the various data collection methods implemented are presented. The case study method, issues of validity and reliability, and the limitations of the methodology are also discussed.

Power Relations

Carmen Diana Deere, in Diane Wolf's *Feminist Dilemmas in Fieldwork*, explains power relations in fieldwork as "the unequal power hierarchy between the researcher and those researched in defining the research agenda, the research process, and the research outcome" (1996:viii). Wolf's book was instrumental in my exploration of feminist issues in doing fieldwork. I agree with Wolf's observation that fieldwork is particularly challenging for feminists when the research focus is on women in the Third World, which "entails 'studying down,' that is, studying women who are poor, powerless, and marginalized" (1996:ix). Most, if not all, the women and men I studied were poor, powerless, and marginalized in the context of the gendered social order in Nepal and in the rural context of Jiri. Thus, it became all the more important that I develop a research project grounded in individuals' lives, prioritizing their stories and valuing their everyday knowledge in my attempts to problematize the social construction of gender in the Jiri community. I needed to remain cognizant of the varied individual standpoints in that particular socio-historical context.

As a feminist researcher, I needed to acknowledge power differentials between the research participants and myself. Not only were there power differentials embedded in my race, ethnicity, social class, and educational standing, but as a Western researcher attempting to implement feminist methods in a "Third World" context, my nationality also added another vector of power asymmetry. I needed to acknowledge that it was I who constructed topics of inquiry, it was I who maintained power throughout fieldwork, and it was I who ultimately benefited from the research process. I also needed to understand that as a Western researcher, I had the means to undertake the fieldwork in the first place.[2]

DEVELOPMENT OF THE RESEARCH STUDY IDEA

Power relations shape every stage of the research process, with the researcher holding the reins of power. This begins with the formulation of the project idea. Diane Wolf reflects, "Despite my good intentions, I was making a situation for myself based on the structures of poverty and gender inequality" (1996:x). From conceptualization to writing, I, admittedly, have done the same. I designed a study fueled by a research agenda ultimately benefiting me, not the people I studied. As a result of my efforts, I was awarded a graduate degree. I knew even from the onset of this project that very little, if any, change would come into the lives of those with whom I worked and studied. As hard as it is to accept, most feminist studies end up benefiting the researcher more than those studied (Wolf 1996). It was my hope that the type of research I implemented and how I presented what I learned in the field would have more of an impact than simply fulfilling my own goals.

ASSUMPTIONS BROUGHT TO THE FIELD

Grappling with one's assumptions is a part of the process of attempting to understand the world in which study participants live. Garfinkel (1967) noted that some understandings are only progressively realized through continued engagement in the field. Davison (1996) explains that everyone involved in the research project (from the researcher to the research assistants to the research participants) comes to the project with a set of assumptions about the other(s) that may or may not turn out to be accurate. Differences in age, cultural orientation, race or ethnicity, class, and marital status feed into these assumptions.

As fieldworkers, we enter the field as more than researchers. Our identities and life experiences shape the political and ideological stances we take in our research (Kleinman & Copp 1993). Part of examining my assumptions was being keenly aware of my own "positionality"—including my gender, age, race, nationality, and ideological orientation (Davison 1996:14). Considering who I was (a white, middle class, American woman in her late 20s) and what I believed (a multicultural feminist ideology) was imperative when I did this fieldwork. Otherwise, I might not have seen how I shaped the story. First and foremost, I needed to be cognizant of the fact that I brought my Western perspective to the field. Even though I had been to Nepal three times prior, I brought my own biases to the field about food, lodging, cleanliness, and dress. While I wanted to respect local customs, I had the privilege of deciding how I dressed, what I ate, how clean I wanted to be, and where I would sleep at night. In essence, I had relative control over my space; I had relative control over my body.

ENTRY INTO THE COMMUNITY AND GETTING ORIENTED IN THE FIELD

Through earlier visits and prior research conducted in Nepal (1992, 1994, 1996), I had a general understanding of the Nepali culture, language, the environment and the system of education. Further, I was not perceived as a complete stranger to the community of Jiri, having conducted a preliminary survey there in 1996. For my 1999–2000 field study, I made my initial field contacts from the United States in the year preceding the project. This was essential to my ability to transition into the field context with an established knowledge base and an understanding of important cultural nuances.

Upon arrival in Nepal in October 1999, the Research Center for Educational Innovation and Development (CERID) at Tribhuvan University in Kathmandu offered me a research affiliation. When I arrived in Jiri three weeks later, I wrote a letter stating the purpose of my research to the Jiri VDC Chair and then met with him to answer questions and become acquainted. He subsequently approved the project and later sent notification letters to all the schools in the VDC, requesting that they offer assistance. In the initial phase of the research, I was very fortunate to meet a British volunteer and her Nepali counterpart, who, together, developed workshops and trainings for primary teachers in Jiri. They were helpful in inviting me to go along on their site visits and introduced me to the head teachers and teachers at the various schools.

I was confident that my previous contact with villagers in Jiri would facilitate my reentry into the community and that my personality would lend itself to building trust and openness between the participants and me. However, I needed to be careful so as to not take things for granted. I needed to make my role as a researcher very clear, and I needed to maintain a keen sense of my positionality. That is, in conducting observations and in-depth interviews, I needed to remain aware of my gender, race, country of origin, socio-economic status, marital and parental status, educational background, age, and ideology as a feminist researcher and activist. As an ongoing practice, I had to acknowledge and accept the power differentials that existed between the research subjects and me.

Partnership in the Field

My partner Chris and I decided to go into the field together. We knew that it would be challenging to our relationship, but we also wanted to share the experience and spend those nine months together. We also decided to present ourselves as a married couple, although we were not married at that time.[3] I should note that my ability to make such a decision and then carry it through was, again, a privilege of my positionality.

Chris played an integral role in this research project as he has a background in sociology and anthropology. He was able to offer insightful commentaries and feedback about the data collected and the greater community in which we had immersed ourselves. He was a tremendous source of emotional and intellectual support for me, but he also provided friendship, camaraderie, and good jokes for the research team, which consisted of two Nepali research assistants and myself.

People in Jiri readily accepted him as my "husband." At the same time, he independently made friends with community members and their children soon after our arrival. And, perhaps most importantly, he proved to be a "gender trouble maker" himself, as he was often seen at our homestay family's house, washing clothes and sweeping the front step, as I, "his wife," left to go out to collect data.

Chris devoted much of his down time to some writing projects he had planned to finish while in Nepal. Most days, Chris would walk down to the bazaar to drink coffee and write in a local restaurant or tea shop. This different kind of "work" puzzled many of the older men in the village who knew he was married and wondered why Chris spent so much time doing something that did not look like "work," that is, something that did not require labor and sweat. Chris would set out for the bazaar at mid-morning with a backpack slung over his shoulder. The bazaar was nearly two miles away. On the path, he would be frequently questioned about where he was going. Though Chris' Nepali was good, he had troubling explaining how reading and writing could be conceived of as "work." Furthermore, he sensed from a few Nepalese men that they regarded his explanations as frivolous or weak. In this way, he caused more "gender trouble."

Research Assistants

I had hoped to hire and train local research assistants for help with interviews and observations. I had also hoped to hire both women and men research assistants and assign them to interview respondents of their same gender. After intensive interviewing, the two highly educated women from Kathmandu I hired had qualifications that surpassed all other candidates. No men candidates who possessed the necessary credentials to work on this project were available.[4]

I trained the two research assistants (RAs) in specific data collection methods for this project. The training focused on interview probing, sensitivity, informed consent procedures and confidentiality, as well as basic methods and guidelines for qualitative research. The RAs, in turn, helped me further develop my cross-cultural and language skills. These skills were critical in terms of negotiating the politics of daily life.

While I designed, planned and implemented the project and analyzed the data, the two research assistants were integral to the data collection for this research project. Either with me or on their own, the two research assistants conducted interviews, collected life history narratives, observed families at student home visits, observed interactions in classrooms, and administered surveys. They also transcribed and translated all collected data. Thus, wherever in the text I put forth "we," I am referring to the research team: the two research assistants and myself.

Consent Procedures

From the beginning, we informed and explained the purpose of the study to all of the teachers, head teachers, students, parents/guardians, and community members who were active participants in this project. We gained written consent from each active participant (and from their parents/guardians, if participants were under-age) before proceeding with an interview or observation.[5] It was important to explain the benefits and potential liabilities of participating in this research. Particularly, we needed to explain how the research goal of wanting to come to an understanding of day-to-day activities and life in Jiri differed from wanting to evaluate or judge the people of Jiri and their lives.

A research assistant read the consent form to each participant in Nepali, and then if the person chose to continue, she or he signed the consent form in agreement. Signing a document is considered very formal in Nepali culture and is rarely done. Therefore, if a participant was hesitant to sign the document, but was willing to make a verbal agreement (recorded on audio-cassette), we understood and respected her or his wishes. Further, some participants were non-literate; in these cases, her or his verbal agreement was documented and recorded on audio-cassette. As a researcher in a fluid cultural context, I needed to be flexible. In the end, only one or two individuals whose participation we solicited refused to participate.

Most of the interviewees, however, wanted to know why we were interested in speaking with them. Many people, especially the school administrators, wanted to know what I planned to do with the information I obtained. Others wanted to know how they might benefit from participating in the study (*i.e.,* what kind of financial reward they would receive). Lofland and Lofland (1984) insist that this is a trade-off: People who are tolerating an observer/interviewer in their midsts have every right to ask, "What do I get in return?" With each participant, we reviewed the potential benefits and risks in their participating. We also emphasized that confidentiality was of the highest priority. To preserve confidentiality, each participant has been given a pseudonym in this book.

Participatory Learning Action (PLA)

In order to gain a better understanding of the central issues that concern the people of Jiri, as well as to develop a rapport with the community, I initiated some preliminary data collection methods, including Participatory Learning Action (PLA) strategies and interviews with community leaders, at the beginning of the research project. PLA research strategies draw on focus group interviews and needs assessments tools. I introduced these activities early in the research process to assist in developing other data collection tools. The PLA research strategies for this project were loosely structured to elicit discussion about community needs and the gender gap in school. Fairly homogenous groups (by age and by gender) of approximately five to eight participants were asked to participate in a series of PLA strategies such as social mapping, needs assessment matrices, and time allocation charts.[6] We also facilitated focus group discussions with these same groups. Ideally, these processes helped link the participants' individual interpretations of the problems to the broader context, including the structural conditions of their social reality (Maguire 1987). Further, the PLA strategies used helped me compile questions and themes to be investigated.

Figure 3.1. Social Mapping Exercise. Photograph by author.

Interviews with Community Leaders

For the same reasons, I purposively selected and interviewed eight Jiri VDC community leaders. Building relationships with community leaders through these interviews not only helped me to gain entry into the community, but also gave me access to information about the socio-cultural, economic, political, and topographical context of Jiri and its educational system.[7] Additionally, these meetings frequently provided me with access to government records. Therefore, initiating PLA strategies and conducting interviews with community leaders at the beginning of the project helped me to gather and analyze qualitatively the central issues that concerned the people of Jiri. They also fostered my (and the researcher assistants') gaining entry into the community as I built relationships with community members and leaders through these procedures.

Collection of School and Other Government Records

To supplement and cross-check the data collected through interviews and observations, I also gathered statistical data on the setting and participants, as well as other documents. These other documents included school records of enrollment and attendance; school testing results; demographic makeup of school staff and students; copies of textbooks and curriculum; government school evaluations; and Jiri VDC demographic, economic, and historical records. I also researched the historical context of the setting through various documents collected.

Selection of Schools

My plan involved focusing on two schools while also collecting some data and making observations at each school in Jiri. I purposively selected the D School[8] as one focus school because it was located in the bustling market area of Jiri VDC and was the center of the most economically productive and populated ward. This school was one of only two schools with Pre-kindergarten (Nursery) Class through Class 8. The other nine primary schools in Jiri VDC were limited to Pre-kindergarten Class through Class 5. The D school had a higher enrollment of girls than boys. Further, at the time of this project, the D School enrolled students from a wide variety of Hindu castes and other religions, as well as socio-economic backgrounds.

I selected the J School as a focus school because it was located in a heavily populated ward with equally wide diversity. This school was the only school in Jiri that offered classes up to the School Leaving Certificate (SLC) level with a 10+2 program. Some students walked for two hours everyday to go to this school. Other students lived in distant villages and stayed in hostels in Jiri to attend this school.

Drawing students from a wide variety of ethnic groups and religions, these two schools offered a good cross-section of the entire community. I chose to observe Class 5 at the D School for several reasons: Both women and men teachers taught at this level, the class size was manageable for observations (the average class size was 40 students in attendance), and the students were old enough to interact with the teacher and with each other to effectively code and analyze their gendered interactions. Further, there were more girl students enrolled in Class 5 than boys.

I chose to observe students enrolled in Class 9 at the J School for a variety of reasons as well. The students enrolled in this class came from very divergent backgrounds—all of the ethnic groups and Hindu castes in Jiri VDC were represented in this class. Further, Class 9 students ranged in ages from 14 to 22. Unlike Class 5, Class 9 had an average class size of 80 students, yet the school did not split Class 9 into two sections, as they did with Class 7, which was even larger than Class 9. I wanted to observe how the teachers of Class 9 managed such a large class size. Furthermore, Class 9 is a pivotal year for Nepali students as they prepare to take the SLC exam the following year.

The faculty and staff at the two focus schools were very accommodating. They made sure we (the research assistants and I) were introduced to the student body as well as the faculty and that everyone knew what we

Telling the Story 63

were doing. The head teachers at these two schools requested that everyone do their best to help us. The school staff helped us to arrange student home site visits, interviews with focus class teachers (Classes 5 and 9), and classroom observations.

In addition to on-going observations at the focus schools, we also spent a day at each of the other nine government schools in Jiri VDC, except for one.[9] All of the schools we visited complied with our need for observations and interview requests. The schools' faculty and staff were very accommodating and welcoming. Many participants seemed honored to take part in the project.[10]

Selection of the Interviewees

For this study, interviewees from five separate sub-groups were selected. These sub-groups included: teachers, head teachers, community members, parents/guardians of students selected for home visits, and students (Table 3.1).

Table 3.1. Interviewees

Type of Interview	Who was Sought for the Interviews	No. of Expected Interviews	No. of Actual Interviews
Teacher Interviews	All the teachers from the two focus classes (Classes 5 and 9) at the two focus schools (entire population)	Class 5 teachers (N=7) Class 9 teachers (N=5) Total (N=12)	N=12 (W=2) (M=10)
Head Teacher Interviews	All the head teachers at each of the government schools (entire population)	N=11	N=10 (W=2) (M=8)
Community Member Interviews	Community members from each of the nine wards (purposive sampling)	20 women and 20 men from each of the nine wards Total (N=360)	**Ward 1:** N=12 (W=4) (M=8) **Ward 2:** N=39 (W=21) (M=18) **Ward 3:** N=41 (W=20) (M=21) **Ward 4:** N=37 (W=21) (M=16) **Ward 5:** N=41 (W=21) (M=20)

(continued)

Table 3.1. Interviewees (continued)

Type of Interview	Who was Sought for the Interviews	No. of Expected Interviews	No. of Actual Interviews
Community Member Interviews (continued)			Ward 6: N=34 (W=16) (M=18)
			Ward 7: N=43 (W=23) (M=20)
			Ward 8: N=41 (W=21) (M=20)
			Ward 9: N=40 (W=20) (M=20)
			Total: N=328 (W=167) (M=161)
Life History Interviews	Selected women, older girls, men, and older boys from each of the nine wards (purposive sampling)	1 woman or older girl and 1 man or older boy from each of the nine wards (N=18)	Ward 1: N=1 (W=1) (M=0)
			Ward 2: N=1 (W=0) (M=1)
			Ward 3: N=2 (W=1) (M=1)
			Ward 4: N=2 (W=1) (M=1)
			Ward 5: N=1 (W=1) (M=0)
			Ward 6: N=1 (W=0) (M=1)
			Ward 7: N=3 (W=2) (M=1)
			Ward 8: N=4 (W=3) (M=1)
			Ward 9: N=2 (W=1) (M=1)
			Total: N=17 (W=10) (M=7)
Student Home Visit Interviews	Randomly selected students from Classes 5 and 9 at two focus schools and their families (probability sampling)	5 girl students and 5 boy students from each of the two classes (N=20) and their parents/guardians (N=40)	Class 5 students: N=10 (G=5) (B=5)
			Class 9 students: N=10 G=5) (B=5)
			Parent/guardian total: N=38

Within the schools, I interviewed all of the head teachers at each of the 10 government schools observed. In addition to collecting some data and making observations at these 10 schools, I conducted ongoing observations of two classes, Class 5 at the D School and Class 9 at the J School. I also interviewed the Class 5 and Class 9 teachers (N=12) at these focus schools. From these interviews, I hoped to glean teachers' and head teachers' attitudes and behavior towards girl students' and boy students' attendance, participation, and success in the classrooms.

Ten head teachers from throughout Jiri VDC were interviewed to ascertain how they contributed to constructing, maintaining, and reproducing gender within the schools. Most of these head teachers were men (80%), and half, including the two women head teachers, were of the Hindu caste Chhetri. Four of the head teachers interviewed were Jirel, the predominant ethnic group in Jiri VDC. Nine out of 10 reported having had some teacher training. These head teachers interacted with students not only as administrators, but also as teachers. All 10 taught at least one subject at their schools. Because they played an important leadership role for the staff and students within the schools they headed, we asked them similar questions to those posed to the community member and parent/guardian samples that addressed the social construction of gender.

To gain a better understanding of how gender was constructed and reinforced within the classroom, all seven of the Class 5 teachers and all five of the Class 9 teachers were interviewed. Of the total 12 teachers, only two were women. Seven teachers practiced Hinduism, four practiced Buddhism, and one, a Tamang man, practiced both Hinduism and Buddhism. Notably, there were more Hindu teachers than Buddhist teachers, yet the mountain region in which the Jiri Valley is located is predominately Buddhist. Of the seven Hindu teachers, two were Brahmin (the highest caste), two were Chhetri (2nd highest caste), and three were non-caste Hindus. Some of the teachers had limited educational backgrounds. Three of the teachers (one woman and two men) had only SLC pass education. Furthermore, whereas all of the head teachers had had some teacher training, four out of the 12 teachers interviewed had not had any training at all. Five said they had had "some government training."

For the community member interviewees, I used a combination of purposive and quota (non-probability) sampling, or what Wendy Luttrell describes as a "stratified, selective sampling" (1993:509). I selected interviewees with the intention of having a sample varied by gender, caste, race, region (ward), age, occupation, income, and educational level. A total of 328 community members were interviewed. From these interviews, I hoped to learn about community members' attitudes and behavior towards girls' and boys' academic potential as perceived by intelligence and their participation and success in school and how these attitudes and behaviors varied by gender of the interviewee.

As a separate sample, all of the parents/guardians living in the homes of the students selected were interviewed (N=38) during student home visits. From the interviews in this sample, I also intended to establish a portrait of the overarching attitudes and behavior towards daughters' and sons' attendance, participation, and success in schools and how these factors varied by gender of the interviewee. In order to elicit context and understand perceptions of gender constructed in both the home and at school, we also conducted life history interviews with 17 individuals. I was eager to uncover and explore, in-depth, individuals' own experiences. Like the community member interviewees, I used a combination of purposive and quota (non-probability) sampling to select the life history interviewees, with the intention of having a sample that varied by gender, caste, race, region (ward), age, occupation, income, and educational level.

For student home visit interviews, I used informal probability sampling.[11] Ten students (five girls and five boys) from each of the focus schools were selected. In the student interviews, I was interested in learning how students perceived gender constructed at home, in the community, and at school. I hoped to learn how students perceived processes of gender as either constraining or bolstering their access, participation, and achievement in school, and how these perceptions varied by gender. I was also interested in understanding the ways in which students pushed or resisted gender constraints. Specifically, in my interviews with students, I asked the students questions pertaining to their attitudes, specifically attitudes toward intelligence by gender and preference for who should be educated by gender, as well as individual likes and dislikes of subjects and the best subject for students by gender. I also included questions to address their perceptions of educational and career aspirations, their use of time, and their thoughts regarding gender differences in attendance and persistence in school.

Of these students, eight were Jirel, the predominant ethnic group in Jiri VDC. Other ethnic groups represented in this student sample were Newar, Tamang, Sherpa, and Chhetri, Brahmin, and Biskokarma of the Hindu castes. In total, 11 students were Buddhist, and nine were Hindu, which was not reflective of Nepal's overall religious profile (86.5% Hindu and 7.8% Buddhist) but was representative of Jiri VDC. The average age of the Class 5 (at the D School) boy students selected was 13 years old, and the average age of the girl students was 15 years old. The average age of the Class 9 (J School) boy students was 17, and the average age for the girls was 16.[12]

Various factors prevented me from obtaining some of the sampling goals. For instance, I could not interview the head teacher of the C School for security reasons. In regard to the community member sample interviews, the remoteness of some wards prevented accessibility to some extent. A case in point was Ward 1, where we did not reach our sampling goal (N=40). With the rugged terrain and sparse population, finding people willing to be interviewed proved difficult. To a lesser extent, this was also true for Wards 2, 4, and 6. However, despite these limitations, the sample of community member interviewees still varied by gender, caste, race, region (ward), age, occupation, income, and educational level. Finding willing and able participants for the life history interview sample was also challenging for similar reasons of remoteness and distance (e.g., Wards 1, 2, 5, and 6), and we did not reach our goal of one woman or older girl and one man or older boy from each of the nine wards for a total of 18 life history interviews. Also, when arranging community member interviews and life history interviews, I found it difficult not having a phone where I could be reached. Sometimes I arranged our meetings ahead of time; other times we would just stop in (e.g., people's homes, stores, fields), with the hope of finding someone who was willing and able to participate in an interview.

Data Collection

Qualitative methods, including focused observations, oral interviews, and life narrative collection, which are often used in case study research, "seek to understand social action at a greater richness and depth and hence, seek to record such action through a more complex, nuanced, and subtle set of interpretive categories" than in quantitative methods (Feagin, Orum, & Sjoberg 1991:17). Qualitative methods typically provide rich descriptions. Because I was seeking in-depth data that illustrated the complex nuances of my topic, a qualitative approach was by far the most fitting for this study. Furthermore, as many of the people in this particular community were nonliterate, qualitative approaches provided a means for giving voice to the people of Jiri in a way otherwise unavailable in quantitative approaches. Collecting life history narratives, for example, was one way to capture the pasts of less literate and more marginalized groups whose histories may not otherwise be transcribed (Wolf 1996).

VALIDITY AND RELIABILITY

Qualitative data are considered to have greater validity, or in other words, are more likely than quantitative data to reflect accurately what happens in the social world (Williams 1991; Babbie 1995). One way to assess validity is to implement a triangulation of data collection methods. If the triangulation of methods yields the same data, then the data are most likely valid or accurate (Ragin 1994). Qualitative projects have often been critiqued for lacking reliability. Reliability is usually interpreted as the "ability to replicate the original study using the same research instrument to get the same result" (Feagin, Orum, & Sjoberg 1991:17). I implemented the following procedures to address the issue of reliability: (1) I maintained the same interview schedule—asking different people the same questions;[13] (2) I used a team of observers and interviewers—the same people carried out observations and the same people conducted interviews; and (3) I cross-checked data using a triangulation of methods—checking collected data with alternative and independent sources of information.

Unlike quantitative research, however, my research is not replicable in the sense that Feagin, Orum & Sjoberg (1991) describe. My race, gender, age, nationality, personal history, personality, and belief systems affected how I was received in the Jiri VDC community and Nepal, in general. My positionality determined what I sought, what I obtained, and what I considered important to note in my observations. Additionally, the study participants' perceptions of my history, personality and gender affected how they presented themselves to me. Such variables affect the study's potential to be replicated, as do variables within the community studied.

DATA COLLECTION METHODS

I had at my disposal a broad array of techniques to assess the nature of gender inequality as well as the motives and interests of Jiri community members. A variety of data collection methods were, more or less, implemented simultaneously. The data collection methods included direct observations of the focus school classrooms and content analysis of materials used in teaching Class 5 and Class 9; observations of the daily lives of students; structured interviews with community members, parents/guardians, teachers, school head teachers, and students; and collection of older girls and boys and adult women and men life narratives.[14] In this section, these data collection methods will be discussed in turn.

Direct Observations of School Classrooms and Content Analysis of Materials

The classroom-centered part of the research asked two primary questions: (1) Did educational curricula and textbooks convey what could be considered "traditional" Nepali messages about women's reproductive functions in the household and in the family or were the messages more gender equal? How were these messages conveyed? (2) Were girls taught to be passive and dependent or assertive in a classroom setting? Teachers who interact differently with boys and girls highlight the enormous energy that goes into creating gender differences based on presumed "natural" distinctions between girls and boys. Collecting data on the social construction of these perceived gender differences and their maintenance through the education system fostered an understanding of how and to what effect the process of gender inequality was reinforced and reproduced in schools.

We conducted intensive, all-day observations of two classes in two government schools two to three days a week, over a period of seven months. In addition, one-day observations were made in eight other government schools over a period of seven months. For their studies of schools in the USA, David Sadker and Myra Sadker[15] developed a classroom coding model for analyzing gender equality. Using the Sadkers' method, along with tools developed by Jean Davison for her observations of Malawi classrooms (Davison & Kanyuka 1990), I developed a coding plan for the rural Nepali classrooms observed. Teachers' interactions with individual students were counted and coded by gender, using two indicators of teacher interaction with students: One was frequency of times a teacher called on a student in an observation period,[16] and the other was teachers' responses to the students' answers—praise, criticism, acceptance, or remediation. This coding of not only the quantity of teacher-student interactions but also the quality of those interactions offered face validity[17] for the conclusions drawn in regard to the teachers' attention given to the students according to their gender.

Teacher-student interactions were coded on classroom observation response sheets. When a teacher called on a student or if a student asked the teacher a question,[18] it was marked on the coding sheet. An interaction was coded as praise when a teacher's comment was clearly identified as praise or positive reinforcement. Comments that indicated praise typically included "*Raamro*" ["good;" "very nice"]. Praise was determined not only by the content of the teacher's comment or response but also by nonverbal cues (e.g., facial expressions), as well as the intonation of the teacher's voice as the comment was expressed. For example, we would code an interaction as praise when the teacher said "*Thik!*" ["OK! or "All right!"] to the student because the teacher's voice was very enthusiastic or positive.

Approval was coded when a teacher offered a reaction that accepted a student's answer or behavior as appropriate or correct. Comments as "*Ho*" ["Yes, it is."] or "*Thik*" ["OK"] express acceptance and were coded as such. These comments implied approval, but not clearly and strongly stated as to be categorized as praise. Approval was most frequently coded in cases when teachers implied acceptance by moving on to another student after a student gave her or his answer. The intonation of the teacher's voice and the non-verbal expressions used by the teacher were important in determining whether a teacher's comment was coded as "praise" or "acceptance."

When a teacher noted or implied a deficiency in a student's answer or behavior, the response or comment was coded as remediation. In the case of remediation, a teacher did not accept the appropriateness or accuracy of a student answer or behavior. The teacher might have probed for another answer after the student gave an incorrect answer by asking "*Kina*?" ["Why?"] or "*Pheri Garnos*" ["Try again."]. Or, the teacher encouraged the student to sound the word out. At times, the teacher also specified the corrective action that should be taken. For example, the teacher may have said, "Turn around, and pay attention to your work." Comments of remediation were not so strong as actual and overt criticism. They did not involve explicit negative evaluation or the imposition of penalties. Important to distinguishing between remediation and criticism were, again, the intonation of the teacher's voice and the use of non-verbal expression. Criticism was coded for teachers' reactions that expressed strong disapproval. For example, a teacher might have exclaimed, "*Hoina*!" ["No! That is wrong!"]. Also, when a student was punished for misbehaving, the interaction was coded as criticism.

To provide evidence of the validity and reliability of the conclusions drawn by the researcher, a research assistant was trained to serve as a co-rater to code the teacher-student interactions according to the coding schema described above. After the training, I felt confident the research assistant understood the concepts related to the coding schema. To attain inter-rater reliability, the research assistant would generally have to place the teachers' statements in the same categories as I did.[19] The results of the coding process were positive in that clear patterns emerged in our coding. Although our coding response sheets were not exactly alike, reliability was established as 90% for each of the codes.[20] Given the relative consistency between the other coder (the research assistant) and myself, I felt sufficiently confident in the reliability of the coding schema to proceed with the data analysis.

We made every effort to minimize the extent to which we disrupted and otherwise intruded as non-participants in the classroom (Jorgensen 1989). Being unobtrusive proved to be a difficult endeavor, especially at first, as my light hair and skin color drew noticeable attention. Some students would spend the entire class period simply staring at me. Over time, they seemed to get used to the idea of my being there regularly, and their fascination (and subsequent distraction) dissipated over time.

Observations of the Daily Lives of Students

Dorothy Smith (1987) asserts that as sociological researchers, we must situate social actors within their everyday worlds and then problematize those everyday worlds. Observation of "ordinary" events and activities in the daily lives of students in Jiri was critical in understanding what these events and activities meant to each student and to their families. The meanings and significance of these daily actions to the participants shed light on the processes of maintaining and reproducing gender inequality.

To learn more about students' response to gendering processes within the household context, I randomly selected five girl and five boy students from each of the two classes at the two focus schools (N=20) to observe their home settings. During these home visits, we interviewed the student and both parents/guardians. We also observed the homestead structure and activities within the homestead, noting the student's interactions with family and friends, as well as responses to domestic chores and their demands. We visited each student and her/his family once on a prearranged Saturday. We chose to do our student home visits on Saturdays, as this was the day we would most likely find all family members at home.[21] We spent several hours at each homestead, observing and interviewing. All interviews were tape-recorded in Nepali and then transcribed and translated into English later that same day. Field notes of observations were also transcribed the same day.

Structured Interviews with Community Members, Parents/guardians, Teachers, Head Teachers, and Students

For each of these sub-populations, I crafted and implemented a formally structured schedule of interview questions. Questions were designed to address interviewees' attitudes and subsequent behavior towards education and how this varied by gender. Using a set of predetermined questions for each of the type of interviews, I elicited information about each respondent's thoughts, opinions, attitudes, and subsequent behavior regarding gender and education. I operated under the assumption that the respondents' thoughts were intricately related to their actions. Questions were designed to address the interviewees' meanings and interpretations of gender inequality.

Interviews ranged in length from 30 minutes to an hour and a half, with the average interview being one hour. We tried to make the interviews as convenient as possible for the interviewees, requesting that they tell us when and where they wanted to do the interview. Almost all of the interviews were conducted at the location chosen by the interviewee. The interviews took place in a variety of settings (e.g., people's homes, fields, places of work, teashops). We conducted these structured interviews at all times of the day and on every day except for Sunday (our project day off).We tried to interview individuals in a safe, quiet space. However, there was almost always some sort of distraction (e.g., a crying baby, curious onlookers coming up to touch us and the tape recorder, etc.). As we did with the home visit interviews, these interviews were tape-recorded in Nepali and then transcribed and translated into English later the same day.

Collecting Life Narratives of Older Girls and Boys and Adult Women and Men

Collecting life narratives of five students and 12 community members allowed for a comparison of 17 individuals' lives. In the course of these interviews, I was able to observe women and men, older girls and boys, in an environment outside the context of the schools. In some cases, I was able to meet their families and friends. This enabled me to better "elicit and contextualize the . . . educational experiences, views and values" (Luttrell 1993:508–509) of the life history interviewees. Sandra Harding (1986) suggests that understanding lives by means of a feminist exploration of individuals' experiences and oppressions offers a full and less distorted vision of knowledge. My goal was to facilitate the selected individual in recalling events from the past. Therefore, these interviews did not follow a structured list of questions, but rather, began with a list of open-ended questions that prompted discussion.

The life history interviews generally took place on Fridays. With a research assistant often acting as translator, I usually conducted life history interviews in the mornings or afternoons. Because of the length of these interviews,[22] we tried to be as accommodating as possible with scheduling the time and location. The life history narrators often chose to be interviewed at their homes. We placed emphasis on locations with minimal distractions and high levels of comfort so that each of the life history narrators would feel at ease. Yet, again, it was almost guaranteed that there would be at lease one interruption of some kind during the interview. These interviews were also tape-recorded and then transcribed and translated into English the same day. These taped transcriptions would later "become the basis for the written narrative account—the life history" (Davison 1996:16).

Data Analysis

Although data collection and analysis are often simultaneous activities in qualitative research (Locke, Spirduso, & Silverman 1993; Merriam 1988), the majority of the analysis took place after the data collection phase was completed. As Barrie Thorne explains,

Fieldwork involves extended witnessing and "sense-making;" it also takes shape, as sociological ethnographers finally have come to recognize, through the process of writing (1993:8).

After returning from the field, I set about the analytical task of uncovering both the meanings and the conditions that shaped the lives of the people of Jiri. The data central to the analysis in this study were the interview transcripts and the field notes from observations and interviews. Also important were collected written documents, such as school enrollment records. In my analysis, I treated each interview and each observation as its own text while also looking for themes and patterns that emerged. Glaser and Strauss' (1967) "grounded theory," which emphasizes inductive theoretical developments rather than logical deductive reasoning based on prior theoretical developments and hypothesis testing, informed the coding and analysis of field notes and interview transcripts.

ORGANIZING THE DATA

Qualitative methodologists (e.g., Charmaz 1983; Emerson, Fretz, & Shaw 1995; Lofland & Lofland 1984) whose work details the processes of inductive analysis influenced my coding and analysis. I started by separating, sorting, and organizing field notes and interview transcriptions into files. One set of files were my chronological files, in which I placed the field notes and interview transcriptions in chronological order. The descriptions of Jiri and collected records were also placed in the chronological files. I then sorted the data into another set of files, which served as my analytical files. For these files, I first organized and sorted the data by groups or roles (e.g., a file for teachers and a file for community members). Later, I further divided these folders according to specific meanings and patterns that emerged.

After organizing the files, I read through the data and focused on important questions such as: What is going on here? How do people characterize and understand what is going on? What assumptions are they making? What do these data represent? At the same time, I used what Kleinman & Copp (1993) refer to as "notes-on-notes" and "commentary notes." I accumulated vast amounts of field notes on all that I observed, and in the margins of those field notes, I jotted comments on what I thought those observations meant. Lofland & Lofland (1984) explain that these "analytical memos," used early on in the data analysis process, are a form of explanatory writing that allows researchers to develop and remain focused on particular themes.

INTERPRETING THE DATA

I did not create and adhere to a formal coding scheme. Burawoy (1991) points out that such a systematic approach frequently involves ransacking data for codes and concepts, organizing and reorganizing, often losing the context and depth of the data. The codes I used in this inductive analytical process were loose. I looked for patterns and trends and examples that deviated from those patterns. I implemented what Charmaz (1983) describes as two phases to coding: initial coding and focused coding. The first step was open or initial coding, in which I summarized and sorted the data to facilitate looking at them from many different angles. I considered what interviewees stressed in their responses, what they ignored, and their own vocabulary and definitions. For example, I sorted the head teacher interviewees according to their responses to the question I posed in regard to girls' dropping out of school. Examining these responses in each coding category gave me an initial understanding of the different meanings behind their responses.

Eventually, certain themes appeared over and over again. I then moved to focused coding, which helped me narrow my analysis to the conditions in which the people of Jiri said and did things connected to the social construction of gender. There were many contrasting layers of experience amongst the people of Jiri as revealed in my observations and interviews. The variations of gendered experiences in individuals' lives are discussed in the following chapters.

Chapter Four
Social Construction of Gender in the Family and Community

> How much they study, it's up to them. But if they all go to school, who'll look after the domestic work?
>
> —Jirel woman

The processes of social construction that create gender are a deeply embedded hegemonic feature of social life (Potuchek 1997). Children are first exposed to gender in the family—where gender is continually created and recreated through daily interactions and socialization (gendering processes) and reinforced and maintained through the social structure of the family. This chapter examines the social construction of gender constraints within the context of homes in Jiri VDC. Specifically, I examine how gender was socially constructed in the home and how students' access to and participation in school were subsequently affected.

In order to better understand how gender was constructed and reinforced in the family, my research assistants and I interviewed Jiri community members (N=328). We also visited the homes of 20 students and interviewed their parents/guardians (N=38). As part of my discussion of interviewees' attitudes toward education, I want to first present the educational status of the community member and parent/guardian interviewees, as their level of education influenced their attitudes and perceptions towards the education of girls and boys in the community.[1]

COMMUNITY MEMBERS' AND PARENTS'/GUARDIANS' EDUCATIONAL STATUS

Research has shown that the specific educational background of a child's parents (or guardians) directly affects the child's own educational opportunities

Table 4.1. Educational Attainment of Community Members Interviewed (Percentages)* (N=328)[3]

Level of Education	Women Community Members (N=167)		Men Community Members (N=161)		Percentage of the Total (N=328)
	Number	Percentage	Number	Percentage	
None	121	72.5	91	56.5	64.6
Literate	11	6.6	20	12.4	9.5
ALC Attended	15	9.0	2	1.2	5.2
Class 1–5 passed	11	6.6	25	15.5	11.0
Class 6–8 passed	5	3.0	7	4.3	3.7
Class 9–10 passed	3	1.8	3	1.9	1.8
10+2 passed or test/SLC passed	1	0.6	9	5.6	3.1
IA completed	—	—	2	1.2	0.6
Bachelor's completed	—	—	2	1.2	0.6
TOTAL	167	100.1	161	99.8	100.1

* Note: Rounded to the nearest tenth.

and aspirations.[2] The majority (64.6%) of the community members interviewed for this study had had no formal education (Table 4.1).

Only 21% reported completing a particular class level (e.g., 1.8% completed Classes 9 or 10), and only an estimated 15% of the community members considered themselves "literate," reporting they were self-taught (9.5%) or had attended an adult literacy class (5.2%).

As seen in Table 4.1, more women than men had not had any formal education: 72.5% of the women reported they were non-literate and/or had not had any formal education, whereas 56.5% of men interviewed were non-literate and/or had not had any formal education. While 15 women reported having participated in an adult literacy class (in contrast to only 2 men), the gender gap widened in reports of higher education: Only 9 (5.4%) of the total 167 women interviewed had completed school beyond Class 6, whereas 23 (14.2%) of the total 161 men interviewed reported having completed Class 6 and beyond, including two men with Intermediate (campus level) degrees and two men with Bachelor diplomas.

For the parents/guardians of the Class 5 and Class 9 students we visited at home and interviewed (N=38), the majority (66.7% for Class 9 and 65% for Class 5) was also non-literate and/or had not attended school. Yet, several of the students' parents/guardians had reached higher levels of education (Tables 4.2 and 4.3). Furthermore, approximately 34% of the Class 9 parents/guardians and 35% of the Class 5 parents/guardians reported being literate and/or having completed some level of formal schooling. These percentages were slightly higher than those of the community member sample.

Table 4.2. Educational Attainment of Class 5 Student Home Visit Parents/Guardians (Percentages) (N=20)

Level of Education	Women Parents / Guardians (N=10)		Men Parents/ Guardians (N=10)		Percentage of the Total (N=20)
	Number	Percentage	Number	Percentage	
None	7	70.0	6	60.0	65.0
ALC	1	10.0	—	—	5.0
Class 3	—	—	2	20.0	10.0
Class 7	1	10.0	—	—	5.0
Class 9	—	—	1	10.0	5.0
Test-pass	1	10.0	—	—	5.0
Intermediate Level	—	—	1	10.0	5.0
College Level	—	—	—	—	—
TOTAL	10	100.0	10	100.0	100.0

Table 4.3. Educational Attainment of Class 9 Student Home Visit Parents/Guardians (Percentages) (N=18)

Level of Education	Women Parents/ Guardians (N=10)		Men Parents/ Guardians (N=8)		Percentage of the Total (N=18)
	Number	Percentage	Number	Percentage	
None	8	80.0	4	50.0	66.7
ALC	1	10.0	—	—	5.6
Class 2	—	—	2	25.0	11.1
Class 3	1	10.0	—	—	5.6
SLC	—	—	1	12.5	5.6
College Level	—	—	1	12.5	5.6
TOTAL	10	100.0	8	100.0	100.2

Fifty percent of the Class 9 men parents/guardians considered themselves literate or educated, in contrast to only 20% of the women Class 9 parents/guardians. While 30% of the women Class 5 parents/guardians reported being literate or having completed a certain level of formal education (versus 40% of the men Class 5 parents/guardians reporting in the same categories), one woman Class 5 parent/guardian had completed Class 7, and another woman had reached the test-pass level.[4] The Class 5 and Class 9 students' enrollment and participation in school may have been partially attributed to their parents'/guardians' literacy status. With limited to no education or schooling, many members of the community and parent/guardian samples had little to no frame of reference for judging intelligence or academic performance. Interviews indicated that this lack of knowledge worked to girls' disadvantage.

We asked community member interviewees who they thought was more intelligent—girls or boys—to gain an understanding of their attitudes and subsequent behaviors regarding intellectual potential by gender.[5] A little less than half (44.5%) of the total community members reported that both boys and girls were equally intelligent. Notably, only a little over a third of the women (37.7%) reported children as having equal intelligence, whereas over half of the men (51.6%) said children were equally intelligent. The existing Nepali gendered order limited many of these women in terms of educational opportunity (72.5% of the women community members reported being non-literate).

Almost 31% of the total number of community members interviewed said boys were more intelligent than girls, but there was a notable gender difference, as a higher percentage of women (35.3%) than men (26.1%) thought boys were more intelligent. Again, the discrepancy between women and men community member respondents was perhaps a product of their own experiences of gendering, which limited women's educational opportunities and resulted in lower rates of literacy than men.

Of the community members who believed boys were more intelligent than girls, 75.3% were non-literate. Specifically, the majority (78%) of the women community members who said boys were more intelligent had not had any formal education. The same was true for the men community members who gave this response (71.4%). When we asked the parents/guardians of 20 Class 5 and Class 9 students we visited at home the same question, more than half of the parents/guardians (55.3%) reported that sons and daughters were equally intelligent. Similarly, almost all of the parents/guardians of Class 5 and Class 9 students said that both sons and daughters should be educated.[6] It appears that the parents/guardians, with a higher level of education or literacy as a group than the community member sample, more readily favored educating both boys and girls and were more likely to view both girls and boys as equally intelligent.

We asked community members who they would send to school if they could only afford to send one child, and of the total community members who said they would educate a son if they could only afford to educate one child, 66.7% were non-literate. Of the men community members who prioritized sons, the majority (60%) was non-literate. The same was true for the women community members who gave this response (71.7%).[7] Similarly, of the total nine parents/guardians (women and men) who said they would send a son in this case, seven had not had any formal education. Again, it is clear that educational level influenced respondents' preference for whom to send to school.

We also asked interviewees to suggest the best subject for students to study by gender. A majority of the community members replied that they didn't know, explaining, as two non-literate Jirel women said, "I am blind [ignorant]" and "I haven't studied in school." Such lack of knowledge relates to the importance of parents' literacy or education in decisions about education. Parents or guardians who had never attended school themselves did not understand what the education process entailed. Consequently, the less parents knew about schooling, the more guarded they tended to be in their attitudes towards the benefits of education. Little to no education also contributed to many adult interviewees envisioning gender as an inevitable and natural "fact," rather than as a *learned process*. This disconnect between social constructions of gender and educational equity worked to constrain girls in particular.

CONSTRUCTING GENDER CONSTRAINTS IN THE HOME

Adults' Internalization of Gender Processes

Analyzing the data from the community members and parent/guardian samples revealed socially constructed gender processes. Living and socialized in the gendered context, the adults in this study had learned to divide girls and boys, women and men, into socially constructed feminine and masculine categories. I found that the responses of interviewees from all four adult samples often included gender stereotypes, indicating the influence of gender processes in their own lives.

More women community members than men community members said they would prefer to send boys to school. These women reflect a normative gendered social order into which they had been socialized at a particular point in time in Nepal (including the high probability that they did not receive much in the way of formal education). For most women, gendered expectations went without question. However, men also perpetuated gender inequality with their attitudes. Men had also been socialized into believing gender and its consequences were not, in fact, socially constructed constraints, but rather, were part of the existing natural and inevitable gendered order of society.

Many women and men respondents from both samples offered learned stereotypical explanations for their answers. For instance, a non-literate Chhetri/Brahmin woman community member explained, the "minds of girls are very soft. Girls are only dreaming . . . . Boys are stronger, courageous. If anything happens, girls will cry. Girls' tears are in the sides of their eyes." Similarly, a Jirel woman from the parent/guardian sample noted, "Sons are more fearless. Daughters are a bit weak by heart." From the existing processes of gendering and gendered social structures in Nepal, these interviewees had learned to divide boys and girls into separate categories based on socially constructed feminine and masculine characteristics. Specifically, interviewees had learned that girls are obliged to perform domestic responsibilities. A woman community member espoused, "Girls are the ones who really care about their parents' sorrow. They're also more helpful in household work. Daughters help mother in the household work and field work." Her explanation reflected what she herself had been taught were the expected roles and responsibilities for girls.

ADULTS CONSTRUCTING AND REINFORCING GENDER INEQUALITY IN THE HOME

Through interviews and observations, I found that women and men both played an important role in the construction, reproduction, and maintenance of gender inequality within the home. Across religions and castes, many interviewees from both the community member and the parent/guardian samples talked of the following family arrangements: Sons married and lived with their parents, whereas daughters went to "others' house," meaning they went to live with their husband's family once their marriages were arranged. With these socially constructed arrangements, sons provided security for parents in their old age, and interviewees often indicated this as a justification for educating their sons more than (or instead of) their daughters.

Interviews revealed adult's reinforcing social constructions of gender. Specifically, most women and men respondents from both samples offered answers that were based on gender constructs. For instance, a non-literate Sherpa man in the community member sample replied that boys were more intelligent because,

Social Construction of Gender in the Family and Community 81

> A son is a son. He's brave. When you get ill suddenly or have an accident, son would be there to take you to hospital or anywhere. But if it happened in [the] presence of [a] girl, they can't do anything. They will just cry and cry and worry. But sons are strong. They have a business mind. They can also start a hotel business. They know how to earn money, but daughter knows only one thing—that is to look for a man so as to get married. Isn't it?

In accordance with stereotypical feminine characteristics for girls and masculine characteristics for boys, adults defined daughters as less intelligent because they were considered to be emotional and weak, whereas they defined sons as more intelligent because sons were considered to be brave and strong.

Both women and men community members typically said the most appropriate subject boys should study would be one that would lead to a good job.[8] For example, respondents from this sample suggested science and health as best subjects for boys so that they could one day become a doctor. This illustrates an emphasis on boys' future careers. Men community members, more so than the women community members, viewed studying health as important for both girls and boys. However, it should be noted that only four men recommended health for boys, whereas 21 men suggested girls study health. The highest percentage of both women and men community members thought girls should study health, but far more men community members (21) chose this subject for girls than did women community members (13), demonstrating that men more often identify girls and women with subjects that benefit family and children than do women. Also, a much higher percentage of men community members (10.6%) thought girls should study English than did women community members (2.4%). The most common explanation for why girls should study English given by men interviewees from this sample was so that girls "could talk to foreigners."

Interviewees' explanations for their choice of best subject by gender were often laden with gender stereotypes. Subjects for girls were frequently selected based on their perceived level of difficulty:

> For girls, I like nurse line [health]. That is suitable for girls and easier too.
> —Jirel woman with a Class 10 education

> Nepali and English are the most important subjects for girls because these subjects are very easy for girls to study.
> —Non-literate Chhetri woman

> Girls can't take English because it is too difficult for them.
> —Non-literate Sherpa man

> Girls are not clever like boys, and they can't grasp things quickly.
> —Non-literate Jirel man

Many community members believed girls to be limited in their ability to grasp subjects. These interviewees explained girls' limited abilities in socially constructed terms:

> Girls should study home science because they don't have to go far. They can earn their living by staying near us.
> —Literate Newari man

> I don't know about the subject but it'd be better for girls to become nurse, do the job in the bank. Girls should get any kind of ordinary job, which shouldn't hamper your [their] physics [body; physical condition].
> —Non-literate Sherpa woman

This woman community member alluded to the difference in physical strength by gender: She indicated girls should get a job suited to their physical abilities. Community members also selected subjects for girls for instrumental reasons:

> I think health science is suitable for girls. Because if they study health science, it will be easier for them to take care of themselves as well as the family. They can be cautious about their health and tell others also what they have learned.
> —Jirel man with a Class 8 education

> Health education. Women are the ones who have to deal with the household work. One day she'll be a mother and give birth to a baby. That deals with the health.
> —Literate Jirel woman

The selection of the most suitable subject for girls was based on its benefits to others. By studying health, these interviewees asserted girls would become better mothers and family caretakers.

In contrast, community members generally considered boys capable and not restricted by physical limitations. For example, a non-literate Chhetri woman, who suggested that science and mathematics were most important for boys, explained,

They can study more than girls. They are more free to go anywhere, they can go anywhere to study. It will be easy to come home from anywhere, at any time.

This community member's comments implied that girls had more social constraints placed on them than boys. A literate Jirel woman believed English to be "good for them [boys]. Boys do not stay at home when they get older. They start to go away to other countries. They don't give much attention to the house and [are] not aware of the household business [work]." She saw boys as free to do as they pleased, without constraints. Notably, she also did not foresee boys staying at home with their parents, as did many other community members.

A literate Jirel man said the best subject was the one a boy chose himself. He elaborated, "Boys can do what they like. They have [the] capacity to do whatever they like if they have the talent." Unlike girls, who were heavily bound by socially-constructed gender obligations beginning at an early age, the Nepali construction of gender allowed boys greater agency in the decisions they made for themselves.

Similar to the community member sample, parents/guardians suggested boys study science and English. However, only one parent/guardian (a man) said boys should study math. In accord with the community member sample, parents'/guardians' explanations for their choices were typically career-oriented for boys and instrumental (e.g., taking care of others) for girls.

Both women and men community members generally agreed that boys should aspire to study up to a high level of education. Nearly a quarter (24.1%) of community members interviewed hoped boys would "study completely," whereas 20.7% of the community members hoped girls would "study high" or "much." Approximately 34% of the 328 community members reported wanting boys to study up to the Intermediate or Bachelor's level, while 21% of the total community members hoped girls would study up to the same level. These statistics demonstrate the gender perceptions community members had in relation to Nepali socially constructed expectations for girls and boys. As future wives, mothers, and housekeepers, they believed girls needed less education to fulfill those gender obligations. This contrasts with expectations for boys who were obliged to be future breadwinners for their extended families and consequently were assumed to need higher levels of education.

Specifically, community members' rationales for boys' higher academic achievement were described in terms of seeking a better economic future: The higher the education boys achieved, the greater the potential for finding a good job, being financially secure, having more choices, and establishing oneself as a respected and successful member of the community. For example, a literate Chhetri man said that boys should study "as far as possible, Master's. According to this modern age, if they study highly, they can get a job in higher position such as lawyer, pilot, etc." Similarly, a non-literate Jirel woman insisted that boys should study "as much as they can. They should study completely . . . . They can get a job, and they can travel to anywhere." This implies women do not have the mobility that men do in Nepali society. Another Jirel woman—also non-literate—explained that if boys study "completely," "they will have [a] happy and comfortable life." In other words, with much education, boys were more likely to secure a good-paying job, rather than having to do arduous subsistence agriculture or low-paying manual labor as their parents had to do.

Conversely, community members' responses to the best educational level for girls were linked to their socially prescribed roles as a mother and farmer or as the lynchpin for managing domestic and agricultural work:

> She must have good education on how to raise the children in a proper way and about agriculture and health.
> —Jirel man with SLC level education

> If girls study in Class 4 [or] 5, they would be able to read and write letters and understand. I wish [hope] that my girls can teach their own children in their future.
> —Non-literate Sherpa woman

> 15–16 Class [higher education] if they can, but if they go to school, who'll work at home? They need to work at home and in the field. We need to eat, [and] without working in the house or field, the food won't be available. Therefore, they need to work at home.
> —Non-literate Sherpa woman

> Up to 5–6 Class . . . After that, they should work at home and [in the] field. They should look after the animals, goats, sheep. Go to collect the fodder for [the] animals. That's the work for the girls.
> —Non-literate Sherpa woman

These interviewees assumed girls' roles to be those of mother and agricultural and domestic provider. Assuming girls would fulfill these prescribed roles was the everyday reality in the gendered context in which they lived. Unfortunately, making these gendered assumptions limited girls' educational aspirations and influenced what girls studied as well.

Figure 4.1. Women Working. Photograph by author.

EFFECTS OF SOCIAL CONSTRUCTIONS OF GENDER ON STUDENTS

Socially constructed gender processes determined students' education. Specifically, the division and organization of Nepali social life by gender influenced students' ability to attend, participate in, and succeed in school. Across all samples of this study, interviews illustrated this proposition. In terms of access, what people said was not always what they put into practice. Fifty-one community members interviewed (16%) said that they would send both sons and daughters to school, but at the time of their interview, they had school-age daughters who did not attend school and worked at home instead.[9] An example of this discrepancy was a Dalit ("untouchable") farmer/blacksmith with a Class 4 education who, in explaining why both should be sent to school, said, "Boy eats the same and the girl eats the same. Both are the same." Through my triangulation of data collection methods, I learned that this same man had a daughter who did not attend school and a son who was enrolled.

Another example came from a non-literate Brahmin grandmother, who, when asked, said both boys and girls should go to school because "if we cut the finger, both bleed." However, her four granddaughters did not attend school, whereas her grandson did. The 12-year-old daughter of a non-literate Jirel man did not go to school, but he told me, "Both are equal. There's no question of educating only girls or only boys." Perhaps these interviewees thought it would be appropriate to tell me both girls and boys are equal, but in reality, gender constructs in their own homes prevented girls from attending school.

When community members were asked later in the interview who they would send to school if they could only afford to send one child, fewer reported that they would send "both" (69.2%) than when asked their preference of whom they would send (86.6%). Given the economic stipulation, a higher percentage of community members (24.7%) said they would first send a son to school than reported earlier (9.8%). As seen in other studies in Nepal (e.g., Ashby 1985; Shrestha, *et al.* 1986), these community members would send a son rather than a daughter if sending a child to school were an economic burden.

Likewise, given the same economic constraint, a higher percentage of parents/guardians said they would send their son over a daughter (23.7%) than those preferring to send their son to school when they were asked the same question earlier (5.3%). Similar to community members, fewer parents/guardians reported they would send both son and daughter (71.1%) than when they were asked their preference with no economic limitations (94.7%). However, the vast majority, nearly three quarters, said they would still educate both. Again, this may have been due to the slightly higher level of education in the parent/guardian sample as compared with the community member sample.

Given an economic constraint, community members and parents/guardians often rationalized sending a son instead of a daughter in terms of direct and indirect (opportunity) costs. For example, a literate Jirel woman community member said she would send her son because, "If I send the girls to school, we won't [be able to] afford her [school] expenses."[10] A Sherpa man from the community member sample complained that in sending his two daughters to school and not his son, "After Class 5, we have to pay the fee. Who can afford?" Many respondents echoed the beliefs of a non-literate Dalit man from the community member sample, who said that he would not send his daughter to school in this case because "there is no one to look after the house and do the work at home." For this man, the opportunity costs of sending his daughter to school would be too great. I would argue that perceived direct and indirect (opportunity) costs saved by not sending a daughter to school were more of a matter of socially constructed gender constraints than inevitable economic limitations.

Within the social constructions of gender, sons were considered future breadwinners for the family, and consequently many parents/guardians more willingly incurred direct educational costs for sons rather than daughters (ABEL 1996; O'Gara, *et al.* 1999; Ashby 1985; Shrestha, *et al.* 1986). A non-literate Sherpa man from the community member sample explained that he would send his son to school because, "Son is the only support for us. He'll take care of us . . . . He'll bring money home." A Jirel man community member, with an SLC pass education, explained, "We have had a belief since time immemorial that he'll [the son will] be the one to look after his parents [and] if he studies, then he'll certainly take care of us." A non-literate Jirel woman spoke for many of the 46 women community members who preferred sending a son to school. She explained,

> Boys are ours. Girls will go away with [a] man. She has to obey him [her husband] and do whatever he tells her to do. But boys are the ones who stay with us. They'll look after the guest that comes to the house. He will try to serve them nicely. Daughter will be taken away.

She implied that investing in a son's education would pay off for her in the future, as educated sons would bring financial security and respect to her house. Because daughters did not remain in their natal homes, this woman did not see the benefit of investing in a daughter's education. Thus, sons were equated with future economic security, whereas daughters were linked to present economic security.[11]

The family, as a gendered institution, placed unequal constraints on the girls' and women's time as compared to that of the boys and men, and this adversely affected girls' participation in school. In my interviews with community members and parents/guardians, both women and men noted that girls did more domestic work than boys on a given day. When we asked parents/guardians to describe their sons' and daughters' daily activities, mothers and women guardians thought girls woke up much earlier than boys. One mother explained that her Class 9 daughter "wakes up at 3 a.m. if she has to study. She has to study hard now because the final examination is approaching . . . . She [also] helps me in the kitchen both in the mornings and evenings." Women and men parents/guardians acknowledged that girls did a lot of housework, but women parents/guardians mentioned more work for girls than did the men parents/guardians. A Newari mother explained, "After having breakfast, she [daughter] goes to school and after returning, she helps with our work so she doesn't have much time to study." Notably, this mother (and many other parents/guardians)[12] referred to girls' household work as "help." Help implied a choice; in actuality, girls were obligated to their domestic responsibilities and typically did not have a choice in the matter.

Women parents/guardians said boys slept longer. The mother of a Class 9 student confessed, "If we're not busy [with the family business], then I let him sleep longer since he will have stayed up late the night before studying." Neither women nor men parents/guardians alluded to boy students doing much work around the house. A Chhetri mother noted, "We haven't made him [son] do much of the housework. He goes to school, comes home, eats, plays, studies, does homework. That's all." According to members of the parents/guardians sample, boy students were afforded more time to study and do homework than were girl students.

Also, women and men community members cited workload at home as a primary reason for girls dropping out of school.[13] Their explanations linked to Nepali social constructions of gender: Girls dropping out of school because of the central role women and girls play in maintaining the family and household served to reinforce Nepali women's perceived roles and responsibilities in society. Interviewees assumed household work was girls' "given" role:

> They have more work at home to do. When they become [a] mother, they have to look after their children, kitchen and the whole household work.
>
> —Non-literate Jirel man

> In villages, there are so many [so much] work. Maybe [because of] the heavy loads of work, they can't go to school. When they return from the school, they have to go to graze the animals or go to collect the firewood or the grass.
>
> —Non-literate Jirel woman

> The reason is simple. They [girls] have to work in the house. Mother needs a friend [helping hand] at home. She'll [the mother will] be alone to do all the household work. So daughter will be good helping hand for the mother. They have to watch the house, graze the goats, or work in the field. They remain busy at home.
>
> —Non-literate Sherpa man

As the last interviewee stated, "The reason is simple. Girls have to work in the house." Girls' socially constructed obligations to domestic responsibilities, their role as a "good helping hand," went unquestioned.

Gender processes in the home also restricted girls' achievement in school. Some community members (but none of the parents/guardians) included stipulations by gender when they reported that they would educate both their sons and daughters. For example, although a non-literate Sherpa man from the community member sample stressed the importance of educating both sons and daughters, he said, "Son should be educated much, but for daughters, only 5, 6 standards [Classes] will be enough." Similarly, a Jirel man with a Class 2 education explained, "[A] son should be educated up to [a] high level, and it's OK for daughters to study up to [a] low level." A non-literate Tamang woman from the community member sample said she would prefer to send both son and daughter to school "because they are all equal," but she stipulated that "if I send the son to [a] boarding [private] school, then I would try to send my daughter to [a] government school." She continued by saying that she "loved them equally," yet her stipulation implied a discrepancy in the quality of education she would give her son and her daughter.

Socially constructed expectations for girls often place heavier and earlier obligations on them, which could potentially have an adverse effect on their schooling (Sibbons 1999; Mathema 1998), particularly their achievement in school. A non-literate Chhetri man from the parent/guardian sample explained that girls "are the ones who look after the house . . . . Most of the time boys are away from the home . . . playing games, playing cards." His comments and those of others raise an important point: Girls were not only considered better at fulfilling their socially constructed gender obligations (e.g., domestic responsibilities), but community members and parents/guardians noted that girls were also needed to fulfill these obligations in the present, which happened to coincide with their being school age. Conversely, school-age boys had few responsibilities in the existing Nepali gendered order. The heaviest expectation for boys was to take on the role of the breadwinner for the family in the future. Until that time, boys were often able to "play" and do as they please. Unlike girls, delayed expectations for boys affected their schooling positively, as they were able to stay in school longer and attain higher educational levels.

Adults not only offered evidence of social constructions of gender constraints affecting students' access to and participation in school, but the students' themselves also provided evidence. For example, I asked the student interviewees to describe a typical day for them, and a compilation of their responses demonstrates gender differences in the allocation of work (Table 4.4). Among the 20 students interviewed, the girl students were obligated to do more chores at home than boy students. The gendered division of labor left the girl students with less time than boy students to do homework and to study. On average, because of her domestic responsibilities, the girl student woke up earlier and went to bed later. Assuming girls would fulfill certain domestic roles was the reality of the girls' gendered lives. However, making these assumptions consequently limited the extent of girls' education and influenced what and how much girls would study, as well as girls' expectations for themselves.

Table 4.4. Composite of Typical Time Allocations for Students by Gender

Time of Day	Girl in School (N =10)	Boy in School (N = 10)
6a.m.-7a.m.	Wakes up, washes face	Sleeping
7a.m.-8a.m.	Washes dishes, makes tea for self and others, and does household work (e.g., cleaning, prepares meals, feeds animals)	Wakes up, washes face, and studies for a while
8a.m.-9a.m.	Dresses for school and has snack	Eats morning meal and then gets dressed for school
9a.m.-10a.m.	Walks to school	Walks to school
10a.m.-12p.m.	Attends school	Attends school
12p.m.-1p.m.	"Tiffin" (snack) break	"Tiffin" (snack) break
1p.m.-4p.m.	School	School
4p.m.-5p.m.	Walks home from school	Walks home from school
5p.m.-6p.m.	Chores (e.g., brings fodder to cattle, fetches water and fuel wood, cleans)	Has snacks and tea and studies
6p.m.-7p.m.	Helps prepare evening meal/helps mother in kitchen	Studies/does homework
7p.m.-8p.m.	Eats "lunch" (light meal) Does dishes	Eats evening meal and watches television (if student has access to television)
8p.m.-9p.m.	Does homework	Goes to bed
9p.m.-10p.m.	Goes to bed	Sleeping

Figure 4.2. Children Working. Photography by author.

This is exemplified by the story of Sanu Kumari. At the time of her life history narrative, Sanu Kumari was studying at the J School in Class 9. She was from an impoverished Chhetri (Hindu) family. Her parents were farmers. She was the oldest child and had two sisters and one brother. At the time of her life history interview, one of her younger sisters was in Kathmandu where she was learning stitching and knitting:

> In my childhood, I used to run away [from classes] and play with our friends. Sometimes we even went to the forest to hide ourselves to avoid the work at home. That's all I can remember . . . . [Thinks for a while . . . .] My father had gone away. *Where?* I don't know but some foreign land [out of Nepal] and there was nobody at home to help my mother since I was the eldest. So due to the household work, I had to stop going to school and I missed my studies for Class 5. Now [at this time] I would have given my SLC [if she had continued with her schooling consistently], but later when my father returned he told me to go back to school and I started from where I had left [Class 5] . . . . I wake up early in the morning [and] wash my face. Tidy up my room. Have tea, then prepare lunch [morning meal of *daal bhaat* (rice and lentils)], serve it to my family, attend class, then return home in the evening. Then have tea and snacks, and then do my homework or study for a while, then prepare dinner for the family. Then after dinner, I also study for a while, and go to bed. Then on holidays [days with no school like Saturdays] I go for herding, fetching grass and firewood. On school days I only go to fetch firewood and cut grass for the livestock. I don't have to go herding because it would make me late to go to school.

Similar to many of her girl classmates in the student sample, social constructions constrained Sanu Kumari: She was expected to fulfill her gender obligations of household work, limiting the time available for studying. Although she started her homework and studied as soon as she returned home from school, her domestic responsibilities of preparing and serving meals, cleaning the house, collecting firewood, and cutting grass for livestock (in addition to the herding and collecting of grass and firewood she did when school was not in session) consumed the majority of her time at home. She was aware of these constraints as she spoke of "hiding in the forest to avoid work at home," and she knew she would be further along in her studies were it not for having to drop out of Class 5 to help her mother with the household chores. She felt she was behind in her education because of it.

Girls in Nepal are more prone to repeat a grade than boys, and girls are also at a greater risk of dropping out of school than boys (Sibbons

1999). Among the 10 girl students we interviewed, seven had to repeat at least one grade. Of the 10 boy students interviewed, only one boy student had repeated a grade. He had to repeat Class 2 after breaking his leg. This was a significant gender difference that had consequences for girls' achievement and completion of the educational process.

For Sita, a Class 5 student, domestic responsibilities were to blame when she had to repeat Class 4. She explained, "I didn't have time to study and couldn't prepare well for the examination." Similarly, Minu failed Class 8 because she didn't have time to study. Class 9 student Krishna Kumari had to repeat Class 2 because she had to take care of a younger sister. With the internalization of gender processes, some students understood their repeating a grade as linked to their academic inabilities, rather than constraints on their time. For example, Class 5 girl student Kamala had to repeat kindergarten because "I didn't know much."

When asked why they thought girls in Nepal drop out of school, 60% of the student interviewees believed that girls drop out of school because of the workload at home. More girl students than boy students cited this as a reason for girls dropping out of school. Sita explained that based on her own experience, there often was no time for girls to study because of household work. Man Kumar, a Class 9 student, noted that girls and women in villages had so much work to do that "they don't have time to go to school." His classmate, Chhetra, observed that girls "give first priority to their housework, so they are always compromising work with school." He assumed that girls placed greater priority on housework themselves, rather than it being the highest priority of girls' parents, who themselves were a product of a gendered society that valued women's domestic role as their greatest contribution to the family and Nepali society. Among the students, there appeared to be an unconscious acceptance of the gendered division of labor without understanding how it came about. However, one Class 9 student, Leela Maya, put it well when she observed, "They [parents] make the daughters do all the household work. They have the notion that girls shouldn't study and [want to] get them married [arrange daughters' marriage]."[14]

ECONOMIC CONSTRAINTS—PUSHING GENDER CONSTRAINTS FURTHER

As discussed in Chapter Two, poverty often constrained Nepali students and their parents/guardians in terms of education. The majority of community members interviewed lived at (or below) the subsistence level; many told us that their crops only yielded enough food for 3–6 months of

Figure 4.3. Typical Jiri Home. Photograph by author.

the year. The construction of most community members' homes typically consisted of thatched, straw, or tin roofs; earthen floors; and walls made of stone and packed mud. A majority reported not having a permanent toilet on their homestead; typically, families used the closest river or forested area instead. During the interviews with community members, many cited limitations in educating their children due to their economic situation. They lamented the high costs of providing school fees, uniforms, and school supplies for both their daughters and sons.[15] Even if villagers in Jiri desired education for their children, it might have been impossible.

The interviewees from the parent/guardian sample also struggled with economic constraints in educating their children. For example, nine parents/guardians (five men and four women) talked about economics being a factor in their daughters,' as well as their sons,' reaching an ideal level of educational achievement. The parents/guardians expressed great disappointment that their children would not be able to study as "high" as they had hoped because of their limited economic means.

As an economic indicator, we assessed the condition of parents'/guardians' homes, and we found the structure of their homes to be very similar to the homes of the community members interviewed. However, more parents'/guardians' homes had wooden flanks and cemented walls than did the homes of community members. Homes of interviewees from the parent/guardian sample had an average of 2–3 storeys, with families sharing an average of four rooms. Seventy percent of the parents/guardians reported having electricity in their homes. The homes without electricity reported using lanterns, "torches" (flashlights), or a *tuki* (oil lamp). Not having electricity made it difficult for students living in these homes to study in the evenings.

Fifty percent of the parents/guardians interviewed had a water tap on their homestead, whereas 40% carried water from a community tap in the village. One mother explained that her family had to carry water from the nearby stream. Only one family from this sample had piped water inside their home. Fifty percent reported having to boil their drinking water. Half of the parent/guardian interviewees lived on homesteads or in homes with toilets, but several said they were in poor condition. Those without toilets used a nearby river or forested area.

Another indicator of economic constraints was the sparseness of educational materials observed in the interviewees' homes. In terms of a place at home to study, all parent/guardian interviewees reported students studying on either a bed or the floor—only nine homes had either a bench or a table on which a student could study or do homework. Very few students had books or study materials at home. We observed books in six out of the 20 homes and newspapers in five of the homes. Only one home had a map. Reading materials at home provide an opportunity for students to practice the literacy skills learned at school. Without such materials, a student may struggle twice as hard (Davison & Kanyuka 1990).

Social Construction of Gender in the Family and Community

Gender constraints are exacerbated by economic constraints, and girls inevitably suffer the most. For example, a Jirel man community member enrolled his son in school, but not his daughter. He gave his reasoning in economic terms:

> We don't get any aid from foreigners for textbooks and stationeries [school supplies]. We poor people can't afford buying all these and can't educate all the children. We don't have that capacity.

Similarly, a Jirel woman from the community member sample lamented, "We parents can't think about educating them. We don't have money to afford [to send sons and daughters to school] because we need money to buy their clothes [school uniforms], textbooks, pens." Nonetheless, four of this woman's sons attended school, but her daughter did not. Although initial decisions to send a boy or girl to school may have been indirectly influenced by economic considerations, these and other examples discussed earlier in this chapter demonstrate that determining how to spend limited household incomes on education was often a gendered decision.

CONCLUSIONS

In this chapter, I have argued that in the context of my case study—Jiri, Nepal—gender was continually created and recreated through daily interactions and socialization (gendering processes) through the social structure of the family. I have attempted to show that adults in this particular community reinforced gender constructs that constrained school-age children and teenagers, especially girls. In order to understand how adults learned to reinforce social constructions of gender, I looked at their own experiences of gendering—most explicitly displayed by their level of (or lack thereof) education. Across both the community member and parent/guardian samples, women generally had less education than did the men in both of these samples (e.g., 72.5% of the women community members reported being non-literate). I argue that differences in attitudes towards educating girls and boys were related to differences in educational status. For example, more women community members than men community members said they would prefer to send boys to school. As a result of having grown up in a gendered social order themselves, the women were generally not given the access to and opportunity of education as compared to the men. With no education or schooling, these individuals had little to no frame of reference for understanding or assessing the educational process.

Men also lacked formal education experiences, particularly in the community member sample, and in instances of little to no education, I again suggest a correlation between educational levels and attitudes toward education by gender. Interviewees' attitudes towards education revealed how community members and parents/guardians differed in constructing gender. The less community members, parents, and guardians knew about schooling, the more reserved they were in their attitudes towards the benefits of education. This skepticism had implications for current and future students, especially girls, as girls tended to be the last enrolled among parents with limited education and financial capabilities and were the first to be withdrawn or drop out of school when household incomes faltered.

The community members, parents, and guardians had learned to divide boys and men and girls and boys into socially constructed "feminine" and "masculine' categories, and as consequence, the adults in this sample constructed and reinforced gender for children. Their interview responses revealed socially constructed gender processes they had themselves experienced and learned. For example, sons were considered "brave," "fearless," having "a business mind" and were, therefore, considered more intelligent, whereas girls were emotional and "weak by heart [nature]."

Interviews across samples illustrated that socially constructed gender processes determined students' education. Specifically, the division and organization of Nepali social life by gender influenced students' ability to attend, participate in, and succeed in school. When I asked interviewees from both samples questions regarding their attitudes towards educational attainment by gender, many community members and some parents/guardians believed that girls, as future wives, mothers, and housekeepers, needed less education to fulfill their gender obligations. In contrast, many interviewees asserted that boys needed higher levels of education, as they were expected to be future breadwinners for their extended families, including aging parents. Adults may have been less inclined to educate their daughters to a high level because they would marry and "go to another's house," whereas, sons would stay with them and provide security in their old age (Reinhold 1993).

Furthermore, interviewees repeatedly mentioned poverty as a constraint to girls' enrollment and persistence in schools. Although many community members and parents/guardians in Jiri were legitimately constrained by poverty, the social expectations placed on sons as a source of future economic security (future breadwinners for the family) and daughters as providing current economic security (through their domestic labor) were more likely the impetus for many parents and guardians in Nepal to incur direct educational costs for sons, rather than daughters (Sibbons 1999; Mathema 1998). Although girls were no more naturally inclined to do their assigned tasks than were the boys, social constructions of gender obliged girls to domestic responsibilities to a greater extent than boys. These gendered expectations were learned at a young age and reinforced over time. And, assigning the girls and women in the family the majority of the domestic responsibilities ensured that the household tasks would get done (Stromquist 1990).

This relates to broader contexts in that the family, as a gendered institution, places unequal constraints on girls' and women's time as compared to that of boys and men. Much of the existing literature regarding low number of girls enrolled in schools centers on the *obstacles* to girls' schooling. But these analyses, I argue, are incomplete. While identifying the obstacles to girls' education (e.g., parents' socioeconomic status, religion, distance to school, cultural attitudes, poverty, availability of schools, parents' education, and unsuitable curriculum) is important, analyzing these obstacles in a disconnected fashion without examining the significance of gender as a social construction "confuses immediate with ultimate causes and fails to understand gender as an institutionalized expression of power in society" (Stromquist 1990:108). In other words, perceived differences between the abilities for boys and girls form the basis for the aforementioned obstacles within a family context.

Analyzing the obstacles without accounting for assumptions about gender may negate the potential for change at this level and within family institutions worldwide. Examining socially constructed gender processes in families helps us unpack and understand how gender affects students, particularly girl students, in terms of access to, participation in, and achievement in schools. Therefore, I argue, development programs focusing on educational equity must critically examine how social constructions of gender created and maintained in families constrain students.

Although many of the interviewees' responses in this study indicated institutionalization of gender and cyclical processes of gendering, the gendered social order is fluid and dynamic, with existing gender constraints being continually constructed, negotiated, and reconstructed (Potuchek 1997). For example, some community members, who did not send their daughters to school in the past, reported they were sending their school-age daughters to school at the time of their interview. The social constructions of gender, which children were first exposed to within the context of the home, was also reinforced and maintained in the social structure of the education system, which is discussed in the next chapter.

Chapter Five
Reinforcing Gender in Schools

> In my opinion, boys are more intelligent than girls because girls cannot think as much as boys can. Even if they think, they cannot bring into behavior [practice], so I think boys are more intelligent than girls.
>
> —Amrit, Class 9 boy student

Collecting data from both the home and the school helped uncover how pervasive the existing gendered social order in Nepal was. This chapter examines the construction of gender constraints within the context of schools in Jiri VDC. Specifically, this chapter examines how the construction of gender that was created, reinforced, and negotiated within the context of the home was also reinforced and maintained within the social structure of the education system. This chapter also explores how these gender structures constrained students to "do gender" (West & Zimmerman 1987) in culturally defined ways.

SOCIAL CONSTRUCTIONS OF GENDER REINFORCED IN SCHOOL: A GENDERED EDUCATION

In order to better understand how gender was constructed and reinforced in Jiri schools, we interviewed 10 head teachers (school principals), all of the Class 5 teachers at the D School, and all of the Class 9 teachers at the J School. We also analyzed the textbooks for both Class 5 and Class 9 and conducted direct observations of the Class 5 and Class 9 classrooms. Interview and observation data collected provided evidence of gendered educational experiences.

Head Teachers Reinforcing Social Constructs of Gender

Head teachers reinforced social constructions of gender through their gendered expectations for students. Our first interview question asked head teachers about the academic performance of students. The five head teachers who selected boys as having better academic performance couched their explanations in terms of gender roles and responsibilities. Said one Chhetri man head teacher,

> They [the girls] have to look after their [younger] siblings, herd the cattle and goats, collect leaves and twigs [fodder and firewood] so in comparison to boys, girls do more work. They have the feeling of helpfulness more. So the parents have the urge of greed to keep their daughters at home because they are great helping hands. Another thing is that they are so used to doing their household work that they feel guilty to go to school, leaving all the housework to be done by their parents so they themselves also don't feel like going to school.

Notably, this head teacher was projecting his own gender bias onto his answer with his statement that girls "don't feel like going to school." He assumed the girls felt guilty if they left the housework to go to school. Further, he did not question the socially constructed assignment of housework to girls exclusively rather than to both girls and boys. Also, similar to many community members and parents/guardians, this interviewee referred to daughters' work at home as "help," implying that girls had a choice when they were actually obligated to their domestic responsibilities.

Similar to many of the interviewees from the community member and parent/guardian samples, head teachers agreed that girls' domestic responsibilities and the opportunity (indirect) costs of girls' going to school were major factors in girls' academic performance. One Jirel man head teacher, in contrast to most community members and parent/guardian interviewees, observed that,

> Boys, they are more interested in games than [in] studies. Girls, they work very hard and study day and night to pass their exams. But boys show less interest in studies in comparison to girls . . . . The girls themselves have started realizing that they need to study and they study hard, whereas boys are naturally naughty. They only like to play and make excuses for studies.

This head teacher, however, spoke of gender differences as being "natural," when, in actuality, they were socially constructed. As consequence, not only were gender stereotypes and traditional attitudes toward gender difference then reinforced, but these beliefs in regard to gender difference presumably also influenced his administrative decisions pertaining to educational equity.

Reinforcing Gender in Schools

The men head teachers typically gave gender stereotypes as explanations for why they selected a particular subject as most appropriate for boys or for girls. For girls, five men head teachers named subjects associated with domestic roles (e.g., home science, health, sewing), and none suggested these for boys.[1] One Jirel man head teacher lamented, "We do not have subjects like sewing and weaving for girls [at this school]." Another man Chhetri head teacher concurred, suggesting that sewing and knitting would be good to teach the girls because he had seen,

> Little girls while going to school plus in the playground are engaged in knitting. I see them making gloves [mittens], bags, etc. So it would be better to have those kinds of subjects.

Following gender stereotypes, a man Chhetri head teacher with a Bachelor's in Education opined that girls should take home science:

> In my opinion, this is the first [top priority] subject. Then nursing, teaching would best for the girls. *Why?* Because these subjects would be very relevant for them. They are the ones who have to spend most of their time at home so if they take home science, then it would help them a lot. It suits them . . . . Girls are encouraged to take up teaching because it is said that they have an inborn quality for that; in other words, they are very kind, they are soft-hearted, dutiful. In comparison to boy, girls are found [to be] more dutiful in every work [chore]. They are very honest/sincere to [towards] their work. That's why if they take nursing, they can take good care of the patients. So in my opinion, home science, nursing, teaching would be very appropriate for girls.

And for boys, the same head teacher espoused that,

> For boys . . . technical subjects would be very appropriate. *Like?* Like overseer, engineer, teacher [laughs]. Because technical subjects would be best for them and vice versa.

By assigning "inborn" qualities to girls and to boys, this head teacher reinforced gender constructs that constrained students, especially girls, to "do gender" in culturally accepted ways. He assumed not only that girls were naturally inclined towards care giving, but he also allowed little room for girls' choice. He assumed girls, without question, would want to take up household responsibilities and care giving. To justify his gender opinions, he took the *same* subject—teaching—and categorized it as a "caring" subject or career for girls, but as a "technical" career when applied to boys.

The head teachers also stressed the importance of boys studying up to a high level so they could get a job. For example, a man Chhetri head teacher, with an SLC education, stated boys should study at least until they could pass the SLC exam. He explained,

> Then they would be able to join any kind and whatever line [of work] to earn their living. So in my opinion, they have to pass until SLC [School Leaving Certificate level].

Another head teacher, a Jirel man with SLC qualifications, reiterated that point, emphasizing that the educational demands in the job market were continually increasing:

> Let's say according to the demand of time, it is changing day by day. In my case, I studied till SLC, and in my time, to study till SLC was very good/high. We immediately got job. Then there was a high facility to get job if you passed till SLC. But now SLC is considered the minimum level. Now we have higher secondary schools, and the population is increasing. For any kind of job, if there is a seat for just one candidate, thousands fight for the post so it is very hard to get a job. Now it's not like in our time. So to get a job tomorrow, boys at least should have to complete their diploma level, if not certificate level. Better at least until diploma or even more.

Because the existing social construction of gender in Nepal assigned adult men the role of breadwinner, boys' marketability was considered critical. These two head teachers argued that boys needed to be highly educated for the ever-increasing competition in the job market. Yet, when discussing ideal educational level for girls, two head teachers stressed that girls needed fewer qualifications than boys because, they theorized, girls would be hired before the boys:

> If for the boys . . . diploma level and above, for girls at least certificate level is a must . . . . Girls, even if they have done their certificate level, they give them the chance to work, whereas boys have to have more than that [qualification] so in that sense, I said diploma for boys and certificate for girls.
>
> —Jirel man head teacher with SLC education

> Nowadays, they give more priority to girls than [to] boys. If they can get up to that level [SLC], they will be able to try luck anywhere. They can get any kind of ordinary jobs. They can apply for trainings. So and so forth.
>
> —Chhetri man head teacher with SLC education

These explanations were couched in overly simplistic terms. Although women might get hired at a younger age, with fewer skills, the head teachers failed to note that these lower-skilled jobs paid less. With less education, there is less of a chance for upward mobility in a position. Boys, who stayed in school longer, would have more education, more qualifications, and more skills and would subsequently get better paying jobs than the girls.

The gendered perceptions the head teacher possessed had serious consequences for the students at her/his school. By espousing traditional beliefs in regard to gender and education, head teachers reinforced the social constructions of gender students had first learned in the home. Furthermore, although most of the head teachers wholeheartedly endorsed girls' education in their interviews, they did not appear to take action to make their schools more "girl friendly" by hiring more women staff. I observed very few women teachers (and at some schools, none) employed at the schools these teachers headed. If such a situation is to be changed, the leaders of these schools must take active steps to assure gender equity in teaching staff.[2]

Social Constructs of Gender Reinforced in the Classroom

To gain a better understanding of how gender was constructed and reinforced within the classroom, we also interviewed all seven of the Class 5 teachers and all five of the Class 9 teachers. Teachers' explanations for their interview responses often illustrated gender bias. When asked who had better academic performance—girls or boys—a woman Newari teacher seemed to prefer girls because they were quiet, unlike the "disruptive boys" who challenged her. Her response had more to do with behavior than the academic performance of students. Of the four men teachers who thought boys performed better than girls, a Chhetri teacher explained,

> Boys are active in class activities as well as in study because in [on] exam, they score high [higher] marks than the girls. They're quick to tell [give] the answers. Girls are shy and [more] inactive than the boys.

This teacher's observation conformed to gender stereotyping and reflected many of the community members' and some of the parents'/guardians' responses: Girls were considered "shy" and "inactive," whereas boys were active and quick. Recognizing girls for being quiet and well mannered or focusing on girls' "good" behavior rather than on their test scores and class rankings might have overshadowed their academic work. Such observations only reinforced socially constructed gender expectations of girls.

Like the head teachers, most of the Class 5 and Class 9 teachers drew on gender stereotypes to explain why they selected a particular subject for boys and for girls. For instance, the woman Newari teacher explained that the most important subjects for boys were those that would enhance their future marketability:

> Math and English. It [learning both those subjects] helps in business also. Most of the boys do [their own] business [rather] than the job. Here, in our school, most of them come from the business family.

Another teacher, a Brahmin man, echoed her sentiments, stressing the importance of English for boys:

> Especially, it is very essential for the shopkeepers because they [the foreigners] go to buy the things in their shop, and in that case, if he [the shopkeeper] speaks English, then he'll have good business, and if he doesn't know English, he'll lose the business. Being the sons of businessmen, they [boys at this school] have to go to foreign country, and at that time, English is very necessary.

A man Tamang teacher stressed that boys should study math and science because "Math and science are important to produce the technicians." Four teachers gave family-related reasons for their choice of subjects for girls. For example, a Brahmin man teacher observed, "Nepali language is important to write the letters to her husband. She can express her feelings." Like many of the interviewees from both the community member and parent/guardian samples, a man Ansari teacher said girls should study health so that they could become a nurse. He rationalized that girls would not "have to compete with the boys in this field." Being competitive in the job market was encouraged for boys and their studies; in contrast, this teacher wanted girls to go into a field where they would be protected from competition.

And when asked about ideal level of educational achievement for boys, a man Chhetri teacher explained, boys needed to study up to Master's degree so that they could achieve advanced job-related skills and help build the nation:

> There are very few [low amounts of] manpower in [the] technical field and administrative field. Engineering [is] also a good field for

Reinforcing Gender in Schools

the development of [the] nation. Therefore, [a] high level of education should be achieved.

In comparison, three teachers argued for an ideal educational level for girls in domestic terms: Girls needed to study up to higher level because they would be mothers in the future. A man Brahmin teacher argued,

> Those who have money should educate their daughters up to SLC. Because to educate the girls means an educated mother. If the mother is educated, then she can bring her child in [to] the educated atmosphere. She teaches her child to learn and write and [she] helps them with the [their] studies . . . . For them [the children], mother is their first teacher.

A woman Newari teacher opined,

> Girls are the main members of the family. [A] Mother plays an important role in their children's life. Children can learn both the good and bad thing[s] from their mother. It's up to mother for their upbringing. [An] educated mother helps her children to learn and study. Therefore, I think it is necessary for the girls to study.

Although this teacher couched her explanation in socially constructed terms, she did point out the pivotal role women could potentially play—"as the main member in the family and an important role in their children's life."

A man Tamang teacher concluded that,

> It's OK if they [girls] study up to degree [Master's], but mostly when girls get married, they are trapped in their family life. And have to focus in [on] their domestic life. Boys also [are] trapped in their domestic life after they get married, but not so much [as] the girls. Therefore, they [the girls] should study up to diploma [Bachelor's] or at least up to certificate [intermediate] level because they are physically not so strong and can't work outside [in the public sphere] in comparison to the men. They [the women] can't go far away to work. Besides, the young babies need to be taken care of by their mother. Mother plays the important role in rearing the children. Due to this, they [the women/mothers] can't go elsewhere, leaving their home and children just to work or study.

As discussed in Chapter Four, girls were often more bound by gender norms and obligations than were boys. Because of this, girls may have been obliged to forego their educational pursuits in order to fulfill their socially constructed gender obligations. The teacher recognized the constraints on girls, but he did not question their utility. Gender construction theorist Barbara Risman (1998) maintains that we take these social constructions of gender for granted because,

> Gender at the interactional and institutional levels so thoroughly organizes our work, family, and community lives that even those who reject gender inequality in principle sometimes end up being compelled by the "logic" of gendered situations and cognitive images to choose gendered strategies (1998:34–35).

Assigning girls and women to domestic roles ensured stability in these social arrangements.

Interviewing head teachers and teachers provided evidence of their gendered attitudes towards students' ability, performance, and potential. Yet, interviews did not tell the whole story. For example, a man Jirel teacher opined, "Girls perform best in class. Girls have high [higher] thinking, [are] more ambitious than the boys. Girls are laborious [work harder] and [more] obedient than the boys,"[3] yet, this was not what I observed in the classroom: Girls talked and acted out like boys, but were not as loud as the boys. Thus, observation data supplement the interview data.

Figure 5.1. Younger Students in Jiri Classroom. Photograph by author.

Reinforcing Gender in Schools 107

Figure 5.2. Older Students in Jiri Classroom. Photograph by author

Davison and Kanyuka (1992) explain that once students are inside the school, teachers influence students' ability to learn by their behavior towards them. The way teachers interact with students shapes girls' and boys' academic participation, retention, and achievement. In order to examine how gender processes within gendered institutions affected students' learning and achievement, Classes 5 and 9 classrooms at two selected schools were regularly observed (2–3 times/week) over a period of seven months. Excerpts from observation fieldnotes illustrate a typical day in the classrooms of Class 9 students at the J School and Class 5 students at the D School:

Class 9 Observation at the J School (December 13, 1999)
Assembly: When we reached the school, the students were already in their respective class lines for the assembly. These class lines were divided by gender for each class. Then, the whole school sang the national anthem. Afterwards, a man teacher read the headlines/news. The head teacher [a man] then called four teachers [all men] in front of the assembly. A Japanese woman volunteer, who was standing next to me, explained that because teachers, more than students, didn't come to school on time, the school administration wanted them to be scolded publicly. They wanted the teachers as well as the students to be punctual. The head teacher criticized the four teachers and said they needed

to be punctual or they might lose their jobs. Then, the head teacher told the school captain [a boy student] to order the assembly to turn-about and go to their classrooms.[4]

Notably, all of the leaders of the assembly were either men or older boy students. Also important to note is that the teachers who were scolded for being late were all men—the two women teachers typically arrived early or on time.

> 1st period (Math, man teacher):
> The classroom is divided into two sections—the girls sit in eight rows of benches on the right side, and the boys sit in eight rows of benches on the left. There are typically six to eight students per bench, but because there are more boys than girls, the boys are more crowded on the benches.[5] The students huddle together on these wooden benches and use wooden tables as desks. The benches we sit on are very wobbly, as are the desks. From my Western perspective, I find the benches to be terribly uncomfortable. The rows of benches face the front of the classroom, where the teacher typically stands [This teacher does not have a desk.].
>
> . . . . We were already 10 minutes late because of the extra activities in the assembly. Behind the teacher were nubs of chalk and a slate chalkboard built into the stone wall. The teacher started taking attendance at 10:15. He called each student out by her/his roster number, and if present, the student stood and responded by saying, "*Ho*" ["Yes"]. Today, there were 35 girls and 43 boys present. At 10:20, he started the class. The teacher did some mathematical problems on the board, and the students copied them from the board into their notebooks. The teacher did not call on any of the students. The teacher ended the class at 10:45. Two girls from the bench where we were sitting then asked us to leave the classroom because they said they had to clean it. The wind kicked up a lot of dust and dirt. When I asked, one of the girls said that they had a total of 20 students [both boys and girls mixed] for the daily cleaning. They each brought in a bucket of water and splashed it all over the classroom floor.

While cleaning duty was assigned randomly by student roster numbers, so in theory, both boys and girls cleaned, over time, I observed that the boys didn't really do any of the cleaning—the girls typically did it all. Albeit subtle, this reinforced students' understanding of social constructions of

Reinforcing Gender in Schools

gender: As part of their gendered education, both girl and boy students learned that girls were the ones who did the cleaning.

2nd period (Population, Health, and Environment, man teacher):
When the teacher asked, nobody had brought their homework—neither the boys nor the girls. They all said they forgot, but the boys were far more vocal in telling the teacher about the forgotten homework. The teacher looked a bit annoyed and told them to do it right away in class. The topic of the debate was "The More Children, the More Income." After some time, the teacher pointed to the boys sitting in the first row of the boys' side and instructed them to come up front, one by one, to argue their point. After all of the boys had had their turn, he moved to the girls' side of the room, where he pointed to the six girls sitting in first row of benches. Each girl made her way to the front of the classroom to do her presentation, turn by turn, row by row. Despite the large number of students in the class, this process went rather quickly, as each student did not have much [or anything] to say. Ten of the girls stood up front and did not say a word. Five of the boys mumbled, inaudibly, for 30 seconds. The 2nd period ended at 11:25. Then, we had another 10-minute break, and all the students went out of the classroom, with the boys scrambling to be the first ones outside.

4th period (Education, man teacher):
As the teacher wrote today's lesson on the board, "1. National Education System's Planning 2028" and "2. Construction of Education," students outside, from other classes [two boys and one little girl], peered into the classroom, through the doorway [a doorway without a door to close]. Some boys passed by, singing loudly, and the boys inside this classroom laughed. One boy on the last bench put his head down on the desk and slept. All the boys on the second to last bench were talking amongst themselves, even as the teacher faced them and read the lesson from the textbook aloud. A girl from outside the classroom came up to the window near the second to last bench on the girls' side, and stretched her hand in to give something to one of the girls. She stayed and talked with some of the girls through the window for a while. The teacher said, "Don't make noise," but still no one seemed to listen to him. Nobody paid attention to the teacher's lesson. The primary level students were already out in the field, and they were distracting the class. Suddenly, one girl next to Bal Kumari [research assistant on the other side of me] asked the time, very loudly, and all the boys started laughing, as they stared at her and teased her. She must have been getting hungry. A boy

in front of me called out to the teacher and said, "That is enough for today." The teacher asked why. The boy said, "We are cold and ma'ams [referring to the research assistant and me] are also feeling cold, that's why." The whole class laughed. The teacher just laughed, said "OK," and ended the class.[6]

After periods 1 through 4, there was lunch, which was referred to as "tiffin break" (snack break). Lunch break was long—over an hour—which I imagine was an especially long time for those students who did not have food to eat. A few brought snacks in tin pails. Without a playground or adequate sports equipment, students often became bored during this time, and some ended up just going home. Two more periods typically followed the "tiffin break," but canceling classes was commonplace. Further, teachers (all men) frequently conducted short class periods, sometimes as short as 15 to 25 minutes. When no one did her/his homework, as in population, health, and environment class, even less time was spent on teaching. Teachers often complained that the large numbers of students (78 students in the Class 9 described above) in the classroom prevented them from tracking and grading homework assignments. Teachers often lacked control of the classroom too—a case in point being the boy student in period four who declared class over for the day.

The crowded classrooms also contributed to students (both girls and boys) not paying attention. With anywhere from six to 10 students to a bench, generally 4–5 feet long, students found it hard to stay focused. Teachers scolded students for talking with each other or for sleeping, but the students generally ignored the teachers' retributions, even when corporal punishment was applied. Teachers hitting students, particularly boy students, was commonplace.[7] Not all teachers hit the students, however. For example, the 6th period teacher told the students to sit down if they stood and answered incorrectly. Overall, the quality of the classroom instruction seemed sub-par, despite the fact that we (a research assistant and I) were there to observe.[8]

The Class 5 classroom at the D School was quite similar to the Class 9 classroom, only Class 5's classroom was smaller in its dimensions and much darker. The tin roof overhead let in hardly any light. Like the Class 9 classroom at the J School, the walls were made of stone and packed mud, and the floor was packed mud. Discarded papers, candy wrappers, and other types of trash littered the floor of this classroom. It was slightly less cold in that room, as the school had just installed new glass windows. Only one side of the classroom had glass in the windows; the other side had boarded-up windows. This Class 5 classroom was divided into two sections—with five rows of benches on the right side and six rows of benches on the left side. The girls sat in five rows of

Reinforcing Gender in Schools 111

benches on the right side (furthest from the doorway), and the boys sat in three rows of benches on the left. Because girls were greater in number in this class, 10–12 girls sat in the front benches on the boys' side. There were typically four to six girls per bench and three to five boys to a bench. To be noted, the D School prided itself on having a greater number of girls enrolled in school than boys and had won several regional awards for this "reversed gender gap." However, upon closer inspection, I learned that many boys in the community had been taken out of this government school and had been sent to private schools by their families for a "better, higher quality education." While on the surface it appeared gender equity had been attained, in actuality, social constructions of gender dictated boys should receive a better quality education than girls.

The Class 5 students used wooden tables as desks. These benches and desks were very low to the ground and small. The rows of benches faced the front of the classroom, where the teacher typically stood (The teacher did not have a desk). Tucked in the front wall were a few homemade erasers ("dusters"), pieces of chalk, as well as a slate chalkboard built into the stone wall.

Class 5 Observation at the D School (January 10, 2000)
1st period (**Math, man teacher**):
The class officially started at 10:25—20 minutes later than the scheduled time. First, the teacher had the class sing their class song. Then, he took class attendance by calling out the students' roster numbers. Today, 24 girls and 17 boys [total: 41] called out "*Ho*" when their numbers were called. The teacher marked those present in his record book. The teacher then asked all the students to come forward to submit money for their exam fees. I asked the girl sitting next to me what it was for, and she said they had to pay 45 rupees per subject to sit for their exams. Then, the teacher talked to the girls sitting in the front bench for a while. They were too far away for me to hear what he said to them, but by his body language, I assumed it to be a casual conversation. Then, he said because they had very little time left, the students should study for a while. He sent one of the girls to get a duster from another classroom. He then started the lesson for the day [a mathematical equation from their textbooks]. The teacher went over the equation for just 15 minutes. He asked the students to "mug up" [memorize] the lesson and memorize the formula because he would be asking them about it the next day. Then he left the classroom, 15 minutes early. While the students waited for the next teacher, they grew restless [e.g., boys punching and pinching each other, girls talking with friends]. It quieted down when the students saw the next teacher

approaching. Today, I noticed that there was a broken windowpane in one of the windows.

I often observed teachers calling on a girl student to retrieve something. Girls might have been included in the roster and sat in the same classroom as the boys, but they received quite a different education than the boys: Even in school, they were expected to fulfill their gendered roles as caretakers and housekeepers.

> 2nd period (Environment, man teacher):
> This period started at 11 am—15 minutes late. The teacher came in and wrote the title of the lesson on the board. He started with his lesson on gases. The girls sitting next to me were talking and giggling. The girls sitting in front of them warned them that they would get into trouble. The teacher struck the boy in the 3rd bench for not paying attention. With his hand, the teacher hit the boy's head, and the boy cowered and raised his arms above his head, in an attempt to protect himself. The teacher then returned to lecturing about different types of gases. As he read aloud from the textbook, the students followed along in their copies of the text. There were no individual student-teacher interactions. He asked the whole class some questions: "CO2?" And the class answered, "CO2." And then he said, "*Ho?*" ["Yes?"]. After finishing explaining, he wrote two questions from the lesson on the board to answer as homework, and then left the classroom. Then again the students [boys and girls] started talking with their friends. A few boys had gone outside and were calling the boys inside to come out so those boys went outside too.

In this instance, my research assistants and I could not code for gendered teacher-student interactions as there were no interactions at all. At the time of this study, teachers in this village commonly implemented rote responses and rote memorization as teaching practices. Also to be noted, we observed both girls and boys were misbehaving.

> 3rd period (Optional English, man teacher):
> The class started 10 minutes late. After the teacher came in, he started checking the assignment he had given the day before. He circulated the room, row by row, and checked each student's work individually. He indicated they had done it correctly by moving on to the next student. Then, he went on with the lesson entitled "Make Some *Chapatis,*" from their Level 3 English textbook, suitable for two grades below them. He

read aloud from the textbook. Some students didn't pay attention [e.g., Some students (one girl and one boy) were playing with their pens, and the girl in front of me continually turned around to see what I was doing], while others read aloud from the book with him. Then, he went on to do the questions at the end of the lesson in the book. When he wrote the first question on the board and asked some students [five girls and one boy] for the answer, none of the students could answer. He helped those who tried to answer [one girl and one boy guessed] and then wrote the answer on the board. Meanwhile, one girl was complaining to the teacher, saying that her friend was bothering her, but her complaints went unheard. He instructed the class to do the rest of the questions by themselves for homework and bring it for the next class. Then, he left the classroom.

4th period (Physical/Health Science, woman teacher):
This was the last period before the lunch or tiffin break. The teacher started explaining different kinds of games. She talked about creative and active games and discussed the activities of some of the group games in this category. Yesterday [last class] she taught three different games: (1) duck walk in a group; (2) elephant walk in a group; (3) the eagle's fly. Today, she reviewed the actions in each of these games [e.g., how to walk like a duck]. One of the boys in the back row on the boys' side mocked the teacher's voice, but she didn't react. Some boys were pulling their friend's hair while the teacher wrote on the board. A few boys had trouble controlling their laughter. Then suddenly one of the girls started laughing. The teacher turned around and asked what had happened, but no one said anything. She then asked the students to copy what she wrote on the board into their exercise books. Then the class ended, 15 minutes early.

6th period (Nepali, man teacher):
The teacher came into the classroom and lectured [read aloud, directly from the Nepali textbook] from the front of the classroom for about 15 minutes. Throughout the lesson, the boys in the back two rows on the boys' side and the girls in the last row on the girls' side talked with their friends. Then, he made the whole class do "mind reading" [reading to themselves]. After the students read silently for a while, the teacher began to ask questions about the meaning of words. As he walked around the room, a girl in the front told the teacher to hit the boy next to her for shouting in her ears and saying "*Kooo.*" Everybody laughed. The teacher called on seven girls—Two answered his questions

correctly, and the teacher acknowledged their answers by moving on and calling on another student. Five girls could not give an answer when called on [They just stood silently]. The teacher did nothing but told them to sit down [He did not coax or help them to come up with an answer]. The teacher called on six boys—The three who answered correctly were asked to sit down. The three boys who could not give an answer were also asked to sit down. After asking students questions, the teacher went back to the textbook and read aloud from it. Four boys and three girls in the back rows continued to talk to each other. Then he assigned some class work. A few girls complained to the teacher that their friends were disturbing them, while the other girls were busy working on the class assignment. The teacher only smiled and looked on. The girl in front of me, who was next to me before the lunch break, turned around and said, "This teacher is very kind and doesn't beat anyone so nobody listens to him." As soon as the teacher left the classroom, the students started running around and shouting.

While the third period teacher ignored the girl student's complaints, a woman teacher in 4th period teacher let the boys who mocked her voice go undisciplined. Perhaps unaccustomed to women teachers, these boys were attempting to challenge her. In regard to punishment and discipline, this varied from teacher to teacher. I never saw either of the two women teachers hit a student. Although no child wants to be punished, it was interesting that the girl student in 6th period noted that no one listened to that teacher, who was a man, because he did not use corporal punishment, which she accepted as the norm for misbehavior.

7th period (*Mero Desh* ["My Country"]—Social Studies, woman teacher): We saw this teacher only occasionally; she did not come to school everyday. The teacher started reading from the textbook right away. All the students were very attentive. Suddenly, one girl burst into laughter. The teacher asked the girl why she laughed, and she didn't answer. The teacher warned her that she would throw her out of the class if she laughed again. Then the teacher went on with the lesson. As she read straight from the textbook, she jumped from one lesson to another. At the end of each lesson, she asked if anyone had questions and if they understood. All the students [boys and girls] nodded to indicate that they understood, but I am not sure they all did. No one seemed to want to raise her/his hand. After finishing the lessons, she told the class to read and to come prepared for the next time. After teaching for 15 minutes, she left the classroom.

Shorter class periods (e.g., the 15–20 minute 1st period math class) were typical at both the D School and J School. Similar to Class 9 at the J School, classes at the D School often started late, and then logistical activities—roll call, singing the class song—consumed the little time remaining. Although the Class 5 students stayed in the same classroom throughout the day, the teachers moved from classroom to classroom. However, all five buildings on the D School campus were in close proximity to one another; there appeared to be ample time for teachers to move from classroom to classroom in between periods.

Observations at the J School and the D School also provide a glimpse of the expenses students faced. Both schools required students to wear uniforms everyday. Further, students had to provide their own school supplies and textbooks. And on top of that, they had to pay examination fees. Paying close to 300 rupees twice a year was a large sum of money for almost all residents of the Jiri Valley. Attending a private school would have cost even more. So, here again, while the D School had a greater number of girl students enrolled than boy students, parents' sending their sons to private schools, rather than the less expensive government schools, reinforced gender constructs. These gendered actions implied girls needed less education as future housekeepers, wives, and mothers, whereas boys, as future breadwinners, needed more and better quality education to succeed.

In addition to taking fieldnotes, teacher-student interactions in Class 5 and Class 9 classrooms were coded for more accurate analysis. I selected two indicators of teacher interaction with students: One was frequency of times a teacher called on a student (by gender) in an observation period, and the other was teachers' responses to the students' answers—praise, criticism, acceptance, or remediation. I found these observed teacher-student interactions to be gendered. Specifically, teachers generally gave more attention (e.g., calling on, as well as giving praise, criticism, remediation, and acceptance) to boys than they did to girls. As Sadker & Sadker (1994) argue, praising, probing, questioning, and correcting students sharpen their ideas, refine their thinking, and help them gain confidence. Gendered interactions in the Jiri classrooms only reinforced what students had learned at home.

We made 21 all-day observations of Class 5 at the D School, with a varying number of times observing particular subjects.[9] As aforementioned, class periods varied in length; some teachers taught for 15 minutes in a period, and others for 45 minutes. There were more girls enrolled in Class 5 than boys: The average number of Class 5 boy students in attendance on any give day was 16, whereas the average number of Class 5 girl students was 24. Class 5 boy students generally had more interactions with their teachers than did the Class 5 girl students, despite the fact that more girls than boys were enrolled in this class. We observed the teachers calling on boys an average of 8.14 times per observation, whereas girls were called on an average of 6 times per observation.

Because girls constituted 60% of the class, gender equity in the classroom would indicate they would be called on by their teachers 60% of the total number of times a teacher calls on a student. We did not observe this to be the case. Only the Optional English and Environment teachers called on girls and boys proportionally. The Social Studies, Math, and Nepali teachers called on boys disproportionately more (45.2%, 48.2% and 46.9%, respectively). While the woman Physical Education teacher called on girls at a higher rate (83.3%), it should be noted that this was based on a very small total number of times the teacher called on students.

Further, teachers generally gave more attention to the boy students, particularly praise and criticism, than to the girl students.[10] In contrast to boys, teachers generally interacted with girl students in a more "accepting" way: They acknowledged the girl students' answers with either a passive (not critical or praising) response or by not responding at all and moving on to the next student. Although the man Optional English teacher gave more praise to both girl and boy students than any other teacher, he also gave far more acceptances to girls (77) than he did to boys (27). Except for the Math class, the two women teachers not only had fewer interactions with boys than did the men teachers, but they also had fewer interactions with girls. Just as teacher-student interactions influence students' academic performance, academic achievement, and perceptions of their abilities, the women teachers not interacting with students or interacting with the students very little could also have influenced students and their educational experiences.

We made 24 all-day observations of Class 9 at the J School, and again, the number of times observing particular subjects varied.[11] It should be noted that all of the Class 9 teachers were men. Similar to Class 5, the average class period ranged from 15 to 45 minutes in duration. In contrast to Class 5, there were more boys than girls enrolled at this level. The average number of Class 9 boys was 46, whereas the average number of Class 9 girls was 34. Boys constituted 58% of the total students enrolled in Class 9, and girls constituted 43%. As noted in Chapter Two, girls' enrollment numbers in Nepal have historically diminished with increasing grade levels.

Similar to Class 5 boys, Class 9 boys had more interactions with their teachers than girls. We observed teachers calling on boys an average of 7.1 times per observation, whereas girls were called on an average of 5.6 times per observation. Similar to the results from Class 5 observations, teachers called on boys disproportionately more, with the one exception being the Education teacher, who called on more girls. Social Studies, Optional Geography, and Science teachers called on students fairly proportionally.

Class 9 teachers generally gave more attention to the boys in all coding categories (praise, criticism, acceptance and remediation) than they gave to the girls. Notably, in Population, Health, and Environment classes, girls received 1 ½ times more criticism than boys, even though they were fewer in numbers. In that same class, boys received 10 times more punishment than girls, and eight times as many acceptances. Similarly, the Education teacher gave more criticism and fewer praises and acceptances to girls than to boys. This same teacher also called on girls more times than boys. And in the Science class, the man teacher was observed doing the following:

> The teacher told two boys to bring a table to the front of the classroom. He asked three other boys to bring in a scale and a spring balance with a long wooden ruler from the school's science lab.[12] The teacher called on a boy and made him weigh a rock on the spring balance. Then, the teacher called on another boy to put another rock on the scale and to check its weight. The teacher called on a girl and made her walk from one corner of the room to the other. She hesitated at first, but I imagine she figured she had no choice but to follow the teacher's instructions. He noted with his watch the time it took for her to walk. The teacher called on another boy and had him measure the distance with the ruler.

Notably, this teacher called on more boys than girls—he only called on one girl. Further, the girl acted as a demonstration, whereas the boy did the practical exercise. Attention from the teacher is critical to the individual student's learning and self-perceptions—even extra criticism can be helpful to the student's academic development. However, to be gender equitable, this teacher would have given both boys and girls equal amounts of praise, criticism, acceptance, and remediation. All of the gendered interactions described above served to reinforce what students had learned at home.

Reading and learning about women in socially constructed gender roles increases the likelihood girls will limit themselves to stereotypes. My research also included examining, coding and analyzing Class 9 and Class 5 textbooks for gender bias. Using Sadker, Sadker, & Lewit's (1995) guide,[13] we coded textbooks for invisibility of women, cultural stereotyping, and gendered linguistic bias. Using these indicators, we assessed both written text and illustrations. The Class 9 Nepali textbook had the greatest gender bias with a composite score of 33.5%. Although we found that the Class 9 Science and Math textbooks had low percentages of gender bias, it should be noted that there were very few illustrations in these books. Further, all of the illustrations in the Science text featured boys or men except for one. In the Class 9 English textbook, women were generally portrayed as emotional and dependent: For example, a writing exercise asked the reader to help Chandra—"She can't do well in science in spite of her hard work." Another scenario depicted a sobbing wife, whose irritated husband said, "Oh! Please be quiet Priya!"

Of the Class 5 textbooks, the Compulsory English text had the greatest percentage of gender bias (41.5%), followed by the Environment text (28.1%). Stories in the English text also portrayed men and women in stereotypical roles. Men and boys were portrayed as active and independent, whereas women were portrayed as docile and, in the case of a story with a monster and a little girl, in need of rescuing. The gender stereotypes conveyed in the students' textbooks reinforced the social constructions of gender students first learned in their homes.

STUDENTS "DO GENDER"

The school climate, the administration, the teachers, and the instructional materials all reinforced the existing prescribed gender roles for girls and boys. Maintaining these gender prescriptions only further constrained students, especially girls, to "do gender" in ways that ultimately limited their educational opportunities and prospects for the future. Specifically, the social construction of gender affected students' interactions, attitudes, perceptions, use of time, and school attendance and participation. During class, free periods, time in between classes, and the lunch breaks, boys and girls, as well as women and men teachers, all "did gender." For example, at lunch break, the women teachers typically sat in the sun and knitted, while the men teachers played football (soccer) with the boy students or wandered into town to see friends. Observations of classrooms in Jiri revealed incidents of both girls and boys "doing gender." As observed in the Class 9 Population, Health, and Environment class,

> The classroom was very noisy when we re-entered at 11 a.m. Girls were talking to other girls, and boys were talking loudly with other boys. The boys' voices could be heard above all the girls' conversations. Last class, the teacher had instructed the students to write and bring in a few points for an in-class debate. But when the teacher asked, nobody had brought their homework—neither the boys nor the girls. They all said they forgot, but the boys were far more vocal in telling the teacher about the forgotten homework.

This was also illustrated in the Class 5 Math class:

> He asked the students to "mug up" the lesson and memorize the formula because he would be asking them about it the next day. Then he left the classroom, 15 minutes early. While the students waited for the next teacher, they grew restless. The boys started punching and pinching each other, while the girls chatted with friends.

The social construction of gender in home and school, as reinforced by parents and teachers, not only influenced students' behavior, but also influenced students' attitudes towards education and their perceptions of their own educational and career aspirations, as well as their hopes and plans for the future. While the majority of student interviewees stated that girls and boys were equally intelligent, five students responded that boys were more intelligent than girls. Of these, four were girls. This means that girls may have been more likely to view themselves as less intelligent than the boys, though the sample was small (N=20). Equal numbers of those four were from Class 5 (2) and Class 9 (2). Class 9 boy student Amrit explained,

> In my opinion, boys are more intelligent than girls. *Why do you think so?* Because girls cannot think as much as boys can. Even if they think, they cannot bring into behavior [practice], so I think boys are more intelligent than girls.

Leela Maya, a Class 9 student, rationalized that boys "are very active and good at games and other activities" and were therefore more intelligent than girls. She added that boys "are superior to girls in many ways." Her classmate Nima said, "Sons are very brilliant and champions." Certainly, girls were not less capable than boys (as their statements imply), but rather, because boys have had more opportunities, their successes have been more apparent. Boys having more opportunities was an aspect of the social order—a part of the everyday reality in the gendered context in which both the girls and boys lived.

Of the students who remarked girls were more intelligent, gender was implicit in their explanations. Class 9 girl student Krishna Kumari explained that daughters were more intelligent than sons because "the daughter will understand the problems of the house and the mother." This defining of girls' intelligence in gendered terms (e.g., domestic responsibilities for girls) reflects the responses of many men and women interviewees from both the community member and parent/guardian samples.

Eighteen out of the 20 students interviewed said it was important for both girls and boys to be educated. Specifically, all Class 9 students interviewed said both girls and boys should be educated, and all but two of the Class 5 students believed it was important for both girls and boys to attend school. The exceptions were Ram Prasad and Sanjita. Ram Prasad said that parents should give priority to boys because "they have to work to earn money and look after their family. They have to go for the war. So they have to know so many things." Ram Prasad conceptualized men as the breadwinner and the protector—socially constructed conceptualizations of men that came from gender processes built into Nepali society. Sanjita, a girl, also said it was more important for boys to go to school. When asked why she felt this way, she became very shy and did not give a reason as to why. Through the gendered interactions and socialization that were part of her daily life, she most likely had come to presume boys were valued more and therefore should be educated ahead of girls.

Other than Ram Prasad and Sanjita, the student interviewees said children, regardless of their gender, should be educated equally. Dal Bahadur gave reasons for both boys and girls to go to school based on the existing Nepali gendered social order of which he was part:

> It is important for both of them [boys and girls] to go to school. Because daughters also, if they study well, it will be good for their own future. Then, the sons also, if they study now, it will do them good in the future. They can do trekking [get into the trekking business]. Daughters, if they stay at home and their husband sends [a] letter from [a] foreign land, she will be able to read out the letter by herself.

Similar to so many interviewees from the parent/guardian, community member, and school staff samples, when Dal Bahadur spoke of sons, he couched his comments in job-related terms. Also, like many other interviewees, when he spoke of daughters, he described school as beneficial to them in domestic-related terms. Even though Dal Bahadur viewed education as important for girls and boys, the purpose for educating them differed in his mind. He had come to accept and embrace different social roles and aspirations for women and men in Nepali society.

Social constructions of gender also affected students' perceptions of educational achievement and particular areas of study. Some students explained that health was a suitable subject for girls because it was related to caring for a family, and it might help a girl to become a nurse. Two boy students and one girl student explained that if girls study health, they would then be able to look after their families if someone got sick. Boy student Amrit further explained that, "After marriage, girls need to know how to raise their children." Linking girls with health care followed the general belief in Nepal that women were "naturally" inclined to be caretakers and nurturers when, in actuality, these were actually socially constructed roles. One boy Class 9 student did diverge from the stereotypes by suggesting that science, typically a male-dominated field in Nepal, might be good for girls. However, his reason for this choice was gendered: He explained that studying science was important so that girls "can be aware of their own health and will do good for their families."

Seven students out of the 10 who chose math for boys explained their choice in terms of future careers that were socially defined as "masculine" in Nepal (e.g., engineer, businessman, pilot), pointing to the institutionalization of gender. Six students suggested science as the most appropriate subject for boys. Similar to math, these students stated that boys who studied science could pursue future careers in male-dominated fields (e.g., doctor, scientist). Class 5 girl student Phul Maya and Class 5 boy student Ritesh explained that boys needed to study English in order to travel and get a trekking job with foreigners.[14]

Socially constructed processes of gender also influenced this selected group of Nepali students' perceptions of their own ability to achieve in the educational system. For this sample, more boy students had higher aspirations than did the girl students interviewed. Five boy students hoped to achieve a Bachelor's diploma or better, whereas only two girl students hoped to achieve this level. Socially constructed gender constraints seemed to influence the educational aspirations of girl students more so than the boy students.

None of the students aspired to achieve a Master's degree, whereas many of their parents/guardians, teachers, and community members suggested students (both girls and boys) aspire to this level. Notably, fewer girls aspired to a Bachelor's diploma than either their parents/guardians or community members (or their teachers) aspired for them. Only two of 10 girl students aspired to this level, whereas half of the boys aspired to this level. Again, I would argue that for this sample, the social construction of gender constrained the aspirations of girls more so than boys.

Linked to educational aspirations were students' career aspirations. As a result of the existing Nepali gendered order, students in the sample demonstrated that they "did gender" by selecting occupations that were aligned with socially approved, gendered occupations. Girl students' career aspirations reflected the gender processes that confined women to certain prescribed roles and occupations. For example, Class 9 students Sanjita,

Monica, Krishna Kumari, Leela Maya, and Nima all hoped to become nurses so that they could take care of sick people; they also wanted to be knowledgeable about hygiene and diseases in order to care for their families.

Boy students in the group had career aspirations that also reflected the existing gendered order: Ritesh hoped to join the military, Kedar and Chhetra aspired to become doctors, and Ram Bahadur hoped to be a pilot. Gopal wanted to go abroad for work. Two boy students aspired to become engineers, and another, an electronics expert, but none of the girl students expressed interest in these occupations.

Gender constructs, introduced in the home and reinforced in schools, also determined students' perceptions of their future. Tilak's life history interview illustrates this. At the time of his life history interview, Tilak studied at the J School in Class 9. He was 19 years old. A member of the Jirel ethnic group, he lived with 17 family members in one house, including three older brothers, one younger brother, two older sisters, a younger sister, three sisters-in-law, and a male cousin. Both his parents were farmers:

> When I was small, I used to play around, roam about, eat and sleep. Before I started my school, I only ate and played. But after I was put into school, I started going to school. I would be in school all day and return [home] in the evening. *Tell me about your friends and family.* What to say? . . . . I have many friends. I have different group of friends in my village and different group of friends in school. Some of my friends work, some are studying, some go trekking with the foreigners, and some are working in a carpet factory. Our relatives are all farmers here. Sometimes the men go for labor work and sometimes for trekking and the women stay at home, either doing their fieldwork or housework . . . . *In what ways would you say your life is different, having gone to school?* I feel I am better off than the people who haven't been to school. I feel I have had a good chance in my life by being able to go to school. I can read and understand many things. I think now nobody will be able to cheat me like if I had been illiterate. I can speak and put forward my thoughts very easily in front of people whenever I have to. Now since I will be having my education certificates, I think it will be very easy for me to apply for jobs . . . . *What kinds of things do you do in the community? Are you involved in any sports?* Yes, I am a member of our village club . . . . We are 20 to 30 people of the same village. We all gather and decide among ourselves on which game to play. And play accordingly . . . . *Tell me about your plans for the future.* I will try to

find a job. Then after I start earning money I will look after my parents. Try to help out the poor people in my village and neighbors. I will try to do all the works I can accomplish to help my family.

As seen in interviews with Class 9 boy students, Tilak also appeared to know what was expected of him in the future as a man in Nepalese society: He recognized he would eventually become a breadwinner. However, for the time being, he concentrated on his studies and enjoyed time spent with friends. Tilak provides an example of how the gendered social order typically constrained boys and their plans for the future to a much lesser extent than it did girls. As discussed in Chapter Four, the heaviest expectation for boys was to take on the role of the breadwinner for the family in the future; until that time, boys were often able to "play" and do as they pleased. Unlike girls, delayed expectations for boys affected their schooling positively, as they were able to stay in school longer and attain higher educational levels. As consequence, boy students like Tilak believed they had "a good chance in life by being able to go to school." They looked to their future with optimism and hope.

CONCLUSIONS

Within the gendered social structures of the family and the education system, community members, parents, guardians, teachers, and head teachers socially constructed and reinforced gender for the students in this study. This chapter examined the gendered education students received in the schools of Jiri VDC. Head teachers' and teachers' attitudes and behavior reinforced the gender constructs students had first learned in their homes. As consequence, these gender constructs constrained students, particularly girl students, to "do gender" in ways that ultimately limited their educational opportunities and prospects for the future.

Many head teachers couched explanations for their responses to interview questions in socially constructed gender terms, such as girls as future wives, mothers, and housekeepers, and boys as future breadwinners. One head teacher linked these roles to "inborn" qualities, explaining girls should take home science because "they have an inborn quality for that . . . they are very kind, they are soft-hearted, dutiful." In doing so, he assumed that girls were "naturally" suited for care giving, leaving them with little or no agency. When head teachers turned to taken-for-granted assumptions for explanations, they reinforced the existing prescribed roles for girls. In doing so, they constrained girls' chances for negotiating and changing gender constructs.

Similar to the head teachers, community members, and parents/guardians, most of the Class 5 and Class 9 teachers drew on Nepali gender stereotypes in their explanations for ideal educational attainment level by gender and the best subject for students by gender. For instance, one teacher explained that the most important subjects for boys were those that would enhance their future marketability. Conversely, subjects for girls were more often identified within domestic spheres and future domestic responsibilities. One man teacher argued boys needed to study up to a high level so that they might "help build the nation," and others suggested girls should study up to a high level for the benefit of her future children. Designating men as nation builders and women in domestic terms is a common thread in the social construction of gender across cultures and across histories, and school experiences in particular often provide girls and boys with messages that reinforce rather than challenge the prevailing gendered division of labor (Stromquist 1989a).

My findings are consistent with the literature on gendered education. Throughout the world, there is continuous reinforcement of existing gender relations through text materials and student-teacher interactions (Smith 2000). My observations revealed consistent gendered teacher-student interactions in Jiri classrooms. Teachers seemed to privilege male voices and male activities in the classroom by generally giving more attention (e.g., calling on, as well as giving praise, criticism, remediation, and acceptance) to boys than they did to girls. The praising, probing, questioning, and correcting students most likely sharpened the boys' ideas, refined their thinking, and helped them gain confidence (Sadker & Sadker 1994).

Gender bias in teaching compounded with a gender-biased curriculum only perpetuates the reproduction of gender inequality. In addition to lack of attention from teachers, the Class 9 and Class 5 textbooks frequently imposed stereotypical images of women and girls. Girls' reading and learning about women in socially constructed gender roles in their textbooks increased the likelihood that they would limit themselves to stereotypes. The gendering the girls experienced at home was reinforced in schools, as girls were encouraged to be docile, passive, and dependent.

Students' gendered educational experiences affected students' interactions, attitudes, perceptions, use of time, and school attendance and participation. Consequently, students were constrained to "do gender." This was demonstrated in students' gendered interactions and behavior. Further, responses to interview questions indicated many students had come to accept and embrace *different* social roles and aspirations for adult women and adult men in Nepali society. It is important to note that these social constructions of gender not only affected who went to school, but also students' perceptions of their own abilities, their educational achievement, particular areas of study, and career aspirations. Higher expectations for boys not only affected boys' academic achievement positively, but these gendered expectations also affected their own aspirations in a meaningful way. Conversely, the lower expectations for girls limited their educational achievement and adversely affected their individual aspirations.

IMPLICATIONS

Literature on the benefits of educating girls largely focuses on increasing enrollment numbers and participation rates of girls. It presumes that girls' access to school will lead to equality between girls and boys, and that girls passing through an educational system will guarantee their actual participation in schools and equal participation in the broader society. Furthermore, educational funding initiatives aimed at girls tend to assume girls and boys enter schools that are gender neutral. My findings indicate the girl and boy students enrolled in schools that operated as *gendered institutions* with established gender patterns and processes.

This localized example provides a lesson for the "universal." The embeddedness of gender roles in the context of schools only perpetuates inequalities. By failing to recognize this beforehand, research and initiatives to help girls in school risk missing the point. Analyzing gender inequality in schools should be problematized with a careful exploration of how gender is socially constructed and maintained in *both* school and the home. Then we can begin to understand and devise more effective ways to increase all students' enrollment, participation and success in school.

Importantly, socially constructed gender constraints are dynamic rather than static and can be negotiated. Schools could potentially help girl students *and* boy students empower themselves to negotiate and change these gender constraints and subsequently, transform their lives. Students and others who challenged the gender-constructed social order maintained and reinforced in the gendered contexts of homes and schools are discussed in the following chapter.

Chapter Six
Gender Trouble Makers: Individuals Resisting Gender Constraints

> If I pass [Class 9], I will study further and so on. Then after that I will go to look for some work. I will earn my own living, and then try to support my family since I am the eldest.
> —Sanu Kumari, Class 9 girl student

> It is better to educate both the boy and the girl . . . . They stayed in the same womb, pillowed their heads on the same liver.
> —Sabitri, woman community member

Gender constructs constrain individuals, but that does not mean individuals are without agency, as examples in this chapter will illustrate. Because gender constraints in any society are socially constructed, they can be challenged, contested, renegotiated, dismantled, and reconstructed (Potuchek 1997). This chapter examines students' resistance—students, who I would argue acted as "gender trouble makers" (Lorber 2000). This chapter also presents and discusses other agents of social change. Individuals who pushed gender constraints illustrate the potential for changing the gendered social order.

PUSHING GENDER CONSTRAINTS: EXAMPLES OF STUDENTS AS GENDER TROUBLE MAKERS

Some students in this study challenged existing gender constructs by changing their own aspirations and goals to those that more closely fit their needs, rather than what the prevailing gendered order dictated. Two Class 5 girl students shine as examples. When asked about her future career, Class 5 student Sagun, unlike her fellow girl students, hoped to become a traffic controller with the Nepali police. Thus, she stepped out of pre-existing gendered occupations. She said she loved "everything about that job." In making such a choice, she pushed against the given gender constructs that privileged Nepali men in public security positions. Class 5 girl student Phul Maya hoped to run her own family business—a hotel/lodge business. Phul Maya and Sagun not only challenged the norm that defined their job aspirations as "men's work," but by choosing alternative paths, these girls challenged existing assumptions about their futures and modified the roles expected of them. I argue that in doing so, these girls contributed to the dismantling of the existing gendered social order.

Other examples included Class 9 students Leela Maya and Monica, whose favorite subjects were science and math, respectively. These two students refused to fit into any universal stereotype that math and science are too difficult for girls to comprehend. Monica selected math as her favorite subject because she was "interested" in math and it was also a subject she found easy. She did not link its usefulness to any future occupation. Leela Maya, in contrast, said that even though science was "not that easy," she figured it would help her to get a job.[1] Leela Maya appeared to be looking critically at course options and was cognizant of skills needed to succeed in a market economy. Even within the constraints of a gendered Nepali society and gendered educational system, these girls demonstrated independent agency, thus pushing the gendered norms in academia.

Sita, a Class 5 girl student, had high educational aspirations: She aspired to secure a Bachelor's diploma and wanted to become a teacher. She explained that she wanted to become a teacher in order to "put forward some of my views regarding the environment." Sita's classmate Kamala also hoped to become a teacher because she had been impressed with her teachers at school.

Girl student Krishna Kumari and boy student Dal Bahadur both planned to study up to a high level as well. Class 9 student Krishna Kumari planned to study up to the campus level[2] so that she could get a job and make her own choices about her life. She said, "I'll go to places I wish to visit. I'll try to stand on my own feet [be independent]. Then only I'll marry...later only." Krishna Kumari pushed gender constraints to reorder her priorities. For her, education came before marriage. With education, she would be independent and would make her own decisions as to when she would marry. Similarly, Class 5 student Dal Bahadur wanted to study up to the School Leaving Certificate (SLC) level so he, too, would have more agency. He hoped to achieve a high enough position that would discourage anyone from cheating him. He elaborated, "We become wiser [with education]. People won't be able to mislead or deceive us." Dal Bahadur conceived of education as a tool to empower himself.

As expressed in her life history narrative, Class 9 student Sanu Kumari, first and foremost, aspired to finish her education:

> *Where do you see yourself living in one year?* If I pass [Class 9], I will study further and so on. *Then after five years?* Then after that I will go to look for some work. I will earn my own living, and then try to support my family since I am the eldest. *Then after ten years?* Maybe I will have married and will have kids and I would be busy raising them [laughs] . . . . *Please tell me what you hope for in the future, for yourself and for your family.* I hope they have a good life. Better than now . . . . *Picture yourself as an elected official who will go to Kathmandu to represent the people of Jiri. What issues would you address?* What to say? Umm . . . I would talk about the village problems like water, electricity, and even girls' education.

After finishing her schooling, she intended to look for work and earn her own living. She only planned to marry later. Setting these priorities demonstrated her independence. As the eldest, she planned to help support her family. Although Sanu Kumari's position in her family obliged her to support her family and might have subsequently limited her future choices, envisioning herself as a breadwinner for the family demonstrates resistance to the gender construct, which in the existing Nepali gendered order, viewed men and boys as the providers of economic security in the family. She also resisted the gender norm that girls marry early. She was very committed to completing her education so that she could find a self-supporting job.

It is important to remember that socially constructed gender constraints, created by society and often maintained by schools, are dynamic rather than static and can be negotiated and resisted. The story of a young woman starting her career as a teacher illustrates this point. Her story is significant not only because it demonstrates how individual agency can modify existing gender expectations in education but also because there were so few women teachers in Jiri VDC schools at the time of this study. In 1999–2000, one of Jiri's major needs was for more women teachers to provide positive role models for girls and to encourage them in their education.

At the time of her life history interview, Laxmi was 17 years old. She came from a poor Chhetri (Hindu) family. The fifth of eight children in her family, she had four sisters and three brothers. When she was interviewed, she was studying at the high school in the 10+2 program. She also taught at a primary school. She explained that after passing the SLC exam at the end of Class 9 and joining the 10+2 program, she worried about whether or not she would be able to continue in her studies. She mentioned to a head teacher that she was thinking of one day becoming a teacher. "Come tomorrow and you'll be a Miss [woman teacher]," Laxmi said he replied. Thus began Laxmi's career as a teacher.

I went to observe Laxmi teach on several occasions. Laxmi had attended a series of teacher trainings offered by a British volunteer and her village community member counterpart in 1999–2000, and I observed Laxmi incorporating their suggestions for student-based learning in her teaching. She kept her students engaged with participatory activities and made sure she called on each student, at least once, regardless of their gender. In telling her story, Laxmi began,

> Our parents are not educated. I am heading [hoping] to study further and my uncle's daughter [cousin] is a diploma [Bachelor's] graduate. So seeing her, I also want to study further . . . *Tell me about a typical day for you.* I go to college from 6a.m. to 9:45a.m. Then I hurry back home [rented room] and prepare food for myself very quickly [laughs]. Then I run down to the MS School. Then I reach the school at around 10:10 or 10:15. Then I take [teach] class until 3p.m. Then by the time I reach home, it [is] always getting dark. I reach home at 5p.m. Then I come and start preparing dinner. I sit down to study till 10p.m. Then after [that] I go to sleep. Besides studying, I teach. That's all . . . . *In what ways would you say your life is different, having gone to school?* There is a vast difference in my life because of school. As you might know, the girls in the village areas don't know about society and its whereabouts [aspects] and what would they become tomorrow. But that I have experienced [learned] after studying in school. Back in my house also, my parents are facing all the hardship, and those who did get married or not married are also trapped in hardship. Whereas since I have studied, I can make up my mind on what to become after I finish my studies. I might even be able to help my parents later. My family is very poor. So I will study very hard and after passing my 10+2, I'll join diploma and I'll continue my job as a teacher. That will help the children [her younger siblings], and they will also be able to think about their future . . . . *Picture yourself as an elected official who will go to Kathmandu to represent the people of Jiri. What issues would you address?* Our village people are still backward [not developed], what are the reasons for this? If [the problem is] because of no education, I would put forward the issues of schools and education. Then about women . . . Why they are still behind, why haven't they been able to come out of their situation [of subordination]?...Find out the reason behind these factors and ask them to solve the problems for

the upliftment of womankind. The upliftment of womankind is most important.

Laxmi illustrates that she was very much a product of gender processes in Nepal, while at the same time wanting to change existing constructions of gender. In five years' time, at the age of 22, she predicted that she would already be married and "busy with domestic/household chores." At the same time, she wanted to continue her career in teaching. She also wanted to better the position of Nepali women and girls. To this end, she initiated a girls' club in the village as a beginning.

Laxmi also demonstrates the fluidity of socially constructed gender constraints: Despite the gender expectations Nepali society obliged girls to fulfill, Laxmi shows how these constraints could be negotiated to achieve her goals. Laxmi's pursuits—studying up to a high level of education, working as a teacher, developing a club for girls—and her accomplishments illustrate that gender does not dictate ability and agency. This village's schools and the chances of girls' success in school would be improved if there were more role models in them like Laxmi. But one teacher is not enough. It takes critical mass to effect change in the ways schools construct, maintain, and reproduce gender.

EVIDENCE OF A CHANGING GENDERED SOCIAL ORDER

The gender system is dynamic, continually being challenged, contested, renegotiated, dismantled, and reconstructed, which means gender attributes are not necessarily fixed. The findings of this research confirm that notions of gender are best described in terms of a fluid continuum of traits or qualities. For example, with regard to intelligence and academic performance, a significant number of community members and some parents/guardians reported boys as better students because they "worked hard" in school and girls were less equipped to study because they were "loose," "emotional," "weak," and only "concerned with boys." However, several head teachers and almost half the teachers reported girls had better academic performance than boys because they were more studious and played around less than the boys. Therefore, it appeared that what was deemed most important, by way of traits, was not always circumscribed by gender. Rather, characteristics of being studious, ambitious, wanting to take care of the family, and finding a good job were viewed as positive traits inclusive of both genders. I assert that a greater understanding of how social constructions of gender affect perceptions of academic performance would contribute to the dismantling of established patterns of gender inequality.

Interviews and observations also illustrated how gender systems and social relations in Jiri have changed over time. An 80-year old Jirel woman and life history narrator recalled,

> Honestly, I know nothing. Why do you want to talk with me? The children of today will know everything even when they are in their mother's womb. But I know nothing. I don't even know how to talk. My parents died at an early age. As a girl, I grew up and lived with my grandfather. My grandmother also had died when I was very small. What stories could he tell me? We were engaged in herding only. I used to walk around with the livestock, cut grass, look after them [livestock], eat and sleep. That was all. Then, [at that time] I did what my grandfather told me to do. That was all. So since I was brought up in such environment, I remember nothing. Some big people [older people/adults] came and asked for my hand [in marriage], and I was handed over. I didn't go myself. I didn't see him [her husband] before. Even though I didn't have my parents, the people came to where we were staying, asked for me, and I was given to them. They [husband's family] asked for me, and they [grandfather and relatives] gave me. Then when those people [husband's family] came, they brought *chhyang* [homemade rice wine]. Doing that much only I was given to them. My family walked me to his home; they reached me to them and came back. Today, I just walk to do the plowing, digging, and earn for my survival. Everyday I walk this path. *What about schools in your time?* No, we didn't have a single school in our time whatsoever. Yes, school came much later. About the time, later, when my children grew up. Then [at] that time the *punji–pati* [people with money] sent their children to school and those who didn't have [money] couldn't send their children.

Many community members and parents/guardians spoke of schools being non-existent in their youth. In 2000, there were 15 schools in Jiri VDC. In 1996, when I conducted my preliminary study, there were no women head teachers in the Jiri VDC schools. In 2000, there were two. Two schools without any women teachers in 1996 had at least one woman teacher by the year 2000. Further, many of the community members who in the past did not send their older daughters to school expressed regret that they had not done so, and some noted that they currently send their school-age daughters to school.

Also, the percentage of respondents who said they thought girls and boys should be educated equally increased substantially from my 1996 preliminary study interviews. For example, a literate Newari man community member from the 1999–2000 study spoke for many interviewees who said both girls and boys should be educated when he stated,

> [It is] better to educate both equally. Because son is our child and daughter is our own child too, so shouldn't you look after them equally? Why discriminate them? You shouldn't discriminate children for education.

Others spoke of the changing accepted norm. For example, when asked why she would prefer to send both sons and daughters to school, a non-literate Jirel woman community member stated, "Because these days everybody educates their daughters and sends them to school," and a non-literate Jirel man from the community member sample added, "Everybody in villages educates their children." Many noted that the concept of educating girls was only a recent phenomenon. A literate Chhetri woman from the community member sample explained, "Our parents said 'What is the use of educating the girl?' But now time [norms, practices] has changed. Nowadays everybody educates their children." A non-literate Jirel man community member said that in "the old days, it was a crime to educate girls, but now time has changed." A non-literate Jirel father from the parent/guardian sample gave an almost identical response, commenting that, "The trend of educating girls [and boys] has started."

Perhaps this was a testament to the government radio broadcasts and awareness-raising programs. Community members reported hearing radio broadcasts advocating the education of girls and boys. A literate Jirel woman community member said, "Son and daughter are same. They [government programs] say so. They say so through radio [broadcasts] so many times." As part of the Nepalese government and international agencies' efforts to increase girls' enrollment numbers, there were periodic program announcements encouraging parents to send girls to school. The fact that some community members and parents/guardians had taken these announcements into consideration demonstrates the potential for these government and agency efforts to bring about real change in gendered patterns of behavior and attitudes.

Some respondents from the community member sample and the parent/guardian sample reported that they preferred to send both daughters and sons to school at the time of their interview, but had not felt the same way in the past. For example, an older, widowed, non-literate Chhetri/Brahmin woman lamented that while she now believed that boys and girls were equal and should both be educated, she did not educate her daughter. She said,

> She [her daughter] is now killing me by blaming me for not educating her but only her brother. She says, "You sent me to the jungle to collect the firewood and sent my brother to school. You should have sent me by any means." At that time, I was alone [widowed]. What could I do? Send both of them to school or [keep daughter home] to look after the animals and the housework?

As I have suggested earlier in this book, perhaps perceived direct and indirect (opportunity) costs saved by not sending a daughter to school were more a matter of socially constructed gender constraints than inevitable economic limitations. Encouragingly, a Jirel woman from the parent/guardian sample questioned these perceived greater costs of educating girls. She insisted,

> You cannot get away saying you don't have enough [money]. You cannot say I will educate my son and not educate my daughter because there isn't sufficient [money]. So we will have to educate both the children [both sons and daughters]. So I would educate them even if I had to borrow money from people.

Again, this is symbolic of the continually changing gendered social order. Over time, social constructions of gender change and people interpret gender roles and expectations differently.

Other signs of change included interviewees' awareness and recognition of socially constructed reasons for why girls drop out of school: workload of girls (domestic obligations), early marriage, and persistence of the socio-cultural belief that girls should not be educated. One of the two women head teachers elaborated on how the expectation of girls to do domestic work prevented girls from staying in school:

> They [the girls] have to manage all the housework and then go to school. Because of that, they cannot pass their exams, plus they don't have enough time to prepare at all, but the blame goes on them that they didn't study well so they failed and the people at home tell them to stay back so they are compelled [forced] to quit school.

Also, attributing gendered thinking to the problem, a man Chhetri head teacher stated that,

> Because of the family, they [parents] give more importance to boys because ours is a patriarchal society. They value their sons a lot. So

the girls slowly start disappearing. Now you can clearly see that out of 20–25 staff [members at this school], there is not even a single female staff [member].

[Laughs loudly again].

We are all male teachers here.

Importantly, this head teacher knew and recognized Nepal as patriarchal.[3] Awareness of social constructions of gender, even at the micro-level, could have significant implications for current and future students' schooling, as awareness is the first step to social change.

Further, a few of the textbooks coded in 1999–2000 presented non-sexist and non-stereotypical images in their illustrations and text. Specifically, in our coding we found some positive role models for both girls and boys in some of the textbooks. The Class 9 Population textbook, for example, not only had illustrations of men nurses and women doctors, but also included discussions of women's rights, women's low literacy rates in Nepal, and the Nepalese women's movement. This bodes well for girls in the future if there is a trend towards breaking down old gender constraints and fostering equal job opportunities for women and girls, with potential to advance in job positions. This also indicated some steps taken by the government to integrate gender-aware materials into the curricula. Textbooks that contained images and discussions conflicting with gender stereotypes provided students the opportunity to reexamine their gender beliefs and assumptions; further, textbooks restructured by gender provided students with alternative role models and potentially inspired them to adopt more egalitarian gender attitudes.

CATALYSTS FOR SOCIAL CHANGE

The seeds of change often start with a small group of individuals who push against the existing social order. In addition to the aforementioned girl students who demonstrated a willingness to buck the gendered system, I encountered many other individuals who showed potential to be catalysts for change. For example, Laxmi, as well as Class 5 students Sita and Kamala (who wanted to be teachers), mentioned individuals who served as their role models. For Laxmi, she aspired to study up to a higher level because she saw her older female cousin study up to the Bachelor's level. She explained, "So seeing her, I also want to study further." Similarly, Sita watched her older male cousin reach a high level of education to later become a teacher. Inspired by him, Sita also had high educational aspirations. For Kamala, she aspired to become a teacher because she had been impressed with the teachers at her school.

Further, the research assistants made an impact on both students as well as community members in the process of conducting research for this study. Both girl and boy students were impressed with how much education the two RAs had achieved. Also, one woman community member admitted to first believing boys were more intelligent than girls, but after seeing Manisha in her position as a research assistant, she changed her mind. Another woman community member said to Manisha, "I hope my daughter can also do the job like yours." A 77-year old woman community member said to Manisha,

> These days I think both girls and boys are equal. How did you come here? It's because your father treated you equally like the boys [and sent you to school to be educated], isn't it? You are coming here instead of the boys, isn't it?

In the parent/guardian sample, two women had significantly higher levels of educational achievement than other women in either the parent/guardian or the community member sample. One had a Class 7 education, and the other had test-pass qualifications. These two Class 5 parents/guardians could become role models for students, especially girls, in their communities, and could become future leaders of educational change as well. One Class 9 guardian—a man—was working on his Master's degree. He, too, could serve as a role model for both girls and boys.

In addition to Laxmi, I met and observed other teachers who demonstrated potential to be influential agents of social change. For instance, the woman Class 5 Physical Education teacher strongly encouraged both girls and boys to participate in her class activities. She warned girls who were shy and reluctant to participate that they would be reported to the head teacher's office if they did not participate. She said in an interview,

> In my class, I find both [girls and boys] of them equally performing best. My subject specially [specifically] deals with the sports and drawing, [and] both the boys and the girls perform equally best in class.

There was also the man Class 9 Social Studies teacher, a Chhetri man, who stressed the importance of Social Studies so that girls (and boys) could learn to think critically. He explained,

> All the subjects are equally important to them. But if I have to choose just two, then I'll give more priority to my subjects. And they are Social

Studies, Education, and Nepali. In case of social side, if we want to know, what are our social norms and values? What are [is] [the] social corruption in our society? Since when [have] the boys gotten more priority? And why only the girls are dominated by society from the start? How can we solve these deformities? We can learn these things in social study [Social Studies]. And girls should be treated equally as the boys. They [girls] should get more opportunities. We can learn this type of education in social study [studies]. Therefore, I take this subject [as] very important.

He argued social studies was the most important subject, as it taught students about their society and how gender norms and patriarchy in Nepal have formed. In contrast to most of the other teachers, as well as the head teachers, most community members, and parents/guardians interviewed, this teacher challenged the constraints faced by girls. This teacher not only demonstrated critical thinking of his own, but also stressed the importance of developing critical thinking skills in the classroom. He encouraged his students (both girls and boys) to think critically and consider social relations. Equipped with these skills, students may reconsider the existing gendered norms and work for transforming existing gender relations and social structures.

CONCLUSIONS

The gendered social structures of the family and the education system (and the gender processes therein) socially constructed and reinforced gender. Consequently, students in this study were often constrained to "do gender." However, while students did gender within socially constructed constraints (and some to a greater extent than others), some students challenged existing gender norms by changing their own aspirations and goals to those that more closely fit their needs. The three girls—Sanu Kumari, Laxmi, and Krishna Kumari—who put their education and securing a job ahead of marriage were resisting a powerful gender norm in favor of improving their life opportunities. Laxmi and Sanu Kumari, in particular, challenged existing gender social norms by forming their own goals to those that more closely fit their needs, rather than what the prevailing gender order dictated. In their narratives, these young women revealed that they planned to work before marriage in order to achieve financial security. They aspired to become future breadwinners for their extended families, especially their parents. In doing so, these gender trouble makers resisted and reshaped gender constraints.

But why were these particular students able to push gender constraints? One common link among these examples was a general awareness of not only the gender constraints in place but also an awareness of the opportunities available. For example, similar to many of her girl classmates in the student sample, social constructions of gender constrained Sanu Kumari: She was expected to fulfill her gender obligations of household work, limiting the time available for studying. Although she started her homework and studied as soon as she returned home from school, her domestic responsibilities of preparing and serving meals, cleaning the house, collecting firewood, and cutting grass for livestock (in addition to the herding and collecting of grass and firewood she did when school was not in session) consumed the majority of her time at home. She was aware of these constraints as she spoke of "hiding in the forest to avoid work at home," and she knew she would be further along in her studies were it not for having to drop out of Class 5 to help her mother with the household chores. She felt she was behind in her education because of it. Yet, she wanted to put education and securing a job ahead of marriage in order to achieve independence and greater agency in the decisions she would make in life. Gender trouble maker students like Sanu Kumari and the others seemed to have developed their critical thinking skills to question and even push socially constructed gender constraints. They appeared to have formed what Alexander & Mohanty call a "gender consciousness"—a critical awareness of their social designation as a woman (1997: xxxviii).

IMPLICATIONS

Stromquist (1990) argues that education has the potential to "develop in women the ability to think more analytically." Specifically, through education, women might develop "assertiveness, self-esteem, and egalitarian beliefs" (99). Not only can education equip girls and boys with the necessary intellectual development, but it can also foment a liberating and enabling view of the world. As Kathleen Staudt asserts,

> Comprehensive education has great potential to facilitate awareness of structures of domination and subordination . . . . Education in and outside the classroom provides the space in which to develop solidarity relations for active involvement in community and social change (1998:84).

So, how does education become a tool for empowerment for all students? I assert that this will only happen "through action and reflection, through praxis" (Alexander & Mohanty 1997: xxviii). First, all stakeholders involved need to critically examine existing practices in which education serves to reinforce traditional gendered norms and constraints. Then individuals must act collectively to uncover the social constructions of gender and its effects on educational equity. Also important is reflecting on the examples of role models and agents of change, such as the social science teacher who stressed the importance of developing critical thinking skills in the classroom. And analyses must be rooted in the lives and experiences of women and girls themselves: "Activists and scholars must also identify and reenvision forms of collective resistance that women, especially, in their different communities enact in their everyday lives" (Mohanty 2004: 236).

Comprehensive education for both girls *and* boys has tremendous potential to bring about social change. Education that develops and reinforces critical thinking skills (in and outside the classroom) facilitates awareness of power structures and existing inequalities. Education that allows individuals to empower themselves not only equips them with an understanding of their society and the place that they currently have in it, but also leads to their undertaking efforts to transform existing social relations and social structures.

Chapter Seven
Conclusions: Gender, Education, and Empowerment

Throughout the process of doing fieldwork, writing, and rethinking, I have come to realize the difficulties in trying to evaluate the gendered positioning of individual women, men, girls, and boys in the Jiri community. In analyzing the data collected through interviews and observations, I now know that people's individual lives and their varied gender experiences in Jiri VDC shifted, rather than remaining the same over time. These diverse gendered experiences represented many different aspects of the gender process, a process more open to change than I once thought. At the end, I am uncertain as to my ability to draw conclusions and find I have more questions than when I started.

Gender construction feminists assert that gender is a socially constructed process embedded in social institutions. In this book, I argue that socially constructed gender processes are institutionalized expressions of power, and these processes—enacted by community members, parents, guardians, teachers, and head teachers in Nepali homes and schools—constrained or enabled students according to their gender. In essence, the expectations first learned in the home were reinforced in schools, and consequently, these gender processes imposed constraints on students, particularly girl students, as revealed by student interviewees. However, gender is dynamic—continually constructed and reconstructed. And because gender is a *socially constructed* process, it can be reshaped and resisted by individuals (Lorber 2000; Butler 1990). Students who challenged gender processes, such as Laxmi and Sanu Kumari, illustrated individuals' capacity to negotiate the social construction and maintenance of gender. These gender trouble maker students seemed to have developed their critical thinking skills to question and even push socially constructed gender constraints, and perhaps empowered with a critical consciousness of their gender, these young women initiated the process for dismantling the existing order of gender inequality.[1]

FUTURE DIRECTIONS FOR JIRI VDC

My research has led me to conclude that there are many different avenues that stakeholders in this particular village and in Nepal might explore. These include gender awareness-raising in communities, such as promoting gender equity with posters of non-stereotypical images of women and men posted in various locations in the village, a calendar of famous Nepali women distributed to all schools and posted in every classroom, stories of women and men in non-stereotypical roles on the radio, promoting sporting events at schools for both girls and boys, and facilitating community discussions about gender relations. I would also recommend training for all school staff (at every level) that focuses on the ways gender is socially constructed; increased numbers of women teachers (who could be role models for both girls *and* boys); mentoring programs and clubs for girls and boys; and a critical examination of the ways gender is constructed and reinforced in school programs, curriculum, and textbooks. Importantly, all efforts for change, on the macro- and micro-levels, must consider socially constructed gender processes within the context of gendered social institutions.

Furthermore, future development programs will also need to address the intersections of class, caste, ethnicity, and religion with gender. Within what Patricia Hill Collins calls a "matrix of domination" (1991:225), women and men are constrained and enabled differently not only by their gender, but also by their race, class, and, in the context of Hindu societies like Nepal, by caste. In other words, women and men experience different forms of privilege and subordination, oppression and opportunity, depending on their social locations. Gendered experiences in both the home and school will vary significantly by race, socio-economic status, caste, ethnicity, and other social locations. Therefore, future research on educational equity must take a close look at the intersections of race, class, caste, and ethnicity with gender, particularly in the contexts of family and schools.

IMPLICATIONS FOR BROADER CONTEXTS

So, what does the "particular" of gender constructs and their effects on educational equity in a rural village of Nepal have to do with "universal"?

Conclusions

What significance does this localized analysis have to with larger contexts? Children first learn the social constructions of gender from their families, and the family, as a gendered institution, places unequal constraints on girls' and women's time as compared to that of boys and men. Much of the existing literature regarding low numbers of girls enrolled in schools centers on the *obstacles* to girls' schooling, but I argue this approach is incomplete: Issues related to gender and educational equity need to be understood "as an institutionalized expression of power in society" (Stromquist 1990:108). For example, while girls are no more naturally inclined to do domestic tasks than are boys, social constructions of gender often oblige girls to domestic responsibilities to a greater extent than boys. Assigning girls and women in families the majority of the domestic responsibilities ensures that the household tasks will get done (Stromquist 1990).

Examining socially constructed gender processes in families helps us unpack and understand how gender affects students, particularly girl students, in terms of access to, participation in, and achievement in schools. Therefore, I argue development programs focusing on educational equity must critically examine how social constructions of gender created and maintained in families constrain students. Researchers can assist policy makers in implementing more effective programs by providing evidence that failing to conceive of gender as an institutionalization of power perpetuates gender inequality, particularly in regard to education.

Also commonplace in much of the existing literature and in many of the existing national programs is the presumption that girls' access to school leads to equality between girls and boys. It is also assumed that girls attending school guarantees their participation in school and equal participation in broader society. These assumptions have significant implications for education policy as well as future education programs. Projects that assume schools are gender neutral will only result in short term gains, at best, and more often will fail in the long term. Before spending money on initiatives that may be short-sighted, better use of those monies would be made if those working for change understood the social forces at work that construct and maintain gender inequality. Researchers should analyze gender inequality in schools by examining how gender is socially constructed and maintained in *both* school and the home. Then we can begin to understand and devise more effective ways to increase *all* students' enrollment, participation and success in school.

Change in terms of educational equity will only come from working in solidarity, not from top-down aid coming from the West. Rather, change will come with the active involvement of stakeholders at every level and the valuing of individuals' everyday knowledge. This solidarity should be based on, mutality, accountability, and the recognition of common interests as the basis for relationships among diverse communities. Rather than assuming an enforced commonality of oppression, the practice of solidarity foregrounds communities of people who have chosen to work and fight together (Mohanty 2004:7)

All stakeholders—government officials, policy makers, researchers, and the villagers—need to work together to best develop programs within the framework of gender as a socially constructed process.[2]

BRIDGING SCHOLARSHIP WITH ACTIVISM

Empowerment consists of "having the specific resources that are required to make, pursue and achieve informed life choices" (Dickerson, Hillman, & Foster 1995:183). Education has the potential to enable and empower individuals. Specifically, education that allows individuals to empower themselves not only equips them with an understanding of their society and the place that they currently have in it, but also leads to their undertaking efforts to transform existing social relations and social structures. Bridging scholarship with activism is the mechanism by which we can work to make education a tool for empowerment for all students. I assert that this will only happen "through action and reflection, through praxis" (Alexander & Mohanty 1997: xxviii). This involves scholars, community members, and students themselves working collectively to uncover the social constructions of gender and their effects on educational equity.

One way all stakeholders can work together to deconstruct traditional notions of gender and their policy implications for education is to legitimatize students,' particularly girl students,' standpoints and everyday knowledge. This means "verifying their daily experiences as points of resistance and potential sources of collective action for those who are in positions to expedite social change" (Dickerson, Hillman, & Foster 1995:183). Empowerment "begins when people change their ideas about the causes of their powerlessness, when they recognize the systematic forces that oppress them and when they act to change the conditions of their lives" (Morgen & Bookman 1988:4). In developing an awareness of the systematic forces that oppress them, students and community members are empowered to become activists themselves.

This empowerment framework validates all stakeholders' daily experiences and everyday knowledge. Within this framework, everyone involved is considered a "scholar activist" (Dickerson, Hillman, & Foster 1995). Rather than maintaining traditional power hierarchies in which the researcher is deemed the "expert" and the students and community members "subjects," scholars envision and validate community members and students, particular women and girls, as "researchers themselves in pursuit of answers to the questions of their own daily struggles and survival" (Tandon 1988:7). At the same time, students and community members can teach scholars alternative ways of knowing and understanding; they can clarify information that has been distorted and often hidden in educational and public policies.

As co-researchers, scholars work with community members and students not only in realizing the sources of their daily struggles but also in facilitating solutions grounded within their communities (Freire 1990). This collective of "scholar activists" challenges existing systems of domination and fosters others empowering themselves through the development of a critical consciousness. The partnership of scholars, community members, and students then becomes a "site of resistance" (hooks 1990), as they collectively raise awareness about social constructions of gender and educational inequities.

Empowerment is "a *process* aimed at consolidation, maintaining or changing the nature and distribution of power in a particular cultural context" (Morgan & Bookman 1988:4). Through reflection, dialogue, and action, scholars, community members and students themselves are all vested within the empowerment process. Working in solidarity will best uncover the social constructions of gender and its effects on educational equity and will clear the pathway to making education a tool for empowerment for all students.

As a social construction, gender is fluid, rather than existing in a state of homogeneity, static in time. Because gender constraints in any society are socially constructed and can be challenged, contested, renegotiated, dismantled and reconstructed, I assert we must continue to ground our analyses in people's individual lives and their varied, changing experiences of gender. By grounding our research and policy reforms in the lived gendered experiences and contexts of individuals, and by working in solidarity with *all* stakeholders, we will not only move towards providing girl and boy children in "Third World" countries such as Nepal with meaningful educational experiences and improved life opportunities, but we also move towards transforming power relations within societies' social, educational, economic and political institutions, resulting in a more equitable social order for all.

Chapter Eight
Epilogue: Reflections on the Process

> Wandering the narrow passages of the *Ason* market, watching women wash clothes in big, shiny tubs, calling out to toddlers or selling their wares, I wondered if it were possible for me to ever truly "walk in their footsteps," to understand the lives they lead from their perspective.
>
> —Journal, June 1992

> It was a long, beautiful walk to get to the SP school today. We diverged from the "motorable" road [still very much under construction] and took on the steep paths, over and around large rocks, across a precarious bridge, slippery even now, in the "dry season," climbing higher and higher. We were afforded beautiful views of the valley. I noticed frost on the ground and some frozen water in the streams, which seemed strange as hot as I felt. Sweat dripped from my face. My heart pounded, and I concluded I was very much out of shape. The sure-footed young Jirel girl, who had decided to accompany us today, caught me as I tripped several times. She never once fell. Rather, she moved up the path confidently in her plastic high heels. And not a hair out of place.
>
> —Fieldnotes, January 6, 2000

Doing fieldwork is a circular process: The person doing the research learns about herself as well as about the people she is studying (Reinharz 1992). This chapter focuses on reflexivity—reflecting upon and critically examining the nature of the research process. This epilogue centers on my struggles to put feminist methodologies into practice. I reflect on and discuss issues of privilege and power and how my positionality was often in conflict with my ideology. Specifically, my goal in this epilogue is to offer critical perspectives on how my positionality as a white, relatively affluent (comparatively speaking), western woman researcher affected my efforts to implement feminist fieldwork practices.

Going into the field, I had hoped my methodology would embody my belief in feminism and social change. I designed my research project with the following goal in mind: to work with community members and contribute to the improvement of individuals' lives in this particular community, while simultaneously meeting the requirements for my doctoral degree. Yet, once in the field, I felt largely unprepared, lacking the mental tools to anticipate and negotiate the inherent gap between methods and practice. In the end, I continually questioned the extent to which I put my feminist ideology into practice. The following is an examination of those struggles in the hopes that critical reflection upon these issues might enhance my own understanding of scholar activism and encourage dialogue among others who attempt to put feminist ideology into practice.

As I discussed in Chapter Three, I interpret "positionality" to be the make-up of intersecting identities, including gender, age, race, nationality, and ideological orientation. In attempting to implement feminist methodologies, I found that my positionality left me feeling at times vulnerable and at other moments privileged. This contradiction manifested itself throughout the project, and I grappled with these issues during every phase of the research.

ENTERING THE FIELD: THE IMPACT OF IDENTITIES ON FEMINIST RESEARCH

Critical to an understanding of my privilege and positionality is consideration of *how* I got to the field. Aspects of my positionality, such as class and nationality, enabled me to travel to my field site and transcend national boundaries in ways that my research participants most often could not. As an American, I benefited from economic resources that carry substantial value in almost every world region, particularly in so-called "Third World" countries. This combination of economic and national status allows me to move freely throughout the world. For example, whereas my friends from Nepal have had to petition for years to obtain a visa to visit the United States, I could purchase a visa in advance from the Nepalese Embassy in Washington, D.C., and my U.S. passport ensured my entry into the country of Nepal.

Positionality also affects how and how easily access to communities is granted. Diane Wolf in her 1996 book *Feminist Dilemmas in Fieldwork* notes that there is insufficient attention to feminist fieldworkers' interactions with those in power—for example, government officials—most of whom tend to be men. Feminists have rarely reported the ways in which they navigate these necessary and problematic relationships, in which those responsible for perpetuating systems of inequality and injustice must be appeased in order for the research to be conducted. In some instances, this requires feminist scholars to "play the game" of gendered assumptions and roles in order to secure access. I first encountered difficulty in Nepal when seeking approval of and clearance for my project. I spent several weeks and many hours waiting to receive the paperwork for my research visa and the necessary extensions. I spent entire days sitting and waiting in government offices, and I came to resent (even hate, a little) the high caste men in the immigration office who refused to acknowledge my pleas for expediting the process. My Western expectations inhibited my capacity for patience, and I became increasingly frustrated and angry. Eventually, the men in the immigration office agreed to speak to my "husband" and processed the visas, only after a high-ranking friend (a man) in another division spoke with the immigration division.

I ran into more roadblocks in the village where I was to do my field research. Upon arrival, I went to the local government office and submitted the necessary paperwork, along with a request to conduct my research in the village. I mentioned my "husband" in the documents so they would know Chris would also be in the village for the duration of the project. A few days later, a letter from the village head arrived, approving the project. The village officials had addressed the letter to Chris, as they had assumed the project was his, and they made no mention of me in the letter. Over time, when it became known the project was mine, I think the fact that a woman and a wife led the project rather than her husband, who had been seen at our home washing the laundry, surprised the village officials.[1] My own experience of "getting in" to the field provided a valuable introduction to the rigid gender inequalities I was about to study.

In terms of personal identities, one's gender, race, and nationality most often cannot be hidden, but other aspects of social identity, such as religion, marital status, political perspectives and age are less apparent and can be blurred much more easily than race and gender. If these aspects are critical to negotiating one's position in the field, they can be constructed and reconstructed to the researcher's benefit in particular settings. For example, Diane Wolf encountered deception in her study of Asian women factory workers. She laments that,

> creating and negotiating my identity in the field posed one particular challenge and dilemma. I felt forced to lie about the same topics about which I hoped for honesty from my respondents. I lied about my religious affiliation, my marital status, and my finances, at the same time that the focus of my research was on young women's finances, family

finances, and marriage. This particular representation of myself made me feel dishonest and uncomfortable, but I could not see another way out (1996:ix).

As feminist scholars like Wolf reveal, there is an inevitable struggle with this kind of duplicity: Presenting and representing oneself in the field can create other problems. It is a difficult choice in human and professional terms.

I reconstructed aspects of my identity to "fit in" in the field. For example, after many discussions and advice sought from friends in Kathmandu, Chris and I decided to tell everyone in the village that we were married, when, actually, we were not. We concluded that living together as an unmarried couple, in a tiny village in a remote part of Nepal, would offend people and create barriers between me (the researcher), as well as us (outsiders moving in), and the community. We believed that if study participants thought we were married, then the community would be more accepting of Chris and me. I also hoped that the married participants would find a common link between themselves and me. We even told our research assistants that we were married, and we both struggled with this conscious deception. In the end, we never revealed the truth. In her research of feminist fieldworkers, Wolf (1996) found that many lied about their marital status. She writes that,

> In most of these cases, the harm is minimal, but the guilt for those deceiving their respondents with whom they are attempting to create a bond of empathy may cause considerable anguish. Although many nonfeminist fieldworkers may deceive their subjects and feel bad about it, feminists have expressed considerable distress over this dilemma, because lying directly contradicts attempts at a more feminist approach to fieldwork, which includes attempts to equalize a relationship (1996:12).

I still struggle with the fact that during interviews and observations I revealed little about my self and my background, which contradicted my objective to solicit openness and honesty from study participants.

I also relied upon my ability to transcend social status boundaries in order to access networks that would assure the success of my project. When I needed sponsorship by Nepali university officials for my research visa, I facilitated this process by heightening my educational background and using my connections to people in high-ranking positions. Conversely, in the villages, I withheld my educational status from participants in rural communities, most of whom had not finished Nepal's equivalent to high school.

My living accommodations in the village pronounced my economic status to the village. I rented two rooms, and many people in town were aware of the rent I paid for the rooms—steep by their standards, inexpensive by mine—and from this, the villagers saw me as having considerable means. Yet, to align with rural community members, I tried to make agricultural connections by frequently talking with them about their livestock and noting that my mother and all of her family members have worked as farmers and raised similar livestock.

Throughout my field experiences, my race, economic status, and nationality allowed me to transition in and out of diverse settings with relative ease. At the same time, while I benefited from this ability, it also created substantial internal conflicts and questions about my fieldwork. I realized over time that my ability to shift and reconstruct the malleable aspects of my identity was essential to the success of my project. Yet I was constantly conflicted about the ethics of shifting my identity for my own benefit, and the inherent privilege embodied within these acts.

REFLECTING ON INTERACTIONS IN THE FIELD

Doing fieldwork involves an inherent contradiction: While we need to *distance* ourselves in order to problematize social life, we also need a *closeness* to understand, to answer questions, and to make sense of social life (Lofland & Lofland 1984). In Nepal, the closeness could be experienced everyday and in abundance. The distance was more difficult to find, largely due to social norms regarding personal privacy and the connotations associated with people who spend time alone. Oftentimes, I found myself working in my room with several people, mostly children, but some adults too, peering through windows, not even trying to hide their interest. This sense of being watched and never being alone could be trying at times and made distance a valuable, if rare, commodity. This also represents assumptions about privilege and personal space.

Community at Large

My entry into the community required being friendly and receptive to courtesy. Nepalis esteem guests as gods, and from a Western perspective, they take hospitality to new heights. Practically everyone you meet in Nepal invites you to come to her/his house. Sybille Manneschmidt, a Canadian researcher, gives sound advice in the sub-title of her article, published in the Nepali journal, *Education and Development*, "Ethnographic Survival Skills: Be Ready to Drink A Lot of Tea!" (1995). In the beginning, I sought out every opportunity to sit and chat with anyone interested in the project and accepted every invitation for *chiyaa* (Nepali tea). I drank gallons and gallons of tea in the interest of my research. This was fine until I developed stomach problems, and a doctor advised me not to drink tea or eat certain foods. Thereafter, I found it very difficult to decline offerings of tea or snacks, and I struggled with the possibility that I may have offended my hosts.

Despite having taken over 200 hours of Nepali language training, I still struggled with mastering verbal skills in Nepali and became frustrated with the language barrier in daily communications. I confused many when I referred to a banana as "cheap" instead of "small," or noted the tremendous strides researchers have made in "chicken breast" cancer research in the States. Fortunately, most were amused by my mistakes. The Nepalis I met were always willing to give me a lesson in Nepali and helped me when I struggled over a word or phrase. In reality, the amount of time necessary to become fluent in Nepali far exceeded my own project timeline and resource base, creating another layer of complexity in the extent to which I could fully immerse myself in local village life.

Study Participants

There is certainly no denying the issue of power dynamics between the participants and myself in this study. Although gender united me with roughly half the research participants, race, class, language and religion divided us. Wolf's (1996) research shows that some argue for or attempt to downplaying differences to reach a more egalitarian relationship (Mies 1983, 1990; Bronstein in Reinharz 1992:29), but others believe that such attempts are insincere because the relationship can never be egalitarian or reciprocal (Reinharz 1992). With the participants in this study, I tried to remain aware of our differences, but also emphasize our similarities. For example, I talked with the students I observed and interviewed about my studies and coursework, and we compared strategies on preparing for big exams.

Despite efforts to be cognizant of power differentials, the researcher does control every aspect of the research and is responsible for the outcome. Community members were almost always willing and ready to participate, which subsequently made my job easier, yet I constantly worried about exploiting participants' eagerness. Jean Davison, in her collection of Gikuyu women's life histories (See *Voices from Mutira*, 1996), discusses how she encouraged the "narrator to take the lead" in the interview (Davison 1996:13). I also employed subject-centered methods, such as life history narratives and open-ended interviews, which I hoped created for the participants the potential to define their own perceptions, circumstances and needs, rather than being defined by me.

Uma Narayan (1989) advocates alternative means for communicating and sharing gendered experiences across cultural boundaries. She suggests "nonanalytical" and "nonrational" forms of discourse, like fiction or poetry, to better convey the complexities of life experiences of one group to members of another (264). If I had had the means to do so, I would have liked to have engaged in creative writing, artwork, and photography with study participants. The participatory learning action (PLA) activities, such as social mapping and need assessment matrices, I facilitated at the beginning of my study were somewhat along these lines, but had I had the resources, I would have liked to have done more "nonanalytical" and "nonrational" activities with study participants as Narayan describes.

With the project constantly on my mind, I found it difficult to interact casually with study participants outside the context of an interview or an observation. About interacting with the participants in her research, Leslie Salzinger muses,

> As I chatted with people I sometimes tried to slip my questions into conversation, "By the way, do you identify more as a 'Latino' or as a Salvadoran?" It never worked. It sounded absurd and they looked at me with amused tolerance: "She's a nice girl, if a bit slow." It soon became evident that their identities were—like my own multiple allegiances—flexible, dependent on context (1991:159).

I, too, would try to slip gender and education into casual conversation and ended up feeling foolish. I learned, over time, that the interactions with study participants and other members of the Jiri community depended on the context.

Of course, I knew it to be unethical to offer monetary compensation in exchange for participation in my study. However, some participants would make assumptions about my social position and request financial assistance. For example, many study participants asked me for clothing or medicine. Community member and parent/guardian interviewees regularly requested money and scholarships for their children. One woman begged me to take her daughter when I left to go back to the States so that her daughter might have a better life. During my interviews with them, two head teachers asked me to help their schools, and one sought me out at my home. He lamented,

> All have their own wishes in life. I am doing this job so I have to do my duty honestly. We have lots of problems here. Why not? The whole country has problems. There are so many donor agencies that annually

> help Nepal in various ways. Our country doesn't have good production. You must have noticed visiting other schools that they are all helped by donor agencies. They have thatched their school roofs. They have well managed buildings, toilets, furniture, and office rooms, but this school is in [a] shadow. Nobody has noticed this school. This school has the poorest caste students and lowest caste students as well. If we could only get donor agencies, we could raise our school to the lower secondary level. Once some researchers [came] to this school and had promised they would do something to help the school but that remained a verbal promise only. So I would like to request your help. This is not for my personal benefit. This is for the sake of the entire school.

I explained that there was very little I could do other than making sure the VDC Chair and his office received a copy of my final report. I felt terrible that I could not do more. It was very difficult to convince them that I had nothing to give. I tried to explain that I could not offer them anything except for the opportunity to share their thoughts with me. Ironically, I was actually the one asking something of them. I ask: How does one put feminist ideology into practice in these instances?

Living and Working with Research Assistants

Interestingly, Diane Wolf reports that in researching her 1996 book, she rarely came across any mention of how feminist fieldworkers interacted with their research assistants. One (Regina Oboler 1986) writes that her field assistant sought guidance from her husband and that she had difficulty in establishing authority with a male field assistant. Another (Nita Kumar 1992:116) mentions her anger about her research assistant's laziness. Wolf notes that these admissions are rare.

It was my hope that power differentials would be minimized with the hiring and training of local research assistants. After learning that finding assistants with the necessary qualifications in the vicinity of the research setting would be next to impossible, I conducted interviews with women and men in the Kathmandu area. I intended to hire one woman and one man to be my research assistants, and they would be asked to conduct interviews and observations accordingly. In a gender-segregated society like Nepal, I believed women and girl participants would be more receptive to and comfortable with women interviewers, as well as men and boy participants with men interviewers. Ultimately, I hired two women, as their qualifications far surpassed those of the other candidates.

Bal Kumari[2] came from a well-to-do Brahmin family that lived in an older section of Kathmandu. At age 38, she had acquired a Bachelor's degree, a law degree, a Master's degree, and many years of fieldwork experience. Her most recent job had been a two-year stint in Bangladesh as a field interviewer for an international non-governmental organization (INGO). Bal Kumari's confident and assertive attitude, as well as her experience, impressed me.

Sagun also impressed me with her fluent English and knowledge. After receiving her diploma, she entered a sociology Master's program and wrote her Master's thesis on Tamang women. She often spoke of taking the TOEFL and GRE to get into a Ph.D. program outside of Nepal.[3] Sagun and I were much closer in age than Bal Kumari—Sagun and I were only one year apart in age. Before going to Jiri, she lived with her Tamang family in a town on the outskirts of Kathmandu, but she had spent most of her childhood and early adult years away at boarding schools and later at college. Sagun told me that her father, a former military officer and now a civil engineer, spent many years working outside of Nepal. She explained to me that her Tamang family practiced both Hinduism and Buddhism.

Sagun accompanied me as I first entered the field, and Bal Kumari, having a previous commitment, met us there ten days later. Even though we shared things in common, I was torn about friendships with them in the beginning. These were people I was paying a lot of money to do work for me. Yet, I had always told myself that I was going to be a different kind of research director—not like some of the patronizing individuals I worked for in the early years of my graduate school career—and would stay committed to my feminist ideals. However, I wondered, could the research assistants and I be friends? Early journal entries reveal uncertainties:

> Spending all our time together and living together, Sagun and I are becoming fast friends, but it makes it more difficult to maintain a "leadership" role and to delegate tasks . . . . I am glad I hired her. I think that because we are so much alike, it will be a better working relationship.
> —November 14, 1999

> I think Sagun would like to talk for several hours like we did last night, but I really would prefer to write my notes . . . . Last night we talked, looked at her photo albums, and she told me countless stories about her friends. She said living with me feels like her days living in the hostel with her friends at the university.
> —November 16, 1999

I fretted about my role and theirs. I was relatively inexperienced in terms of management. I am a woman. I was young (and I look young), and I am short. I wondered if these women would take me seriously. Boundary issues were made more complex by our cultural differences:

> I am concerned about shifting into the lead role once Bal Kumari arrives. I certainly don't want to play power politics, but I need/want to be able to assert authority if need be. I think it's important for Sagun's own self-esteem that she sees herself as compatible and on the same level as me.
> —November 18, 1999

> I am not sure what to do about Bal Kumari and Sagun—go easier on them, go harder on them. I know they take cues from me, but it's hard to always be doing a visible task just so they'll get going and do what they are supposed to be doing, what I am paying them to be doing. And I don't know where to draw the line, constantly worrying about cultural difference, cultural understanding.
> —January 11, 2000

I also entered the field assuming that I could "help" Sagun and Bal Kumari. From my Western perspective, I felt I possessed skills that I could pass on to them. For example, I thought I could help Sagun to be more confident. I assumed that she would want to empower herself, and I urged her to be more assertive. Admittedly, in these instances, I enacted what Mohanty (1991; 2004) and others criticize by imposing my Western standards of empowerment upon Sagun.

Sometimes, I worried that the RAs and I were not communicating. I often felt as though Sagun and Bal Kumari were not listening to me when I felt they should be giving me their full attention:

> They didn't seem to be paying attention when I was reviewing the research strategies and sampling plan. They are so reluctant to add any kind of input, especially Sagun. And to think they have both reached the Master's level in the social sciences. I realize I am being unfair, having just shoved several years worth of sociology down their throats in a matter of days, in another language. I just wish they weren't continually nodding their heads when I asked them all week [during the training] if they understood, and they really weren't getting it.
> —November 25, 1999 (Thanksgiving)

> Sagun said it was dusty and cold [at the high school] but didn't say much else at first . . . She spoke more about the boys' disruptive behavior later. Bal Kumari didn't say a whole lot. This evening, I tried to encourage them to talk to me about today and also to tell me if they have had any problems, etc. Let's hope they will eventually feel

comfortable to speak up, if need be. They have been working hard, and I feel bad they used their day off to catch up on things.

—December 13, 1999

Two months after hiring the research assistants, trouble brewed with one of them. From her research on feminists doing fieldwork, Diane Wolf determined that relationships with research assistants tend to require considerable negotiation. Wolf also notes that researchers often discover that their translators are not translating everything, or that they change what they translate (1996). I found both to be true with Bal Kumari's work, and it eventually reached the point that I had to ask Bal Kumari to leave. Firing people is not a common practice in Nepal, so it proved to be an uncomfortable situation. I credit Bal Kumari for handling the news of her imminent departure with maturity and professionalism. She was, however, definitely shocked. After she left, I told everyone in the village that she was called home for an arranged marriage (She and I both would have lost face if I had told the truth), and with Sagun's help, I soon found a very competent replacement. Sagun recommended that I hire her friend from college, Manisha. Although she never would have openly admitted it, I sensed that Sagun was not unhappy about Bal Kumari leaving. I think Sagun found it difficult to live and work with her.

Manisha, a Rai woman in her late twenties, lived in an upscale neighborhood in Kathmandu with her husband. Because her husband was away all the time, working at an uncle's hotel, Manisha said she was very happy to go to Jiri to work with Sagun and me. She also had a Master's in sociology and was very interested in women's issues. I soon learned that we had both majored in biology as undergraduates. She eagerly took on the heavy workload for this project and far surpassed my expectations. Sagun and Manisha were happy to live in the same room again (They had lived in the same hostel in college), and I was glad to see Sagun now had a friend with whom she could live and work.

Sagun and Manisha eventually became good friends of mine, and I treasure our friendship very much. Aside from successfully producing the work I demanded of them, they were truly there for me, especially when I needed a friend. They sympathized with my homesickness and reflected on the harsh reality of their own lives, filled with separations from loved ones. Sagun rarely saw her father, away all the time for his work, and her spending many years away at school. Manisha had not seen her father, working for the Gurkha Army in Hong Kong, or her brother for seven years. She also missed her husband, who we had hoped would come to visit her during her stay in Jiri.

Working with Sagun and Manisha taught me a lot about mentoring. I had a tendency to micro-manage them, and at those times, I failed miserably as a manager. It was when I solicited their ideas, trusted their abilities, and shared ownership of the project that we had the greatest success and productivity. The more interactive and collaborative the running of the project, the more we enjoyed working, and the more we were all changed, for the better, by the work. I am not only deeply indebted to Sagun and Manisha for helping me carry out this project, but I am also indebted to them for teaching me about feminist methodology.

Homestay Family

As a western academic, it becomes second nature, and is our easily exercised right, to speak up in situations of sexism or other forms of inequality. For purposes of filing "clean" research and not offending my hosts, I often felt obligated to keep my personal feelings in check. Yet, sometimes I wondered if this was necessary: Could I make a feminist point without compromising my research? Could I speak against discrimination without compromising my rapport in the community or would speaking out actualize my privilege? In doing so, would I become the embodiment of the Western white liberal feminist critiqued in most postcolonial writings? I found these questions most pressing in my homestay family where the youngest child, an 11-year old niece, was given the lion's share of work everyday, and occasionally kept home from school to catch up on domestic work, while her cousins, two boys, attended school without fail. I felt that our *bhauju*[4] (mother in our homestay family), in particular, treated her live-in niece as an indentured servant:

> *Bhauju*'s exploitation of *bahini*[5] continues. *Bahini* has the worst life Chris and I have ever seen up close. When she tried to catch a few minutes of TV [She never gets to watch TV while the boys watch it all the time], *Bhauju* conjured up some work for her to do. She is never idle. This morning I heard her go get water at 5a.m. She always looks so tired at night. She sleeps on the hard floor, while the boys sleep in beds with mattresses. She has never been to the market area, EVER. *Bhauju* didn't let her go to school yesterday because she wanted someone to watch the teashop while she and her son went to the market together [He is always getting videos to rent]. *Bahini* never has any fun, while the boys play all day long. Here is evidence for my study right here, up close and personal—gender inequality reproduced and maintained, beginning in the home. *Bahini* was devastated when she wasn't allowed to go to school yesterday. She loves going to school.
>
> —April 10, 2000

The boys attended a private school; their girl cousin attended a public school. So, there I was, living amidst processes of gender that perpetuate inequalities—the very thing I was trying to study. I never did say anything. I just swallowed my anger like a bitter pill. Once Chris, also greatly saddened by *Bahini's* plight, lost his cool: The boys shouted down to their cousin to bring them their toothbrushes, with paste already applied, so they wouldn't miss anything on the WWF (World Wrestling Federation) program they were watching via satellite. Chris asked the boys why they thought it was OK to yell at her to do that. He reminded them that their cousin never watched TV.

I found myself desperately wanting to take *Bahini* home with me to the States, rescuing her from her awful living situation. I wanted her to meet my and Chris' parents, to play as she wanted, and to run around in our backyard. I wanted to free her somehow, and now I understand that my wish to do so was an embodiment of my privilege.

Another example was when our homestay family's niece in Kathmandu decided that she wanted to go to the technical school in Jiri. Our homestay *dai*[6] (Nepali for "big brother") had the police chief pull some strings, and she was accepted, despite her poor scores on the entrance exams:

> I was feeling sad tonight anyway, but I just couldn't bring myself to be a part of the niece's "celebration dinner," with Chhetra Dai, the police chief, and Ram Dai drinking themselves into oblivion, dining on the snacks all the women worked so hard to prepare, and congratulating themselves on this great accomplishment of theirs.
>
> —February 8, 2000

I tried to let these instances seep in and learn from them. Keeping my positionality and privileges in perspective was an on-going challenge.

EMOTIONS IN THE FIELD

My own experience paralleled that of Jean Davison, who writes of her ethnographic experiences in Kenya:

> The process of person-centered ethnography...forces the person undertaking it to give up "the comforts of home" in mind and body. Ethnographic research in a rural setting . . . involves giving up electricity, running water, and a toilet seat for an extended period of time . . . . It also means adjusting to a different diet and learning new ways of cooking. It demands that we learn the language and if possible the nonverbal forms of communication, of the particular group in which we

plan to live and work . . . . Another requirement of fieldwork in a rural Gikuyu community is adjusting to the changing rhythms of the agricultural cycle, the community's cultural rituals, and its multiple relational networks (1996:15).

Giving up the comforts of home was quite difficult for me. It would be very self-absorbed of me to complain about living in Nepal and the personal challenges I faced, but I do think that the struggles of everyday life affected my fieldwork. I struggled with issues of space, privacy, homesickness and self doubt. There were many days, especially in the first couple of months in the field, that I felt low and discouraged. While I tried to keep my problems and complaints to myself and not concern anyone else, privacy was really difficult to maintain.

I had the privilege of deciding how I dressed, what I ate, how clean I wanted to be, and where I would sleep at night. Yet, despite this control over certain choices, I still encountered feelings of vulnerability. I began the research process by keeping a daily log of the various stages of the fieldwork. Over time, this logging of the daily tasks expanded into much more. I not only wrote down what we did everyday, but I also recorded my emotions—whether I felt scared, happy, sad, lost or loved. An early excerpt from this daily log (or what I now refer to as my "emotional fieldnotes") reads,

> Because of my emotional rut, I am constantly looking for other things—other than the project—to do. I just wrote five more items down on my food wish list. I guess I am homesick these days. I feel so spoiled about this. But I do miss my mom and her quiet, subtle reassurances. I miss being able to manage my food, so that my stomach doesn't always hurt. I miss being able to exercise and having time to read.
>
> —January 11, 2000

Following Miles and Huberman's (1994) advice to graduate students working on their dissertations, that same day I compiled a list of obstacles. I wrote,

> LIST OF WHAT I AM UP AGAINST: Living in a rural area of a developing country—difficult living conditions in terms of food, lodging, health, clean water, and modern conveniences, as well as community living/having no privacy; we are remote; out of communication with dissertation committee and others who could offer advice; this is my first time as a manager—cultural differences between me and staff...am I delegating too much? How do I know? Developing overall research plan ALONE; language barrier—problems communicating with staff and research participants as well as potential participants in daily living

and community life; translations; staff—young, uncertain, nervous, somewhat inexperienced, not liking the work possibly, taking advantage of me possibly, hard to manage; pressure to be in several places at one time—at the schools, doing interviews, analyzing, reading; very little free time; stomach aches.

—January 11, 2000

I tried to keep my emotions and struggles in check and reflect on how they affected my fieldwork. Sometimes, I was successful, and other times I was not. After four or five months in the field, the "low days" did not disappear altogether, but became fewer in number. The daily challenges seemed less daunting, and I became more comfortable with my work over time. However, in my analysis, I needed to remain cognizant of my personal biases, positionality and emotions, and how they may have continually factored into the course of the project.

NEGOTIATING THE POLITICS IN THE FIELD

My experiences involved considerable "give and take" with individuals in the field and outside of the field. My attempts to implement feminist methodology pushed me into occasional conflict between my wish to do research for change, and expectations placed upon me by academia in seeking accreditation (in my case, seeking a Ph.D.). This conflict is relatively unexplored in the literature. I struggled with the following question: To what extent could I attempt to implement feminist methodologies and my specific research agenda without jeopardizing the approval of my academic institution, even if so much of academic validation processes are rooted in patriarchal institutional power structures? From academics, I heard comments ranging from, "Your topic is sooo esoteric..." to "Your proposed methods...too warm fuzzy," to "It's not like she's researching a cure for cancer..." So, even before entering the field, conflict surfaced between my obligations to fulfill academic expectations and my attempts to conduct what I believed was "activist" research.

Then once in the field, I felt incredibly isolated from my dissertation committee and home institution, yet I felt immense pressure to complete my project. Studying populations with less privilege is common in social science. I wondered: Did studying girls and women in rural Nepal—a marginalized group that might be considered among "the most oppressed of the oppressed"—make my project more appealing in academic circles? For example, in 1996, I applied for a grant to study women's organizations in Kathmandu. One member of my grant award committee thought I should change the project completely and focus on female genital mutilation in

Nepal. I presume she made this suggestion because female circumcision was becoming a popular subject of study at that time. There's just one problem—as far as I know, female circumcision is not practiced in Nepal.

While academia "pulled" me in one direction, negotiating the web of politics in the field "pushed" me in another. Weaving my way through the politics of daily life in the field, I encountered different obstacles and hurdles along the way—in a variety of venues and amongst many different people. My feminist principles were really put to the test as the world in which I lived swirled with patriarchy—the Nepali version of "a good ole boys' club" and *machismo*. Nepalis seemed to be continually searching for an *aaphno manchhe* (Nepali for a well-connected person who will look after you).[7] Wolf (1996) explains that women researchers, regardless of race, are pressured more than men to conform to local gender norms, often creating difficulties and dilemmas for feminists working in highly patriarchal settings. In Nepal, women were expected to defer to men on all matters of importance. That meant that everything—from small, private matters to large, problematic issues—had to be negotiated through a *dai* ("big brother"). This need to depend on a *dai* wreaked havoc on my impetus to work independently and to be free of dependence on even good Nepali men friends. For example, my friend Ram (a man) had to discuss all matters of our living arrangements with our homestay family. He and others strongly discouraged me from even telling our homestay *bhauju* that I could no longer drink tea for medical reasons.

While at times my positionality and presence were honored in the field, I sometimes felt my positionality was more of a hindrance. For example, I was frequently invited to local government meetings and educational caucuses for the district. I felt uncomfortable being introduced at every single one as an "honored and distinguished guest," and at times resented being asked to stay late after a day of school observations to be a "honorary" judge for an intra-school competition. From my Western perspective, I felt my time would be better spent transcribing interviews. Over time, I learned the importance of making these guest appearances and made sure that I thanked everyone. Pleasing and appeasing seem to be par for the course in conducting fieldwork.

DANGERS IN THE FIELD AND POWER DIFFERENTIALS

Although certain facets of social power seem to dominate the majority of applied research contexts, personal danger in field research settings is rarely discussed and is perhaps the strongest manifestation of vulnerability. Despite the power and privilege I possessed as a Westerner working in an

Epilogue

international context, there were times in the field when I felt quite vulnerable. For example, one afternoon my two research assistants and I were talking with community members in a teashop. A rather intoxicated man interrupted our conversations several times. We tried to ignore him, but he made me nervous. Later, when I was conducting an in-depth interview in the teashop, that same man tried to grab me. My self-defense training kicked in, and I pushed the man away from me. Everyone was embarrassed, including myself, and I tried to minimize the scene made. Daily, I became aware of the necessity to negotiate space, in ways that men researchers may not feel or encounter.

Nepali friends advised me never to discuss politics at the schools or with the school staff, as schools in Nepal have historically been viewed as political hotbeds. While I avoided political discussions, the presence of very active political groups and the conflict between the government and certain sects of political groups definitely affected the running of this project, as well as the overall atmosphere in Jiri VDC. As discussed in Chapter Two, the increased Maoist presence and activity in certain parts of the Jiri Valley at that particular point in time forced schools to close on occasion, and when word spread of an upcoming attack, many residents chose to stay at home and not venture out at all.

The handful of violent acts that took place while we were in Jiri definitely cast a spell of anxiety, fear, and paranoia on the research participants, research assistants and me. For instance, I wrote in my notes that "one older man—whom we attempted to talk to and interview twice—told us that with the many political parties around, they all have to be very careful in what they say" (12/17/99). This caution concerned me in terms of the validity of people's responses in our interviews. Another example was the after-effects of a commercial helicopter that was blown up in Jiri.[8]

> Manisha and Sagun got a late start, but they are on their way back to where they went two days ago—Ward 5—to interview the men who weren't available the other day. We heard more news about the Maoists and Jiri as an "affected area." Manisha and Sagun have been warned that Wards 1 and 4 are the most dangerous. They think it would be even more hazardous for them if Chris or I go with them, as it is a well-known fact that Maoists greatly dislike Westerners, especially Americans. They allegedly blew up the Save the Children office in Gorkha, and now there are no foreign offices in all of Gorkha.
>
> LATER—SAME DAY
>
> Chris and I had to go out looking for Manisha and Sagun on the main road because they still hadn't returned home by 7p.m. It ends up they

> passed us in the police van as we were walking down the hill; they had caught a ride with the police doing rounds. They had much to tell us: They went back to Ward 5, where they had gone two days ago, to interview the men who were not available then. What they were found were slammed doors in their faces and a scolding from those who did talk to them the other day. People were frightened to talk to them because shortly after their interviews with Manisha and Sagun, the helicopter had been blown up. Some were connecting the blast with people giving interviews to Manisha and Sagun the day before it happened. Others chastised the people who had given interviews, and then today, people were too frightened to talk to them. Manisha and Sagun were eventually able to convince some people that they had no association with any political groups, that they were simply students doing research.
>
> —February 12, 2000

Although Sagun and Manisha were successful in getting some villagers to agree to interviews, the fear created by the helicopter explosion hindered the research process. As rumors continued to spread, Sagun, Manisha, Chris, and I became increasingly concerned about our own safety.

> I went upstairs to Manisha and Sagun's room earlier today to see if they were feeling better. They showed me a Nepali paper [written in Nepali] that the police chief had brought over for them to read to Chris and me. It said something about President Clinton/the Embassy warning foreigners, particularly Americans, and especially those associated with INGOs/NGOs, not to travel to certain districts in the next week or so. Districts listed included Dolakha [ours] and Ramechhap [next to Jiri VDC]. Apparently, the Maoists have a nationwide plan in effect until Saturday, "Democracy Day."
>
> —February 16, 2000

With government-issued warnings, I began to feel trapped, and worries and fears about Chris' safety, Sagun's and Manisha's safety, as well as my own, started to overwhelm me.

> I had a total breakdown this afternoon because I just feel so damn responsible. What if something happens to Manisha and Sagun in the field? What if someone tries to hijack or bomb our vehicle? I would never ever forgive myself if something happened to Chris or to the RAs. I feel out of control and not informed enough to make a decision. And no one is looking out for us, like the Peace Corps Head office or Fulbright's in Kathmandu. We're on our own, and I am in charge. And that is scary.
>
> —February 17, 2000

Distracted by anxieties, I found myself focusing on other things than the project. After talking with the VDC Chair and some trusted friends, Sagun, Manisha, Chris, and I made a group decision to stay in Jiri and finish the project. We hoped that word would spread that we did not have political ties or ambitions—we were simply students, there to study gender and education.

If things had worsened and we felt we were in direct danger, we were in the (privileged) position of having an "escape" out of the village. While we could "drive out" in a hired car, abandoning the project if necessary, the villagers had no choice but to stay. We always had the choice to leave. We also had the privilege to leave if we became very ill. For instance, I hired a car several times to travel to Kathmandu to have stomach ailments treated by the city doctors. When I contracted pneumonia in the village, not only did the doctors at the village clinic insist that I should be first in line to be examined (which I adamantly declined—others, far sicker than myself, had walked several days to reach the clinic), but I also had the ability to travel to Kathmandu for x-rays and powerful antibiotics. One of my greatest fears while in the field is getting sick. My positionality afforded me access to quality medical attention, and for me, this embodies the privilege inherent in my conducting fieldwork.

LEAVING THE FIELD AND NEGOTIATING THE WRITE-UP—THE NEXT STEP

As eager as I was to return home to my family, and ashamedly, to the comforts of home, I found it difficult to leave the field. I had developed friendships throughout my time in Jiri, and I had grown accustomed to the routine of my daily life there. People brought Chris and me flowers, *tikas* (which is colored paste placed upon one's forehead as a blessing) and Buddhist prayer shawls to ensure a safe journey home. As friends, new and old, asked when we would return, I was reminded of my ability to move freely in and out of communities, contexts, and countries. At times like these, I was reminded, once again, of my privileged life.

It is difficult to say when exactly I *left* the field. It seems as if it is an on-going process. Although I am no longer physically in Jiri, my thoughts were there as I analyzed the data and wrote this book. Many days, I am still there. I am currently working on ideas and new directions in my research that will enable me to return.

I would be remiss if I did not discuss the challenges of the write-up. Returning home to the States, I sat down and struggled with how I would document my findings and present them in a report. Turning once again to what literature I could find, I read Margaret Sutton's (1998) work, which emphasizes the importance of thinking deeply about asymmetrical relations in research settings. Sutton writes,

> Recognizing that science reinforces relations of inequality, what can researchers do to overturn them? Understanding that generalizations about groups of people obscure important differences within groups, how can we represent social life without distortions? (1998:21).

This became my challenge after returning from the field. I asked myself: How could I work to overturn the relations of gender, race, class, and caste inequality in Jiri and in Nepal? How might my research work towards that end? How do I depict community life in Jiri without distorting it? How best to portray the people of Jiri in a written document? Charles Kurzman (1991) suggests sharing one's writing with the research participants—making the write-up a shared enterprise. Unfortunately, this was problematic in the context of Nepal. Distance, non-literacy on many participants' part, and language all served as barriers to my implementing this idea for my own project. Davison (1996) notes, "the elicitor [researcher] has the responsibility to craft the transcribed, translated text into a form that is rendered meaningful to a reading audience outside the culture of the narrator" (1996:17). Also affecting these decisions are academic institutional expectations, which are riddled with gender power dynamics as well.

How would I disseminate my research findings in Nepal? Upon my return from the field, my primary concern was to write a dissertation and complete my degree. This placed certain constraints of style and emphasis on my writing and on portraying those who cooperated as participants in the project. Later, I wanted to write this book to represent the culmination of my work and to reach a body of readers interested in the social construction of gender and feminist methodologies. Even today, after finishing this book, I am still considering how best the research could be returned to the community, to whom, and in what form. In the end, it is my hope that, in some small way, I have given voice to participants' words and lives.

CONCLUSIONS

I continue to contemplate and reflect on the complexities of conducting fieldwork—for past, current, and future projects. To this day, I ask myself: Where is the activism in all of this? Is it possible to be a "scholar activist"? Is it possible to link feminist ideology with practice?[9] Importantly, I must admit that for this project in Jiri VDC I largely failed to reach my goals of putting feminist ideology into practice. While I did write up my preliminary

Epilogue

findings as well as recommendations for both the D School and the J School before I left the village,[10] I did not successfully enact "activist" research in terms of working with community members to develop action plans that would benefit a greater number of individuals in the village. Yet, I sense the project's presence in this particular community and our interactions with individuals—our subtle "gender trouble making" in the field—encouraged community members to think about gender and its complexities.

And I hope you, the reader, have been able to see the "universal" in this "particular" example. By describing and reflecting on my fieldwork struggles with attention to context, personal conditions, and historical moments, I hope to push these disclosures into the space between feminism and praxis. I hope that my discussion will aid future researchers and help advance dialogue among present scholars. As argued in Chapter Seven, we need to work together through reflection, dialogue, and then action. As scholars, community members, and students, we can become "sites of resistance," collectively raising awareness about social constructions of gender and educational inequities so that education may become an empowerment tool for all.

Notes

NOTES TO CHAPTER ONE

1. This book uses Shelley Feldman's definition of "Third World." As Feldman explains, "'Third World' is used . . . to specify postcolonial settings in which aid dependence and structural adjustment characterize the political and economic context of resource distribution and policy initiatives. The term is not meant to homogenize a particular group of countries nor underestimate or ignore their historical and contextual specificities and national capacities" (1998:24).
2. Nepal has had very few resources for improving its educational system. Financially and programmatically, Nepal has depended heavily on international donors and loans for its public schools. This dependence has enabled Nepal to support a public school system, but also indicates that the country has had inadequate means for making institutional-level changes.
3. See Floro & Wolf (1990); Cochrane, O'Hara, & Leslie (1980); Beenstock & Sturdy (1990); Pitt & Rosenzweig (1989); Schultz (1989); Behrman (1991); King & Hill (1993).
4. See Birdsall (1980); Csapo (1981); Chernikovsky (1985); Kasaju & Manandhar (1985); Jamison & Lockheed (1987); Behrman & Sussangkarn (1989); Davison & Kanyuka (1990); Abraha, et al. (1991); Brock & Cammish (1991); Ilon & Moock (1991); Roth (1991); Tietjen (1991); Punalekar (1993); Mukhopadhyay (1994); Post (2001).
5. I am certain that the findings noted here are descriptive of the situation in that particular Nepali village at the particular time of this project. I will use the past tense throughout this book to illustrate that the social constructions of gender described existed in that space, at that time. I follow the lead of Skinner & Holland (1996) who also used past tense throughout their analysis as an effort not to freeze the people in their study in time and out of history.
6. Nepal also provided an ideal setting for this study as the country faces rapid transition. Since 1989, Nepal has experienced a shift from an absolute monarchy to democracy with a growing reliance on capitalist exchange. Nepal

is one of the world's poorest countries, and foreign development programs have attempted to supplement the Nepalese government's economic and political transition, with foreign assistance programs offering aid and making various components of this transition possible.

7. Issues of development and the social construction of gender are central to this project. To better understand the relationship between gender and development, I conducted a descriptive study in Kathmandu on women's NGOs (non-government organizations) in 1994. Following that study, I learned of Jiri Village Development Committee (VDC) through an advisor who was part of a National Institutes of Health (NIH) research team in Jiri. He encouraged me to consider Jiri as a research site, as no ethnographic studies of Jiri's educational system existed. Therefore, in 1996, I conducted an exploratory study of the educational needs of women and girl children in Jiri as a preliminary research for my dissertation fieldwork. I felt this was a timely project, as the United Nations Conference on Women in Beijing China in 1995 raised education and the girl child as two critical areas for concern. After conducting this preliminary study, I developed a dissertation proposal to use a triangulation of methods to collect data through one school year, from October 1999 through June 2000. This text is largely taken from those dissertation findings.

8. The term "gender," as a noun, refers to the social distinctions between girls and boys, and women and men, including the roles that are deemed appropriate to each sex. When I use "gender" as an adjective ("gendered") or verb ("to gender"), it refers to any affect that reinforces gender roles, in other words, an affect that encourages a girl to "act like a girl," and a boy to "act like a boy." The "process of gender" then is the means by which society pushes girls and boys into appropriate roles.

9. See Mohanty (1991); Spivak (1988); Ong (1988); Chowdhry (1995) and Apffel-Marglin & Simon (1994).

10. See Harding (1986); Smith (1987); and Collins (1997).

11. Constraining or confining women to predominately domestic roles also assures patriarchal control. Men express gender as power by exerting control over women's sexuality, marriage, fertility, and decision-making abilities. Women's autonomy to decide if and when they want to become mothers diminishes the construct of a "natural" tendency of women toward motherhood (Stromquist 1990). The high fertility rate in Nepal, an estimated rate of 4.3 in 1999, indicates lack of such autonomy. Control of women's sexuality is achieved by placing a high value on pre-marital virginity, belief in women's limited physical ability, the penalization of abortion, and the association of birth control use with sexual promiscuity. This control over sexuality means women are treated as objects with little to no agency in terms of their own desires.

12. As the world's only Hindu Kingdom, a large percentage of the Nepalese population (86.5%) is Hindu.

13. *Kanyadan* also secures parents a place in heaven, as it is considered to be one of the greatest religious duties that parents can perform (Mathema, 1998).

Notes to Chapter Two

14. "Opportunity cost" refers to the perceived, indirect costs incurred when a child, particularly a daughter, goes to school and is not available to conduct household chores, agricultural work, or income-generating labor.
15. All names have been changed.
16. Students and families incur direct costs through school fees, first initiated in the late 1980s, as well as the purchase of school-required uniforms and shoes or boots. These school costs create a formidable barrier to girls' education (O'Gara, et al. 1999). The determination of how to spend limited household incomes on education is also gendered. Many Nepali parents, especially those in conservative Hindu families, view sons as the future income earners in their families, whereas daughters, through arranged marriages, will marry and go to live at the family homes of their husbands. Therefore, parents/guardians more willingly incur direct educational costs for sons, rather than daughters (ABEL 1996).
17. Parents and community members often worry about girls' safety in traveling to and from school, as well as their safety at school. As a consequence, girls may not be sent to school.
18. A small body of literature argues that education also heightens women's and girl's self-esteem and leads to greater knowledge of their individual rights (e.g., Kurz & Prather 1995). The 1995 Fourth World Conference on Women in Beijing, China cited both education and the girl child as two critical need areas for overcoming inequalities and persistent discrimination globally.
19. Another popular phrase in Nepal is, "If you educate a woman, you educate a nation."
20. El-Sanabary's (1997) report estimated 123,000 newly literate women in 1994–95, 100,000 women who became literate in 1995–96, and projected 140,000 for 1996–97. I could not find further follow-up data, but it appears these programs focused more on women and their empowerment through non-formal education than on girls and formal education.
21. At that time, 80 rupees equaled approximately US $1.59. In 2006, 80 rupees equaled approximately US $1.15.
22. A successful project to note is the GABLE (Girls' Attainment in Basic Literacy Education) in Malawi. GABLE and the government of Malawi rewrote curricula in the lower grades and interjected supplementary gender-sensitive text materials at the higher levels until all grade level syllabi and textbooks had restructured gender, whether in illustrations or text (Bernbaum, et al. 1999).
23. Again, an example to the contrary is Malawi's GABLE project. The GABLE project made gender awareness a top priority in teacher training. GABLE trained key personnel in each school and district, who, in turn, trained their colleagues.

NOTES TO CHAPTER TWO

1. In this chapter, I am describing the situation in Nepal and in Jiri VDC at the particular time of my research study (1999–2000). Thus, I will use the

past tense throughout this chapter to illustrate that the social constructs, particularly the social constructions of gender described, existed in that space, at that time.
2. To calculate the Human Development Index (HDI), the UNDP measures a country's achievements in terms of indicators such as life expectancy, educational attainment, and adjusted real income.
3. Under-five mortality rate is the probability of dying between birth and exactly five years of age expressed per 1,000 live births.
4. Maternal mortality ratio is the annual number of deaths of women from pregnancy-related causes per 100,000 live births.
5. Adult literacy is defined as aged 15 and older and able to read and write.
6. The School Leaving Certificate (SLC) is awarded after a student passes a set of national exams, externally administered at the end of the 10th year of the formal schooling cycle.
7. In 1961, the King of Nepal banned all political parties and instituted a new party-less political system known as the *Panchayat*. This system was based on indigenous village councils. Election to the National *Panchayat*, or Parliament, was indirect, proceeding through a hierarchy of village, district, and zone levels. The Jiri Village *Panchayat* was divided into nine wards. The *Panchayat* system was changed to the Multiparty system in April 1990. Under the Multiparty System, Jiri became a VDC (Village Development Committee), with nine wards (Subedi *et al.* 2000b).
8. All schools and individuals in this study have been given pseudonyms.
9. Because this book is the first ethnographic study of Jiri's educational system, much of the educational information provided in this chapter was gleaned during the conducting of this project. Further, because there are very few comprehensive studies of Jiri extant, there was very little to supplement my own research. The information on Jiri VDC provided in this chapter was all that I have uncovered in the 10 years I have studied Jiri.
10. This study focuses on 10 of the 11 government schools in Jiri VDC; the four private schools were not included.
11. Translation: "Let's make our village by ourselves." This statement refers to the self-sufficiency of the village.
12. I was advised not to travel to or visit the C School in Ward 5 because of the presence of Maoist activists and the presumed potential danger to Westerners.
13. As noted earlier, data on Jiri VDC were limited. Other than the Jirels, data on proportions of ethnic groups in Jiri VDC were not available. Further, a breakdown by gender of Jiri VDC's population and population growth rates was not available.
14. Polyandry is the practice of a wife with more than one husband; these husbands are often brothers.
15. Polygyny is the practice of one husband with more than one wife.
16. An important future study would be to examine the implications of Nepal's heavy reliance on donor aid and the gendered nature of the donor institutions.
17. In comparison, for the years 1992–1999, 2% of central government expenditure was allocated to education in the United States and for those same years, 3% of India's government budget (UNICEF 2001).

18. On June 1, 2001, the Crown Prince Dipendra allegedly killed 10 royal family members, including the reigning King and Queen of Nepal. The Maoists reject the official explanation that Crown Prince Dipendra was the assassin. Instead, they argue a conspiracy to usher in a new King (King Gyanendra). Since the royal family deaths, Nepal has remained unsettled, and analysts have suggested that the ensuing rebel strikes have been an attempt to take advantage of the instability lingering in the country. In July 2001, Prime Minister Girija Prasad Koirala resigned after the royal family massacre and amidst rumors of corruption, further adding to the instability. A suggestion for future study would be to focus on the events of the summer of 2001 and their effects on education.
19. The hills include Kathmandu, which had the highest percentage of girl students passing (72.2%) for that year.
20. Because many Nepali parents are consumed with agricultural and domestic work, taking care of small children is a responsibility expected of older siblings, especially older female siblings.
21. Mo Sibbons' definition of "access" is used here: "Access includes not only the physical availability of schools but also the absence of any constraint to education or anything that prevents girls or boys from going to school" (1998:37).
22. Jiri is located in Dolakha District in the Central Mountain Region.
23. In 1999–2000, 93 students were enrolled in Class/Grade 1 at the H School. According to the Ministry of Education (MOE)'s 1997 report, the average class size for Class 1 in the Dolakha District was 56.6, and the average class size at the primary level was 32.1.

NOTES TO CHAPTER THREE

1. Refer to Chapter One for a discussion of these critiques.
2. See Chapter Eight for further discussion of the power differentials inherent as a Western researcher implementing feminist methodologies in a "Third World" context.
3. See Chapter Eight for a discussion of the dilemmas in how we presented ourselves.
4. These necessary credentials included fluency in Nepali and English as well as social science research (preferably fieldwork) experience. I could not find any local candidates who had these qualifications. The two women research assistants I hired had fieldwork experience, graduate degrees in social science, and high proficiencies in English reading and writing. Several men with these credentials already had jobs and were not available.
5. The American University Institutional Review Board approved all informed consent forms and data collection methods.
6. Social mapping involves villagers drawing a map of their community. For this study, participants drew the local area of the village and included households. On the map, the participants indicated educational participation by gender for each household. With these same participants, we also drew needs assessment matrices, which entailed participants first brainstorming the problems

associated with access to and participation in education by gender. Using objects to symbolize each problem participants suggested, participants then ranked what they believed to be the most pressing problems and placed them on the vertical side of our makeshift matrix. The participants subsequently brainstormed possible solutions, found objects to represent each, ranked the solutions in order of feasibility, and then placed them on the horizontal side of the matrix. The idea is that the participants can later use the matrix to develop an action plan. We also put together time allocation charts, in which the participants described their daily schedules of activities as well as that of other members of their household. We discussed differences in activities and time spent on each by gender. See Eileen Kane's 1995 book *Seeing for Yourself: Research Handbook for Girls' Education in Africa* for more detailed descriptions of PLA strategies such as these.

7. This information was also useful in putting together Chapter Two.
8. Names of people and schools have been changed to preserve confidentiality.
9. Authorities advised us not to travel to or visit the C School in Ward 5 because of the presence of Maoist activists and the presumed potential danger to Westerners.
10. It is important in any discussion of research methods to note the potential for "social desirability," or eagerness to please, on the part of respondents. Critical questions to consider were: (1) What motivated the schools' faculty and staff to be so accommodating? (2) What were the consequences of their being accommodating?
11. To determine which students would be included in the student home visit sample, I assigned a number to each student in the classes observed at the focus schools, and then I drew numbers from a hat.
12. Because I argue in this book that gender is a social construction and is defined quite differently than sex (e.g., female, male), I purposely use gender terms such as "girl student " and "boy student," rather than biological terms such as "female" or "male," even though many of the students in this study were teenagers and some were adults.
13. Life history interviews were an exception to this.
14. Jean Davison's Malawi and Kenya studies (1984, 1990, 1992, and 1993) provided a guide for the interviews and observations for this study.
15. See Sadker, Myra and David Sadker. 1994. *Failing at Fairness: How Our Schools Cheat Girls*. New York: Simon & Schuster.
16. In Nepali classrooms, a student typically stands to give her or his answer when called on by a teacher.
17. Singleton, Straits, & Straits define face validity as "a personal judgment that an operational definition appears, on the face of it, to measure the concept it is intended to measure" (1993:516).
18. Occasionally, students (girls and boys) asked the teacher a question or requested clarification on a particular lecture point. Very rarely did students volunteer an answer. Students typically answered questions when called on, or when the teacher posed a question to the entire class, the students would answer aloud, in unison.

19. This informal method of assessing reliability is used when no statistical method is available for determining reliability for data such as these.
20. In other words, my coding was identical with the co-rater's (the research assistant's) coding 90% of the times teacher-student interactions were coded.
21. Saturdays are the Nepali weekend holiday. There is no school, and many people take it as a day of rest and participate in religious ceremonies.
22. Collecting the life histories took between one to five hours, with the average lasting three hours. One life history interview was conducted with each person.

NOTES TO CHAPTER FOUR

1. I am certain that the findings noted here are descriptive of the situation in Jiri at the time of this project. However, because I consider social constructions of gender as fluid and constantly changing, and in order not to freeze the people of Jiri in time and out of history, I use the past tense throughout the analytical chapters.
2. See Davison & Kanyuka 1992; Laosa 1982; Wolfe & Behrman 1984; Shrestha, *et al.* 1986; and Davison 1993.
3. "Literate" = Self-reported as able to read and write, and ALC = Adult Literacy Class (a government program, usually 3–6 months long). The SLC (School Leaving Certificate) is awarded after a student passes a set of national exams, externally administered at the end of the 10th year of the formal schooling cycle. Test pass is a preliminary test taken before the SLC exam.
4. Notably, there were more educated women in the Class 5 parent/guardian sample than in the Class 9 parent/guardian sample. This discrepancy may have been due to difference in age. Perhaps the Class 5 women parents/guardians were younger than the women parents/guardians of Class 9 students, and as a product of the changing times, had had more educational opportunities than the presumably older parents/guardians from the Class 9 sample. The two parent/guardian samples also differed by region or location: All of the Class 5 parents/guardians lived in Ward 7, the most prosperous of the nine wards, as well as the location for the main market in the Jiri VDC. In contrast, only two Class 9 parents/guardians lived in Ward 7; the others lived in Wards 9, 8, 6, and 5, which were more remote and isolated. This may also have been a factor in Class 9 women parents/guardians having had less education than the Class 5 women parents/guardians.
5. We explained at the beginning of the interviews that this project focused on education and that all of the interview questions related to the academic context.
6. Whereas 86.6% of community members said that both girls and boys should be educated, an even higher percentage of parents/guardians (94.7%) thought both should be educated.

7. There were also differences between religions. Over half of the men who said they would prioritize educating their son were Buddhist (54.3%), whereas just over one third of the men who said the same were Hindu (37.1%). Also, well over half of the women who preferred to send their son to school were Buddhist (60.9%), whereas just over a quarter of the women who reported they would prefer to send their sons were Hindu (26.1%). Future studies should examine the influence of religion on attitudes towards gender and education.
8. "Job," used here and elsewhere in the text, is a loose translation for the Nepali word *kaam*, which literally means "work." When respondents referred to jobs, they may have been referring to full-time employment or short-term, seasonal work, paid in wages or food.
9. Notably, this was not true of any interviewees from the parent/guardian sample who said both boys and girls should attend school.
10. Future studies should examine differences in school costs by gender. For example, do school uniforms for girls cost more than those for boys?
11. See Davison, *et al.* (1994) *Educational Demand in Rural Ethiopia* for similar findings in the context of Ethiopia.
12. For example, a Jirel woman from the community member sample, who was non-literate, stressed the importance of sending a son to school because, "we need daughter as a friend to help at home."
13. Reasons community member gave for girls dropping out of school included heavy workload at home, girl deciding herself to drop out of school, the girl drops out to marry or elope, the culturally given belief that girls should not be educated, and poverty. More women than men from the community member sample reported that girls drop out because of the workload at home, the girl decides herself to drop out of school, or girls run away to get married. Perhaps this was based on their own experiences, including the social obligation of girls and women to perform domestic tasks, as well as their own roles as wives and/or mothers. More men than women attributed poverty as the underlying reason for girls dropping out of school. I would argue that this answer was rooted in their socially constructed role as breadwinners. As controllers of the family purse, these men community members were responsible for school fees and could relate to other fathers who might have felt obligated to remove a daughter from school because of direct and indirect (opportunity) costs.

    Also, more men than women cited the socio-cultural belief that girls should not be educated as a reason why girls drop out of school. Again, this may be attributed to the men interviewees having had more education than the women interviewees and subsequently having had more exposure than many of the women. Parents/guardians were asked the same question. Workload at home (36.8%) and poverty (36.8%) were the most often cited reason for girls dropping out of school. Equal numbers of women and men parents/guardians cited workload at home as a factor, whereas, similar to the community member sample, more men parents/guardians cited poverty than did women. Again, this may have been related to the fact that men were typically the controllers of the family income.

14. In addition to the workload at home, five students (four girls and one boy) cited marriage as a reason for girls' dropping out of school. Notably, four out of ten girls cited early marriage as a constraint to completing education, which is comparable with their parents/guardians' perceptions. Significantly, interviewees across samples noted the linkage between early marriage and girls' persistence in school. This awareness is encouraging, as a step towards social change.
15. After Class 5, students had to pay a class or enrollment fee each year. Further, students had to pay fees for exams. Entrance fees and exam fees increased incrementally according to class/grade level. Yet another expense was a uniform—wearing a uniform to school everyday was mandatory at all class levels for every school in Jiri. Finally, schools did not furnish students with textbooks and school supplies; students were expected to purchase their own texts and other required materials.

NOTES TO CHAPTER FIVE

1. Notably, neither of the women head teachers selected these same subjects for girls. Perhaps the women head teachers knew from their own experience that relegating girls and women to sewing classes would not bring girls any closer to independence or to good jobs with competitive wages.
2. Social desirability on the part of the head teachers was an intervening factor in the research process. We often felt that the head teachers were telling us what they thought we wanted to hear. For example, throughout the interview process, head teachers insisted that girl and boy students were treated the same. One man Jirel head teacher with an SLC education insisted, "We teach in school, we teach both the boys and the girls in the same manner." Observations of teachers in the classroom demonstrated otherwise. Although most of the head teachers considered themselves to be "gender aware," many of their responses to interview questions demonstrated a lack of awareness of the social constructions of gender, indicating a missing component in their teacher training.
3. Notably, this teacher's response was quite different from the community members and parents/guardians who described girls as having "soft" minds and "only dreaming."
4. Both the J School and the D School had regular school assemblies. These assemblies were typically fashioned with military-style drills and formations.
5. In 1999–2000, classrooms in Nepal were typically divided, with boys on one side and girls on the other. Because the classrooms were organized by gender spatiality (teacher/administration-controlled), this construction of gender boundaries (literally and figuratively) reinforced patterns found in temples (Buddhist and Hindu), families, and workplaces.
6. In the winter months, the teachers typically wore sweaters over long-sleeve shirts and long pants. The girls were required to wear skirts that fell far below the knees, but due to the cold, they wore thick stockings or pants underneath, if they owned such items. The boys wore pants and long-sleeve shirts. Only a few owned a sweater, and many of their shirts and pants

were ripped with large holes. I would imagine they all felt quite cold in the classroom during the wintertime.
7. Although most teachers showed gender bias in their interactions with students, teachers delivered corporal punishment to both boys and girls, but typically not as forcefully with the girls.
8. More discouraging, on the days we did not observe, there was anecdotal evidence that the quality of classroom instruction was even more impoverished than the days we were present.
9. Environment was the most frequently observed subject at the Class 5 level (16 observations), whereas Social Studies was only observed nine times. Classes were often cancelled when a teacher was absent. Also, the head teacher frequently declared a holiday in the middle of the day, and students would leave for home.
10. The coding system implemented was based on the coding schema developed by Myra Sadker and David Sadker.
11. Math was the most frequently observed subject (16 observations), whereas Education was only observed 11 times. Again, classes were often cancelled when a teacher was absent, and the school day would frequently end early or be cancelled altogether.
12. This science lab had been built with money from an international donor. Because of its relatively new and pristine condition, it was never used except for district educational meetings and other official gatherings.
13. In Sadker, Sadker, & Lewit's (1995) guide, *Gender Bias in the Curriculum*, they describe different forms of bias in instructional materials: *Invisibility*—omission of girls and women from text and illustrations; *stereotyping*—assigning girls and women and boys and men rigid roles and traits based on their gender as well as portraying girls and women and boys and men in stereotypical images; and *linguistic bias*—referring to women and men in masculine terms, such as "Chairman," regardless of the gender of the Chair.
14. As discussed in Chapter Two, the conflict between the Maoists and the King's Army has hurt the trekking industry in Jiri, resulting in fewer and fewer trekking guide jobs.

NOTES TO CHAPTER SIX

1. None of the Class 5 girls selected math or science. Perhaps they had not yet seen the utility of either subject, or perhaps they had not been encouraged to excel in either subject by teachers or parents/guardians.
2. The campus level is also known as intermediate or "10+2." It is similar to 11th and 12th grade in the U.S. educational system.
3. However, he made no mention to me or to other teachers of plans to recruit women teachers.

NOTES TO CHAPTER SEVEN

1. Students' standpoints need to be further examined, as it is often the individuals themselves who offer the best perspective for effecting social change.

We also need to explore further how and why some students challenge gender constraints and others do not.

2. Consideration should be made of the potential for change at the grassroots as well as the national levels. Future initiatives should examine villages where existing programs are in operation and consider how they can be restructured.

NOTES TO CHAPTER EIGHT

1. Perhaps the greatest contribution my research made in the local context was Chris' presence in the field with me and his own "gender trouble-making." While I—a woman and wife—conducted research in the schools, people's homes, and in the village bazaars, Chris—a man and husband—did laundry with other women, cleaned our rooms, and chatted with others in the local tea shops.
2. All names have been changed.
3. At the time of this study, the highest level of education one could achieve in Nepal was the Master's level. None of the universities in the country offered a Ph.D. program.
4. *Bhauju* is Nepali for "sister-in-law." We addressed the mother in our homestay family as "*Bhauju.*"
5. *Bahini* is Nepali for "little sister." We called our homestay family's niece "*Bahini.*"
6. We referred to the father in our homestay family as "*Dai.*"
7. The literal translation of the Nepali term *Aaphno Manchhe* is "self man."
8. We heard that that particular helicopter was one of the three in Jiri and was the only one owned by the Nepalese government. The rumor was that the Maoists blew up the helicopter as an act of protest against using a helicopter to transport goods to the Solu Khumbu (Everest) region rather than hiring people to carry the loads up the trail for wages. Of course, the Maoists may not be the ones to blame—or to credit, however you might look at this—for this attack. They may not have been involved at all.
9. For an in-depth discussion of putting feminist ideology into practice, see Jennifer Fish's (2006) book *Domestic Democracy: At Home in South Africa*.
10. The head teacher at the D School asked us when we first started our observations to give him feedback from our observations—their weaknesses regarding teaching methods, classrooms, the whole organization of the school, etc. We promised we would do so before leaving Jiri. I wrote up my preliminary findings as well as recommendations for both this school and the J school before I left the village. It was a small token of appreciation for allowing me to observe for such an extended period of time. Several teachers at both schools told me later that my report contained useful information.

Bibliography

ABEL. 1996. *Exploring Incentives: Promising Strategies for Improving Girls' Participation in School.* Washington, DC: Advancing Basic Education and Literacy Project (ABEL). Creative Associates International, Inc.

Abraha, Seged, Assefa Beyene, Tesfaye Dubale, Bruce Fuller, Susan Holloway, and Elizabeth King. 1991. "What Factors Shape Girls' School Performance? Evidence from Ethiopia." *International Journal of Educational Development.* 11(2):107–118.

Acharya, Meena. 1981. *The Mathili Women.* Philippines: Regional Service Center.

Acharya, Meena and Lynn Bennett. 1981. *The Rural Women of Nepal: An Aggregate Analysis and Summary of Eight Village Studies.* Philippines: Regional Service Center.

Acker, Joan. 1990. "Hierarchies, Jobs, Bodies: A Theory of Gendered Organization." *Gender and Society.* 4(2):139–158.

Alexander, M. Jacqui and Chandra Talpade Mohanty. 1997. "Introduction: Geneaologies, Legacies, Movements." Pp. xiii-xlii in *Feminist Geneaologies, Colonial Legacies, and Democratic Futures.* New York: Routledge.

Anderson, Jeanine, and Christina Herencia. 1983. *L'image de la Femme et de l'homme dans les livres scolaires peruviens.* Paris, France: UNESCO.

Apffel-Marglin, Frederique and Suzanne L. Simon. 1994. "Feminist Orientalism and Development." Pp. 26–45 in *Feminist Perspectives on Sustainable Development*, edited by Wendy Harcourt. London: Zed Books.

Ashby, Jacqueline. 1985. "Equity and Discrimination among Children: Schooling Decisions in Rural Nepal." *Comparative Education Review.* 29(1): 68–79.

Babbie, Earl. 1995. *The Practice of Social Research.* Seventh Edition. Belmont, CA: Wadsworth Publishing Company.

Beenstock, M. and P. Sturdy. 1990. "Determinants of Infant Mortality in Regional India." *World Development.* 18:443–53 (March).

Behrman, J. 1991. "Investing in Female Education for Development: Women in Development Strategy for the 1990s in Asia and the Near East." Mimeo, PA: University of Pennsylvania.

Behrman, J. and C. Sussangkarn. 1989. *Parental Schooling and Child Outcomes: Mother Versus Father, Schooling Quality, and Interactions.* Mimeo, PA: University of Pennsylvania.

Bennett, Lynn. 1981. *The Parbatiya Women of Bakundol.* Philippines: Regional Service Center.

Benoliel, Sharon, Lynn Ilon, Margaret Sutton, Dibya M. Karmacharya, Shreeram Lamichhane, Pramila Rajbhandry, Basu Der Kafle, and Sunita Giri. 1998. *USAID Impact Evaluation: Promoting Education for Girls in Nepal.* Washington, DC: USAID.

Bernbaum, Marcia, Kristi Fair, Shirley Miske, Talaat Moreau, Duncan Nyirenda, Johnson Sikes, Joy Wolf, Richard B. Harber, Jr., Ash Hartwell, and Beverly Schwartz. 1999. *USAID Impact Evaluation: Promoting Primary Education for Girls in Malawi.* Washington, DC: USAID.

Best, Ralphaela. 1983. *We've All Got Scars: What Boys and Girls Learn in Elementary School.* Bloomington, IN: Indiana University Press.

Bhattachan, K.B. 1994. "Nepal in 1993: Business as Usual." *Asian Survey.* 34(2):175–180.

Birdsall, N. 1980. "A Cost of Siblings: Child Schooling in Urban Columbia." *Research in Population Economics.* 2:115–150.

Bista, D.B. 1980. *People of Nepal.* Kathmandu, Nepal: Ratna Pustak Bhandar.

Brock, C. and N.K. Cammish. 1991. *Factors Affecting Female Participating in Education in Six Developing Countries.* Education Research Series No.9. London: ODA.

Brock, C. and N. Cammish. 1997. *Factors Affecting Female Participation in Seven Developing Countries.* London: Department for International Development.

Bronstein, Audrey. 1982. *The Triple Struggle: Latin American Peasant Women.* Boston, MA: South End Press.

Burawoy, Michael. 1991. "Introduction." Pp. 1–7 in *Ethnography Unbound: Power and Resistance in the Modern Metropolis*, edited by Michael Burawoy, Alice Burton, Ann Arnett Ferguson, Kathryn J. Fox, Joshua Gamson, Nadine Gartell, Leslie Hurst, Charles Kurzman, Leslie Salzinger, Josepha Schiffman, and Shiori Ui. Berkeley, CA: University of California Press.

Burchfield, Shirley A. 1997. *An Analysis of the Impact of Literacy on Women's Empowerment in Nepal.* Washington, DC: USAID.

Butler, J. 1990. *Gender Trouble: Feminism and the Subversion of Identity.* New York: Routledge.

CBS (Central Bureau of Statistics). 1991. *Population Census 1991.* Kathmandu, Nepal: Central Bureau of Statistics.

———. 1993. *Statistical Pocket Book Nepal 1993.* Kathmandu, Nepal: Central Bureau of Statistics.

———. 1996. *Statistical Pocket Book Nepal 1996.* Kathmandu, Nepal: Central Bureau of Statistics.

———. 1999. *Statistical Year Book of Nepal 1999.* Kathmandu, Nepal: Central Bureau of Statistics.

CERID (Research Centre for Educational Innovation and Development). 1996. *Promotion of Girls' Education through Recruitment and Training of Female*

Teachers in Nepal: A Country Case Study (Phase I). Kathmandu, Nepal: CERID.
Cameron, Mary M. 1995. "Transformations of Gender and Caste Divisions of Labor in Rural Nepal: Land, Hierarchy, and the Case of Untouchable Women." *Journal of Anthropological Research*. 51:215–246.
Charmaz, Kathy. 1983. "The Grounded Theory Method: An Explication and Interpretation." Pp. 109–26 in *Contemporary Field Research: A Collection of Readings*, ed. Robert M. Emerson. Prospect Heights, IL: Waveland Press.
Chernikovsky, D. 1985. "Socio-Economic and Demographic Aspects of School Enrollment and Attendance in Botswana." *Economic Development and Social Change*. 33:319–32.
Chowdhry, Geeta. 1995. "Engendering Development? Women in Development (WID) in International Development Regimes." Pp. 26–41 in *Feminism/Postmodernism/Development*, edited by Marianne H. Marchand and Jane L. Parpart. London: Routledge.
Cleland, J. and G. Kaufman. 1998. "Education, Fertility, and Child Survival: Unraveling the Links." *The Methods and Uses of Anthropological Demography*, edited by A. Basu and P. Aaby. Oxford: Clarendon Press.
Cochrane, Susan. 1979. *Fertility and Education: What Do We Really Know?* Baltimore, MD: Johns Hopkins University Press.
Cochrane, S., D. O'Hara, and J. Leslie. 1980. "The Effects of Education on Health." World Bank Staff Working Papers. No. 405. Washington, DC: World Bank.
Collins, Patricia Hill. 1991. *Black Feminist Thought: Knowledge, Consciousness, and the Politics of Empowerment*. New York: Routledge.
———. 1997. "Comments on Hekman's 'Truth and Method: Feminist Standpoint Theory Revisited': Where's the Power?" *Signs*. 22:375–379.
Connell, R.W. 1987. *Gender and Power*. Stanford, CA: Stanford University Press.
Csapo, M. 1981. "Religious, Social, and Economic Factors Hindering the Education of Girls in Northern Nigeria." *Comparative Education*. 17(3):311–319.
Dahal, Dilli R. 1995. "Ethnic Cauldron, Demography, and Minority Politics." Pp. 148–170 in *State Leadership and Politics in Nepal*, edited by Dhruba Kumar. Kathmandu: Centre for Nepal and Asian Studies.
Davison, Jean. 1984. "Myths and Realities: A Study of Parental Attitudes toward Educating Females in Kenya." Paper presented at the Educational Foundations Seminar Series, Kenyatta University, Nairobi, Kenya.
———. 1993. "School Attainment and Gender: Attitudes of Kenyan and Malawian Parents toward Educating Girls." *International Journal of Educational Development*. 13(4):331–338.
———. 1996. *Voices from Mutira: Changes in the Lives of Rural Gikuyu Women, 1910–1995*. Second Edition. London: Lynne Rienner Publishers.
Davison, Jean and Martin Kanyuka. 1990. "An Ethnographic Study of Factors that Affect the Education of Girls in Southern Malawi." A Report to the Ministry of Education and Culture and USAID Malawi. Lilongwe.
———. 1992. "Girl's Participation in Basic Education in Southern Malawi." *Comparative Education Review*. 36(4):446–466.

Davison, J., B. Honig, K. Tietjen, T. Zewdie, and T. Tadesse. 1994. *Educational Demand in Rural Ethiopia*. Addas Ababa. USAID/Ethiopia.

Dickerson, Bette, Philipia Hillman, and Johanna Foster. 1995. "Empowerment through 'Ordinary' Knowledge/Scholarship/Policy Nexus." Pp. 179–192 *in African American Single Mothers: Understanding Their Lives and Families*, edited by Bette J. Dickerson. Thousand Oaks, CA: SAGE Publications.

El-Sanabary, Nagat. 1997. *USAID/Nepal's Female Literacy Program Technical Assistance: Trip Report, March 12-April 1, 1997*. Washington, DC: USAID.

Emerson, Robert M., Rachel I. Fretz, and Linda L. Shaw. 1995. *Writing Ethnographic Fieldnotes*. Chicago, IL: University of Chicago Press.

Feagin, Joe R., Anthony M. Orum, and Gideon Sjoberg. 1991. *A Case for the Case Study*. Chapel Hill, NC: The University of Carolina Press.

Feldman, Shelley. 1998. "Conceptualizing Change and Equality in the 'Third World' Contexts." Pp. 24–36 in *Women in the Third World: An Encyclopedia of Contemporary Issues,* edited by Nelly P. Stromquist. New York, NY: Garland Publishing, Inc.

Fish, Jennifer N. 2006. *Domestic Democracy: At Home in South Africa*. New York, NY: Routledge.

Floro, M. and J.M. Wolf. 1990. *The Economic and Social Impact of Girls' Primary Education in Developing Countries*. Washington, DC: Creative Associates International, Inc., USAID.

Fournier, A. 1974. "Notes Preliminaires sur des populations Sunuwar dans l'esr du Nepal." Pp. 62–83 in *Contributions to the Anthropology of Nepal*, edited by C. von Fürer Haimendorf. Warminster, UK: Aris & Phillips.

Freire, Paulo. 1990. *Pedagogy of the Oppressed*. New York: Continuum.

Fürer Haimendorf, Christoph von. 1964. *The Sherpas: Buddhist Highlanders*. London: John Murray.

Garfinkel, Harold. 1967. *Studies in Ethnomethodology*. Englewood Cliffs: Prentice-Hall.

Gellner, David N. 1997. "Ethnicity and Nationalism in the World's Only Hindu State." Pp. 3–31 in *Nationalism and Ethnicity in a Hindu Kingdom: The Politics of Culture in Contemporary Nepal*. Amsterdam, the Netherlands: Harwood Academic Publishers.

Glaser, Barney G. and Anselm L. Strauss. 1967. *The Discovery of Grounded Theory: Strategies for Qualitative Research*. Chicago, IL: Aldine.

Hamill, J., H. Sidky, Janardan Subedi, Ronald H. Spielbauer, Robin Singh, John Blangero, and Sarah Williams-Blangero. 2000a. "Some Sociocultural Consequences of Transportation Development in the Jiri Valley, Nepal." *Contributions to Nepalese Studies: The Jirel Issue* (January 2000): 89–95.

Hamill, J. H. Sidky, Ronald H. Spielbauer, Janardan Subedi, Robin Singh, Sarah Williams-Blangero, and John Blangero. 2000b. "Preliminary Ethnosemantics of the Avifauna Vocabulary in Jirel." *Contributions to Nepalese Studies: The Jirel Issue* (January 2000): 53–77.

Harber, Clive. 1988. "Schools and Political Socialization in Africa." *Education Review*. 40(2):195–202.

Harding, Sandra. 1986. *The Science Question of Feminism*. Ithaca, NY: Cornell University Press.

Herz, Barbara, K. Subbarao, Masooma Habib, and Laura Raney. 1991. *Letting Girls Learn: Promising Approaches in Primary and Secondary Education.* World Bank Discussion Papers. No. 133. Washington, DC: The World Bank.
Heward, Christine. 1999. "Introduction: The New Discourses of Gender, Education, and Development." Pp. 1–14 in *Gender, Education, and Development: Beyond Access to Empowerment*, edited by Christine Heward and Sheila Bunwaree. London: Zed Books Ltd.
hooks, bell. 1990. *Yearning.* Boston: South End Press.
Hurst, Leslie and Nadine Gartrell. 1991. "Introduction to Part IV." Pp. 181–182 in *Ethnography Unbound: Power and Resistance in the Modern Metropolis.* Berkeley, CA: University of California Press.
Institute for Integrated Development Studies. (IIDS). 1994. *The Statistical Profile on Nepalese Women: An Update in the Policy Context.* Kathmandu, Nepal: Institute for Integrated Development Studies.
Ilon, Lynn and Peter Moock. 1991. "School Attributes, Household Characteristics, and Demand for Schooling." *International Review of Education.* 37(4):429–451.
Jamison, Dean T. and Marlaine E. Lockheed. 1987. "Participation in Schooling: Determinants and Learning Outcomes in Nepal." *Economic Development and Cultural Change.* 35(2):279–306.
Jorgensen, Danny L. 1989. *Participatory Observation: A Methodology for Human Studies.* London: SAGE Publications.
Joshi, Govinda Prasad and Jean Anderson. 1994. "Female Motivation in the Patriarchal School: An Analysis of Primary Textbooks and School Organization in Nepal, and Some Strategies for Change." *Gender and Education.* 6(2):169–181.
Kane, Eileen. 1995. *Seeing Yourself: Research Handbook for Girls' Education in Africa.* Washington, DC: The World Bank.
Karan, P. and H. Ishii. 1996. *Nepal: A Himalayan Kingdom in Transition.* Tokyo: United Nations University Press.
Kasaju, Prem and T.B. Manandhar. 1985. "Impact of Parents' Literacy on School Enrollments and Retention of Children: the Case of Nepal." *Issues in Planning and Implementing National Literacy Programs*, edited by G. Carron and A. Bordia. UNESCO. Paris: International Institute for Educational Planning.
Kelly, G. and C. Elliott. 1982. *Women's Education in the Third World: Comparative Perspectives.* New York: State University of New York.
Khaniya, T.R. and M.A. Kiernan. 1995. "Nepal." *International Encyclopedia of National Systems of Education*, edited by T. Neville Postlethwaite. Oxford: Pergamon.
Kimmel, Michael. 2004. *The Gendered Society.* New York: Oxford University Press.
King, Elizabeth M. 1990. *Educating Girls and Women: Investing in Development.* Washington, D.C.: The World Bank.
———. and M. Anne Hill. 1993. *Women's Education in Developing Countries: Barriers, Benefits, and Policies.* Baltimore: The Johns Hopkins University Press.
Kleinman, Sherryl and Martha A. Copp. 1993. *Emotions and Fieldwork.* London: SAGE Publications.

Kumar, Nita. 1992. *Friends, Brothers, Informants: Fieldwork Memoirs of Banaras.* Berkeley, CA: University of California Press.

Kurz, Kathleen M. and Cynthia J. Prather. 1995. *Improving the Quality of Life of Girls.* New York: UNICEF.

Kurzman, Charles. 1991. "Convincing Sociologists: Values and Interests in the Sociology of Knowledge." Pp. 250–268 in *Ethnography Unbound: Power and Resistance in the Modern Metropolis.* Berkeley, CA: University of California Press.

Lee, Allison. 1996. *Gender, Literacy, Curriculum: Re-writing School Geography.* London: Taylor & Francis.

LeVine, Robert A., Sarah E. LeVine, and Beatrice Schnell. 2001. "'Improve the Women': Mass Schooling, Female Literacy, and Worldwide Social Change." *Harvard Educational Review.* 71(1) (Spring):1–50.

Locke, Lawrence F., Warren Wyrick Spirduso, and Stephen J. Silverman. 1993. *Proposals that Work: A Guide for Planning Dissertations and Grant Proposals.* Newbury Park, CA: SAGE Publications.

Lofland, John and Lyn H. Lofland. 1984. *Analyzing Social Settings: A Guide to Qualitative Observation and Analysis.* Second Edition. Belmont, CA: Wadsworth Publishing Company.

Lorber, Judith. 1994. *The Paradoxes of Gender.* New Haven: Yale University Press.

———. 1998. *Gender Inequality: Feminist Theories and Politics.* Los Angeles: Roxbury Publishing Company.

———. 2000. "Using Gender to Undo Gender: A Feminist Degendering Movement." *Feminist Theory.* 1:101–118.

Luttrell, Wendy. 1993. "'The Teacher, They All Had Their Pets:' Concepts of Gender, Knowledge, and Power." *Signs.* 18(3):505–546.

Magellan Geographix. 1999. "Political Map of Nepal." http://www.askasia.org/image/maps/nepal1.htm. Downloaded on March 20, 2002.

Maguire, Patricia. 1987. *Doing Participatory Research: A Feminist Approach.* Amherst, MA: The Center for International Education, School of Education, University of Massachusetts.

Maharjan, Pancha N. 1998. *Local Elections in Nepal, 1997.* Kathmandu, Nepal: Center for Nepal and Asian Studies, Tribhuvan University.

Manneschmidt, Sybille M. 1995. "Ethnographic Survival Skills: Be Ready to Drink a Lot of Tea!" *Education and Development,* edited by Bajra Raj Shakya and Gaja S. Pradhan. Kathmandu, Nepal: Research Center for Educational Innovation and Development, Tribhuvan University.

Mathema, Madhuri. 1998. "Women in South Asia: Pakistan, Bangladesh, and Nepal." Pp. 583–592 in *Women in the Third World: An Encyclopedia of Contemporary Issues,* edited by Nelly P. Stromquist. New York, NY: Garland Publishing, Inc.

Mehotra, S. and R. Jolly. (Editors). 1997. *Development with a Human Face.* Oxford: Clarendon Press.

Merriam, Sharan B. 1988. *Case Study Research in Education: A Qualitative Approach.* San Francisco, CA: Jossey-Bass.

Mies, Maria. 1983. "Towards a Methodology for Feminist Research." Pp. 117–139 in *Theories of Women's Studies,* edited by Gloria Bowles and Renate Duelli Klein. London: Routledge.

———. 1986. *Patriarchy and Accumulation on a World Scale: Women in the International Division of Labor*. Atlantic Heights, NJ: Zed Books.
———. 1990. "Women's Research or Feminist Research? The Debate Surrounding Feminist Science and Methodology." Pp. 60–84 in *Beyond Methodology: Feminist Scholarship as Lived Research*, edited by Mary Margaret Fonow and Judith Cook. Bloomington, IN: Indiana University Press.
Miles, Matthew B. and A. Michael Huberman. 1994. *Qualitative Data Analysis: An Expanded Sourcebook*. (Second Edition). Thousand Oaks, CA: SAGE Publications.
Ministry of Education (MOE). 1997. *Educational Statistics of Nepal 1997*. Kathmandu, Nepal: Statistics Section. Ministry of Education (MOE).
Ministry of Education and Culture (MOEC) and United States Agency for International Development (USAID). 1988. *Education and Human Resources Sector Assessment*. Kathmandu, Nepal: Ministry of Education and Culture (MOEC).
Mohanty, Chandra Talpade. 1991. "Under Western Eyes: Feminist Scholarship and Colonial Discourses." Pp. 51–79 in *Third World Women and the Politics of Feminism*, edited by Chandra Talpade Mohanty, Ann Russo, and Lourdes Torres. Bloomington, IN: Indiana University Press.
Mohanty, Chandra Talpade. 2004. *Feminism without Borders: Decolonizing Theory, Practicing Solidarity*. Durham, NC: Duke University Press.
Morgen, S. and A. Bookman. 1988. "Rethinking Women and Politics: An Introductory Essay." Pp. 3–29 in *Women and the Politics of Empowerment*, edited by A. Bookman and S. Morgen. Philadelphia, PA: Temple University Press.
Mukhopadhyay, Sudhin. 1994. "Adapting Household Behavior to Agricultural Technology in West Bengal, India: Wage Labor, Fertility, and Child Schooling Determinants." *Economic Development and Cultural Change*. 43(1):91–115.
Naples, Nancy. 2003. *Feminism and Method: Ethnography, Discourse Analysis, and Activist Research*. New York: Routledge.
Narayan, Uma. 1989. "The Project of Feminist Epistemology: Perspectives from a Non-Western Feminist." Pp. 256–269 in *Gender/Body/Knowledge: Feminist Reconstructions of Being and Knowing*, edited by Alison M. Jaggar and Susan R. Bordo. New Brunswick, NJ: Rutgers University Press.
Oboler, Regina Smith. 1986. "For Better of Worse: Anthropologists and Husbands in the Field." Pp. 28–51 in *Self, Sex, and Gender in Cross-Cultural Fieldwork*, edited by Tony Larry Whitehead and Mary Ellen Conaway. Urbana, IL: University of Illinois Press.
O'Brien, Mary. 1983. *The Politics of Reproduction*. Boston: Routledge and Kegan Paul.
O'Gara, Chloe, Sharon Benoliel, Margaret Sutton, and Karen Tietjen. 1999. *More, but Not Yet Better: An Evaluation of USAID's Programs and Policies to Improve Girls' Education: USAID Program and Operations Assessment Report No. 25*. Washington, D.C.: Academy for Educational Development.
Ong, Aihwa. 1988. "Colonialism and Modernity: Feminist Re-presentations of Women in Non-Western Societies." *Inscriptions*. 3(4):79–93.
Orenstein, Peggy. 1994. *School Girls: Young Women, Self-Esteem, and the Confidence Gap*. New York: Doubleday, with the American Association of University Women.

Pinto, Regina. 1982. "Imagem da Mulher atraves dos livros didaticos." *Boletim Bibliografico de Biblioteca Mario de Andrade.* 43(3–4):126–131.
Pitt, M. and M. Rosenzweig. 1989. "Estimating the Intrafamily Incidence of Illness: Child Health and Gender Inequality in the Allocation of Time in Indonesia." Paper presented at the Conference on the Family, Gender Differences, and Development. Yale University, New Haven CT, September 4–6, 1989.
Post, David. 2001. "Region, Poverty, Sibship, and Gender Inequality in Mexican Education: Will Targeted Welfare Policy Make a Difference for Girls?" *Gender and Society.* 15(3):468–489.
Potuchek, Jean L. 1997. *Who Supports the Family? Gender and Breadwinning in Dual-Earner Marriages.* Stanford, CA: Stanford University Press.
Prather, Cynthia. 1991. *Educating Girls: Strategies to Increase Access, Persistence, and Achievement.* Washington, DC: Creative Associates International, Inc.
Punalekar, SP. 1993. "Structural Constraints in Tribal Education: A Case Study of Tribal Community in South Gujarat." *The Indian Journal of Social Science.* 6(1):19–30.
Raj Lohani, Shiva. 1998. "Financing of Education: Issues and Policy Directions." Pp. 40–56 in *Education and Development 1998.* Kathmandu, Nepal: CERID.
Raj Panday, Devendra. 1999. *Nepal's Failed Development: Reflections on the Mission and the Maladies.* Kathmandu, Nepal: Nepal South Asia Centre.
Ragin, Charles C. 1994. *Constructing Social Research: The Unity and Diversity of Method.* Thousand Oaks, CA: Pine Forge Press.
Reinharz, Shulamit. 1992. *Feminist Methods in Social Research.* New York, NY: Oxford University Press.
Reinhold, Amy Jo. 1993. *Working with Rural Communities in Nepal: Some Principles of Non-formal Education Intervention: Action Research in Family and Early Childhood.* Westport, CT: Save the Children.
Risman, Barbara J. 1998. *Gender Vertigo: American Families in Transition.* New Haven, CT: Yale University Press.
Roth, Eric A. 1991. "Education, Tradition, and Household Labor among Rendille Pastoralists of Northern Kenya." *Human Organization.* 50(2): 136–141.
Rugh, Andrea. 2000. *Starting Now: Strategies for Helping Girls Complete Primary.* Washington, D.C.: Academy for Educational Development.
Sadker, Myra and David Sadker. 1994. *Failing at Fairness: How Our Schools Cheat Girls.* New York: Simon & Schuster.
Sadker, Myra, David Sadker, and Abigail Lewit. 1995. *Gender Bias in the Curriculum and in Classroom Interaction.* Color videotape on effectiveness and equity in college teaching (co-producer). Washington, DC: The National Education Association.
Salzinger, Leslie. 1991. "A Maid by Any Other Name: The Transformation of 'Dirty Work' by Central American Immigrants." Pp. 139–160 in *Ethnography Unbound: Power and Resistance in the Modern.* Berkeley, CA: University of California Press.
Savada, Andrea Maltes. (Editor). 1993. *Nepal and Bhutan: Country Studies.* Washington, DC: Library of Congress. U.S. Government Printing Office.
Schultz, T.P. 1989. *Returns to Women's Education.* Washington, DC: The World Bank.

Sharma, Madhav P. 1989. "Rural Education: A Case Study of Two Districts in Nepal." Paper presented at the Community Development Society Meetings. St. Louis, MO. July 23–27, 1989.
Shrestha, G.M. 1990. "Improving the Quality of Teaching and Learning in Primary Schools." Pp. 33–41 in *Nepal: Improving the Efficiency of Primary Education*, edited by Learning Systems International. Tallahassee, FL: Florida State University.
Shrestha, Gajendra Man, Sri Ram Lamichhane, Bijaya Kumar Thapa, Roshan Chitrakar, Michael Useem, and John P. Comings. 1986. "Determinants of Educational Participation in Rural Nepal." *Comparative Education Review.* 30(4):508–522.
Shtrii Shakti. 1995. *Women, Development, and Demography: A Study of the Socio-Economic Changes in the Status of Women in Nepal (1981–1993).* Kathmandu: Shtrii Shakti.
Sibbons, Mo. 1998. "Approaches to Gender-Awareness Raising: Experiences in a Government Education Project in Nepal." *Gender and Development.* 6(2):35–43.
———. 1999. "From WID to GAD: Experiences of Education in Nepal." Pp. 189–202 in *Gender, Education, and Development: Beyond Access to Empowerment*, edited by Christine Heward and Sheila Bunwaree. London: Zed Books Ltd.
Sidky, H., James Hamill, Janardan Subedi, Ronald H. Spielbauer, Robin Singh, John Blangero, and Sarah Williams-Blangero. 2000. "Social Organization, Economy and Kinship among the Jirels of Eastern Nepal." *Contributions to Nepalese Studies: The Jirel Issue* (January 2000): 5–22.
Singh, Shavitri. 1995. *Statistical Profile on Women of Nepal.* Kathmandu: Shtrii Shakti.
Singleton, Royce A., Jr., Bruce C. Straits, and Margaret Miller Straits. 1993. *Approaches to Social Research.* (Second Edition). New York, NY: Oxford University Press.
Silva, Renan. 1979. "Imagen de la mujer en los textos escolares." *Revista Columbiana de Educacion.* 4(II):9–52.
Skinner, Debra and Dorothy Holland. 1996. "Schools and the Cultural Production of the Educated Person in a Nepalese Hill Community." Pp. 273–299 in *The Cultural Production of the Educated Person: Critical Ethnographies of Schooling and Local Practice*, edited by Bradley A. Levinson, Douglas E. Foley, and Dorothy C. Holland. Albany, NY: State University of New York Press.
Smith, Dorothy. 1979. "A Sociology for Women." Pp. 135–87 in *The Prism of Sex: Essays in the Sociology of Knowledge*, edited by Julia A. Sherman and Evelyn Torton Beck. Madison, WI: University of Wisconsin.
———. 1987. *The Everyday World as Problematic: A Feminist Sociology.* Boston, MA: Northeastern University.
Smith, Dorothy E. 2000. "Schooling for Inequality." *Signs: Journal of Women in Culture and Society.* 25(4):1147–1151.
Spivak, Gayatri Chakravorty. 1988. "Can the Subaltern Speak?" Pp., 271–313 in *Marxism and the Interpretation of Culture*, edited by C. Nelson and L. Grossberg. Basingstoke: MacMillian Education.

Staudt, Kathleen. 1998. *Policy, Politics, and Gender: Women Gaining Ground.* West Hartford, CT: Kumarian Press.

Stromquist, Nelly. 1989a. "Determinants of Educational Participation and Achievement of Women in the Third World: A Review of the Evidence and a Theoretical Critique." *Review of Educational Research.* 5(2):143–183.

———. 1989b. "Recent Developments in Women's Education: Closer to a Better Social Order?" Pp. 103–130 in *The Women and International Development Annual: Volume 1,* edited by Rita S. Gallin, Marilyn Aronoff, and Anne Ferguson. Boulder, CO: Westview Press.

Stromquist, Nelly P. 1990. "Women and Education Women and Illiteracy: The Interplay of Gender Subordination and Poverty." *Comparative Education Review.* 34 (February 1990—Special Issue: Adult Literacy): 95–111.

Stromquist, Nelly. 1992. *Women and Education in Latin America: Knowledge, Power, and Change.* Boulder, CO: Lynne Rienner Publishers.

———. 1995. "Romancing the State: Gender and Power in Education." *Comparative Education Review.* 39(4):423–454.

Subbarao, K. and Laura Raney. 1993. *Social Gains from Female Education: A Cross-National Study.* Washington, D.C.: World Bank.

Subedi, Janardan, Sree Subedi, H. Sidky, Robin Singh, John Blangero, and Sarah Williams-Blangero. 2000a. "Health and Health Care in Jiri." *Contributions to Nepalese Studies: The Jirel Issue* (January 2000): 97–104.

Subedi, Janardan, H. Sidky, James Hamill, Ronald H. Spielbauer, Robin Singh, John Blangero, and Sarah Williams-Blangero. 2000b. "Jirels, Jiri, and Politics: An Overview." *Contributions to Nepalese Studies: The Jirel Issue* (January 2000): 117–126.

Subedi, Pravita. 1993. *Nepali Women Rising.* Kathmandu: Sahayogi Press.

Sutton, Margaret. 1998. "Feminist Epistemology and Research Methods." Pp. 13–23 in *Women in the Third World: An Encyclopedia of Contemporary Issues,* edited by Nelly P. Stromquist. New York, NY: Garland Publishing, Inc.

Tandon, R. 1988. "Social Transformation and Participatory Research." *Convergence.* 21(2–3): 5–18.

Tembo, L.P. 1984. *Men and Women in School Textbooks.* Paris, France: UNESCO.

Thorne, Barrie. 1993. *Gender Play: Girls and Boys in School.* New Brunswick, NJ: Rutgers University Press.

Tietjen, K. 1991. *Educating Girls: Strategies to Increase Access, Persistence, and Achievement.* Washington, DC: ABEL Project, USAID.

Tuladhar, Sumon K. and Bijaya K. Thapa. 1998. "Mainstreaming Gender Perspective into the Education System of Nepal." Pp. 57–81 in *Education and Development 1998.* Kathmandu, Nepal: CERID.

UNDP (United Nations Development Program). 1999. *Nepal Human Development Report, 1998.* Kathmandu, Nepal: UNDP.

———. 2001. *Human Development Report 2001.* New York, New York: UNDP.

———. 2005. *Human Development Report 2005.* New York, New York: UNDP.

UNESCO (United Nations Educational, Scientific and Cultural Organization). 1987. *Coping with Drop-out Rate.* Bangkok, Thailand: Regional Office for Education in Asia & Pacific. UNESCO.

———. 1990. *Women's Participation in Higher Education: China, Nepal, and the Philippines*. Bangkok: Principal Regional Office for Asia and the Pacific, UNESCO.

———. 1991. *Asia Pacific Program for All National Studies: Nepal*. Bangkok, Thailand: UNESCO.

———. 1992. *Promotion of Primary Education for Girls and Disadvantaged Groups*. Bangkok: Principal Regional Office for Asia and the Pacific, UNESCO.

UNICEF. (United Nations Children's Fund). 1992. *Educating Girls and Women: A Moral Imperative*. New York, NY: United Nations Children's Fund.

———. 2001. *The State of the World's Children 2001*. New York: UNICEF.

UN World Food Programme. 2001. "Country Brief—Nepal." http://wfp.org/country_brief/asia/nepal. Downloaded on November 20, 2001.

United Nations. 1996. *Women of Nepal: A Country Profile*. New York: United Nations.

Upadhyay, I.P. 1990. "Efficiency Issues in the Primary Education System in Nepal." Pp. 7–24 in *Nepal: Improving the Efficiency of Primary Education*, edited by Learning Systems International. Tallahassee, FL: Florida State University.

West, Candace and Don H. Zimmerman. 1987. "Doing Gender." *Gender and Society*. 1(2):125–151.

Williams, Christine L. 1991. "Case Studies and the Sociology of Gender." Pp. 224–243 in *A Case for the Case Study*, edited by Joe R. Feagin, Anthony M. Orum, and Gideon Sjoberg. Chapel Hill, NC: The University of Carolina Press.

Wolf, Diane L. 1996. *Feminist Dilemmas in Fieldwork*. Boulder, CO: Westview Press.

Wolfe, B. and J. Behrman. 1984. "Who is Schooled in Developing Countries? The Role of Income, Parental Schooling, Sex, Residence, and Family Size." *Economics of Education Review*. 3(3):231–245.

World Bank. 2000. "For Schools: Exploring Countries and Regions, South Asia, Nepal." http://www.worldbank.org/html/schools/regions/sasia/nepal.htm. Downloaded on August 5, 2001.

———. 2006. "Nepal: Data and Statistics." http://www.worldbank.org.np. Downloaded on April 28, 2006.

Index

A
Aaphno Manchhe, 179
ABEL, 7, 9–10, 86
Academic performance/potential, 66, 99
Acharya, Meena, 3
Acker, Joan, 4–5
Action research, 157
Activism
 bridging scholarship with, 144–145
 scholar, 166
Activists and scholars, 139, 144, 167
Alexander, M. Jacqui and Chandra Talpade Mohanty, 6, 138–139, 144
Anderson, Jeanine, 17
Apffel-Marglin, Frederique and Suzanne L. Simon, 170
Araha, Seged, 162
Armies
 Gurkha regiments of British and Indian, 38
 Royal Nepal, 38
Ashby, Jacqueline, 2, 7, 9, 86
Assumptions
 brought to the field, 56–57
 theoretical, 51–53
Australia, 16

B
Babbie, Earl, 67
Bahini ("little sister"), 158, 159, 179
Beenstock, J. and P. Sturdy, 11, 169
Behrman, J. and C. Sussangkarn, 169
Bennett, Lynn, 3
Benoliel, Sharon, 14
Bernbaum, Marcia, 171
Best, Ralphaela 16

Bhattachan, K.B., 40
Bhauju ("sister-in-law"), 158, 179
Birdsall, N., 169
Biskokarma, 66
Bista, D.B., 24–25, 31, 38
Boys
 roles, 8
 socially assigned roles, 19
Brahmin (priest caste), 31–32, 35, 38, 66
Brazil, 17
Brock, C. and N.K. Cammish, 11
Buddhism and Buddhists, 9, 34, 65, 169, 175
Burawoy, Michael, 74
Burchfield, Shirley, 14
Butler, Judith, 5, 18, 141

C
Careers
 aspirations, 121–122
 men's, 121
Case study method, 51–52
Castes
 Biskokarma, 66
 Brahmin, 31, 66
 Chhetri, 31, 65–66
 Ethnicity and (jat), 31
 Hindu, 62–65
 Jirel, 66
 Sherpa, 66
 Tamang, 31, 34, 65–66
 women from the Dalit caste, 35
CERID (Nepal Research Center for Educational Innovation and Development), 13, 57
Charmaz, Kathy, 73–74

193

Chernikovsky, D., 169
Chhetri (warrior caste), 31–32, 35, 38, 65–66
Chowdhry, Geeta, 170
Christianity, 34
Clans and sub-clans, 31
Classrooms
    condition of and materials in, 48, 110
    direct observation in, 68–71, 107
    punishment in, 114
    social constructs of gender reinforced in the, 103–117
Clinton, First Lady Hillary Rodham, 11
Cochrane, S., D. O'Hara and J. Leslie, J., 11, 169
Coding
    responses, 69, 175, 178,
    two phases of, 74
Collins, Patricia Hill, 52, 142, 170
Columbia, 17
Communist rule, 28
Community
    entry into the, 57
    interviews with leaders of the, 61
    interviews with members of the, 75
Conclusions, 141
Connell, R.W., 4
Consent procedures (for research), 59–60
Critical consciousness, 145
Critical thinking skills, 141
Csapo, M., 169

D

Dalit (ethnic/caste group), 31, 35
Data
    collection methods, 60, 66–68
    interpreting, 74
    organizing, 73
    study participants, 152–154
    validity and reliability, 67
Daughters
    access to school, 15
    education, 105
    enrollment in school, 14
    gendered education, 17
    projects for, 15
    roles, 8
    socially assigned roles, 19
    subjects studied, 105
Davison, Jean and Martin Kanyuka, 2, 5, 56–57, 69, 94, 107, 152, 159, 166, 169, 174–175

Deere, Diana, 55
Development programs, 17
Dickerson, Bette; Philipia Hillman and Johanna Foster, 144
Dilli Dahal, 31
Dipendra, Crown Prince, 173
Domestic work/responsibilities, 124, 128, 131, 170

E

Economic
    constraints, 92
Education
    access, 44–46
    advanced (master's degree), 122, 179
    benefits for girls and women, 3–4, 11–12, 125
    development efforts, 17
    expenditures by sub-sector, 37
    expenses, 115, 177
    financing, 36
    funding, 1–2
    gendered, 15–17, 99–102
    gender perspective, 2
    initiatives for girls/women, 1, 2, 10, 12–15
    levels of women/men, 76, 136
    national curriculum, 48
    Nepalese system of, 41–42
    obstacles/barriers to, 1, 7, 10, 11, 143
    participation rates, 125
    pre-primary, 37
    public expenditures on, 37
    quality of, 37, 48
    teacher, 37, 177
    teacher attendance and training rates, 48–49
    textbooks, 48, 124, 135
    trends in public expenditure on, 37–39
Educational
    access, participation, and enrollment in Jiri, 43, 44–46
    equality, 6
    inequality, 2
    overview of system policies and structures, 41–43
    programs, 13
    quality, 48–49
    status of community members and parents/guardians, 75–79
El-Sanabary, Nagat, 14, 171
Emerson, Robert M., 73

Index

Empowerment, 8, 12, 15, 16, 125, 138, 141, 167
Epilogue
  reflections on the process, 147
Equal Access to Education project, 11
Ethnic Groups (major), 31
Ethnicity, 9
  Caste and, 31–32
Everyday knowledge, 52, 53, 56, 143, 144

F

Family
  as a gendered institution, 7, 87, 97, 143
Feagin, Joe R., Anthony M. Orum and Gideon Sjoberg, 52, 67–68
Feldman, Shelley, 169
Female Education Scholarship Program, 14
feminine/femininity, 4
feminism
  gender construction feminist, 6, 141
  See also Methodology, feminist,
  multicultural feminist ideology, 57
  praxis and, 167
  postcolonial feminism, 52, 157
  standpoint feminism, 53
Feminist(s)
  gendered construction, 141
  ideology, 148, 179
  research and impact of identities on, 148–150
  research methodologies, 52–53
  Western, 6
Field
  dangers in the, 162–165
  emotions in the, 159–161
  entering the, 148
  leaving the, 165–166
  living and working with research assistants in the, 154–159
  negotiating politics in the, 161–162
  politics in the, 161
  reflecting on interactions in the, 151–152
  relationships in the, 58
  work, 141, 151, 173
Fieldnotes, 1, 147, 160
Fish, Jennifer N., 53, 179
Floro, M. and J.M. Wolf, 11, 169
Focus groups, 60
Foreign aid, 36
Fournier, A., 32
Freire, Paulo, 145
Fretz, Rachel I., 73

Furer Haimendorf, Christoph von, 32

G

Gaauns ("villages"), 30
Garfinkel, Harold, 56
Gellner, David, 31
Gender
  access, 43–46, 89
  as in "do gender" or "doing gender," 4, 18, 19, 118, 121, 123–124, 137
  as dynamic, 5
  as an institutionalization of power, 11, 14
  as a process/gender processes, 2, 3, 4, 7, 11, 18, 19, 141, 142
  as a social construction, 2, 4, 19, 141, 142
  awareness, 49, 133, 142
  bias, 17, 178
  behavior, 49
  boundaries, 177
  community and, 10
  constraints, 3, 18–19, 75–99, 125, 129, 131, 138
  constructs/construction/constructionism, 4–5, 122, 125, 127, 167
  construction processes, 12, 79, 98
  differences, 100
  economic constraints and, 92–94
  education and empowerment, 141–142
  effects of social constructions on students, 85–92, 99–102
  equity, 116, 142
  evidence of a changing gendered social order, 131–135
  family and, 75
  home and, 7–11
  inequality, 2, 3, 7, 17, 18, 80, 125, 141, 159
  neutrality, 5
  obligations, 91, 138
  processes, 12, 107
  reinforcing in schools, 99
  resisting constraints of, 127
  role construction, 80
  schools and, 99
  sensitivity awareness, 49
  social constructions of, 3, 4–7, 9, 75, 102, 108–109, 117–121, 129, 135, 139, 143, 145, 169–170, 174

social constructs reinforced in the classroom, 103–117
stereotypes, 12, 17, 101, 124, 178
trouble makers (individuals resisting gender constraints), 58, 127, 167, 179
Gendered
  differences, 69
  education 15, 97, 99–102, 124, 128
  existing social structures in Nepal, 15
  institutions, 7, 15, 87, 97, 125, 143
  interaction, 120
  Nepali society, 128–129
  perceptions, 103
  positioning of men and women, 141
  social order, 8, 12, 16, 56, 134
  social structures, 123, 137
  student responses, 71
  teacher/student interactions, 124
Gendering processes, 7, 11, 17, 19, 30, 71, 75, 78, 80, 95, 97, 124, 170
Girls
  access to school, 15, 43–46, 143
  enrollment in school, 14
  gendered education, 17
  projects for, 15
  roles, 8
  socially assigned/perceived roles, 19, 121
Girls'/women's education, 3–4, 10
GNP (Gross National Product), 35–36
Glaser, Barney G. and Anslem L. Strauss, 73
Government
  Democratically elected, 39
  Schools in Jiri VDC, 28, 63
Gyanendra, King, 173

H
Hammill, J.H., 25, 32–33, 38–39
Harber, Clive, 17
Harding, Sandra, 170
Herencia, Christine, 17
Herz, Barbara K., 11
Heward, Christine, 11
Hill, M. Anne, 11, 169
Hindu
  caste, 8–9, 31, 35, 62–65, 142
  kingdom, 34, 170
  religion, 31, 63, 175
Home visits, 63
hooks, bell, 145
Household division of labor, 9
Human Development Index (HDI), 172

Hurst, Leslie Nadine Gartrell, 2

I
IIDS (Institute for Integrated Development Studies) in Kathmandu, 15
Ilon, Lynn and Peter Moock, 169
INGOs (International Non-Government Organizations), 1–2, 155–156, 164
Indo-Aryan descent, 31
Intelligence, 7
Interviews/interviewees
  See also, Methodology, interviews
  community leaders, 61, 71
  community members, 66, 71
  home visits, 63, 66
  life histories/ life narratives, 3, 66, 72, 175
  observations, 132
  parents/guardians, 71, 120
  questions, 71
  selection of, 63
  students, 71
  study participants, 152–153
  sub-groups, 63
  teachers, 71
  trade-offs, 60
  women, 72
Islam, 34

J
Jamison, Dean T. and Marlaine E. Lockheed, 7, 169
Jat ("caste and ethnicity"), 31
Jiri
  agriculture in, 38
  economics of education, 39
  economy, 38
  educational development in, 26–28
  first school in, 27
  future directions for, 142
  government schools, 28–29, 45, 49, 63
  health care, 25
  hospital, 25
  human development status in, 24–26
  Lamosangu-Jiri Road in, 24, 38–39
  private schools in, 40, 45
  research site, 21
  tourist trade, 39
  typical home, 93
  VDC (Village Development Committee), 3, 8, 12, 19, 21–23, 28, 30,

Index

38–40, 123, 129, 141–142, 154, 163, 170, 172, 175
VDC community leaders, 71
VDC government schools, 28–29, 45, 49, 172
Jirel (ethnic group), 34, 66, 133
Jorgensen, Danny L., 70
Joshi, Govinda Prasad Jean Anderson, 17

K
Kaam ("job/work"), 175
Kami ethnic group, 31
Kane, Eileen, 174
Kanyadan ("gift of a virgin daughter"), 8, 170
Karan, P. and H. Ishii, 31, 34–35
Kasaju, Prem and T.B. Manandhar, 169
Kelly, G. C. Elliott, 11
Kenya, 17
Khaniya, T.R. and M.A. Kiernan, 24, 43–44
Kimmel, Michael, 4
King, Elizabeth M., 11
King Gyanendra, 40
King Prithvi Narayana Shah, 32
Kleinman Sherryl Martha A. Copp, 57, 73
Kumar, Nita, 154
Kurz, Kathleen M. Cynthia J. Prather, 11, 171
Kurzman, Charles, 166

L
Language
  in Nepal , 33
  of instruction, 34
LeVine, Robert A., Sarah E. LeVine and Beatrice Schnell, 29
Lamosangu-Jiri Road, 24, 38–39, 45
Literacy
  adult, 76, 172, 175
  programs, 14
  women's rates, 23, 171
Living accommodations in village, 151
Local analyses, 6
Local School Scholarships program, 11
Lofland, John and Lyn H. Lofland, 73, 151
Lohani, Raj, 36–37, 39
Lorber, Judith, 4–5, 7–8, 18, 127, 141
Luttrell, Wendy, 65

M
Magar ethnic group, 31
Maguire, Patricia, 60
Manneschmidt, Sybille, 151
Maoist party, 40, 163, 172–174, 179
Masculine/masculinity, 4
Materials
  content analysis of, 68
Mathema, Madhuri, 8–9, 88, 96, 170
Matrix of domination, 142
Mehorta, S. & R. Jolly, 11
Merriam, Sharan, 52
Methodology
  See also Feminism
  See also Research
  access, 43–46, 57, 148–151
  action research, 167
  and identity, 148–151
  case study research, 3, 51–52
  classroom observations, 3, 62, 68–71, 107–117
  data analysis, 60–68, 73–74, 152–154
  feminist, 5–6, 52–53, 148–150
  field observations, 68–71, 103–117
  fieldnotes, 147
  fieldwork relationships, 58
  focus groups, 60
  gender construction feminist, 6
  interviews, 3, 60–72, 152–153
  life histories/life narratives, 3, 66, 72, 175
  language, 33–34
  leaving the field, 165–166
  participatory learning action (PLA) strategies, 60, 153
  postcolonial feminism, 52, 57
  power differentials, 56, 162–165
  research design, 51
  research questions, 53–55
  selecting study participants, 152–153
  social desirability, 174, 177
  social mapping, 61
  standpoint feminism, 53
Mies, Maria, 4, 152
Miles, Matthew B. and Michael A. Huberman, 160
Mohanty, Chandra Talpade, 5–6, 156, 170
Morgen, S. and A. Bookman, 144–45
Mortality rate, 172
Mukhopadhyay, Sudhin, 169
Multi-party system, 39
Muluki Ain (National Code), 35

N
Naples, Nancy, 5

Narayan, Uma, 153
National curriculum, 48
Nepal
    CERID (Research Center for Educational Innovation and Development), 13, 57
    democracy in, 28
    Dolakha district, 22, 27, 32, 34, 45, 173
    economy, 35
    education system, 169
    ethnic groups in, 31
    GNP (Gross National Product), 35–36
    gendered processes in, 131, 171
    government, 169
    Hill (or Central) region, 23–24, 44, 173
    Himalayas (Mountain or Northern region), 23
    His Majesty's Government of, 24
    human development status in, 23–24
    Janakpur zone, 23
    languages in, 33
    map of, 22
    national curriculum, 48
    Panchayat period in, 27, 39, 41, 172
    political parties in, 40
    population by mother tongue in, 33
    population in, 29
    Terai, 21
    Tribhuvan University, 57
Nepalese
    Chelbeti Program, 13
    educational system, 41
    government, 133, 170, 179
    Ministry of Education and Culture, 11, 36
    BPEP (Basic Primary Education Program), 13
    School Award Program, 13
Nepali
    census, 30
    classrooms, 174
    gendered order, 129
    language, 34, 43, 152, 173
    Women's Development Center, 14
Newar ethnic group, 31, 38, 133
NGOs (non-governmental organizations), 19, 164, 170

O

Oboler, Regina, 154
O'Brien, Mary, 4
Observations
    classroom, 3, 62, 68–71, 107–117
    daily lives of students, 71
    interviews and, 132
    social constructs of gender reinforced in the classroom, 103–117
Obstacles
    to education, 1, 11
O'Gara, Chloe, 10–11, 170
Ong, Aihwa, 170
Opportunity/indirect costs of education, 9–10, 134, 171, 176
Orenstein, Peggy, 16

P

PACT (Private Agencies Collaborating Together, Inc.), 11
Panchayat
    period in Nepal, 27, 172
    system, 39, 41
Panday, Devendra Raj, 23, 36
Parental attitudes toward gender differences, 7
Participation in schools, 2
Peru, 17
Pinto, Regina, 17
Pitt, M. and M. Rosenzweig, 11, 169
PLA (participatory learning action) strategies, 60, 153
    See also Methodology
Politics
    political context, 39
    negotiating in the field, 161–162
Polyandry, 172
Polygyny, 172
Population
    changes and demography, 29
    distribution by sex, 30
    ethnic group, 32
    Nepal, 33
Positionality, 57, 148, 162–165
Post, David, 169
Potuchek, Jean, 75, 97, 127
Power differentials, 154, 173
    and dangers in the field, 162–165
    in field research, 56
Prather, Cynthia, 11
Praxis, 144
Privilege, 147, 162
Punalekar, S.P., 169

R

Raksi ("alcoholic drink"), 38

Index

Rana regime, 41
Reinharz, Shulamit, 147, 152
Reinhold, Amy Jo, 8, 96
Religion and caste, 34–35
Research
   See also Methodology
   assistants (RAs), 58–59, 70, 136, 155
   assumptions, 51–53
   coding, 70, 74
   consent procedures, 59–60
   data collection methods, 60, 66, 68–73
   design, 51
   development of, 56
   field, 58
   interviews, 3, 60–72, 152–153
   living and working with assistants, 154–159
   methodologies, 55, 73
   observations, 68–71, 103–117, 132
   questions, 53–55
   record (government and school) collection, 61
   reflections on the process, 147
   relationships, 58
   response coding, 70
   results, 75–98
   sampling and sampling goals, 65–67
   social mapping, 61
   study participants, 152–153
   techniques (class observation, home visits, interviews), 63
Researchers/role as researchers, 58, 143
Risman, Barbara, 4–5
Roles
   socially assigned, 19, 120–121
   stereotypical, 48
Roth, Eric A., 169

S

Sadker, Myra and David, 16, 69, 124, 174, 178
Salzinger, Leslie, 153
Sampling, 65–67
SATA (Swiss Association for Technical Assistance) multipurpose development project 1957, 24–25, 38
Savada, Andrea Maltes, 21, 23
Scholar activism, 139, 144, 166
School(s)
   collection of records in, 61–62
   drop-out rates, 46–47, 134, 176
   enrollment, 44–45, 73
   gendered institution, 15
   government (VDC), 28–29, 45, 49
   Leaving Certificate (SLC), 24, 62, 172, 175, 177
   number of by region, district and VDC, 27
   nursery (pre-kindergarten), 62
   participation and persistence in, 47
   primary, 62
   private, 40, 46
   promotion rates, 47
   repeat rates, 46–47
   selection of, 62
   social institution, 17
   source of social change, 16, 138
   staff, 62
Schultz, T. P., 11, 169
Shah kings, 41
Sherpa (ethnic group), 31–32, 34, 38, 66
Shrestha, G. M., 9, 48, 86, 175
Shtrii Shakti, 3, 35
Shudra (untouchable), 35
Sibbons, Mo, 35, 45–46, 88, 96, 173
Sidky, H., et al, 31
Silva, Renan, 17
Singh, Shavitri, 3
Singleton, Royce A., Bruce C. Straits and Margaret Miller, 174
Skinner, Debra and Dorothy Holland, 39, 41, 169
Smith, Dorothy, 16, 52, 71, 170
Social change
   catalysts for, 135–137
Social constructions of gender, 3, 4–7, 9, 75, 102, 108–109, 117–121, 129, 135, 139, 143, 145
Social institutions, 4–5
Social mapping, 61, 173
Sons
   roles, 8
   socially assigned roles, 19
Spivak, Gayatri Chakravovty, 170
Stakeholders, 144-5
Staudt, Kathleen, 2, 16–17, 138
Stereotypes, 48, 81, 124, 178
   See also Gender, Stereotypes
Stromquist, Nelly, 7, 10, 16–17, 97, 124, 138, 143
Students
   See also Gender, as in "Do or Doing Gender," 118–123
   gender trouble makers, 127

Subbarao, K. and Laura Raney, 11
Subedi, Janardan, 3, 9, 30
Sunwars, 31–32, 38
Sutton, Margaret, 165

T
Tamang (ethnic group), 31, 34, 63, 66
Tandon, R., 145
Teachers
    attendance, 48–49
    attention from, 117
    interviews with, 63, 103–106
    observation of, 177
    proportion of women to men, 29
    vacant staff positions, 25
    training, 48–49
    women, 177
Tembo, L.P., 17
Textbooks, 48, 70, 117–118, 124, 135
Tharu ethnic group, 31
"Third World," 1, 5, 6, 145, 148, 169, 173
"Third World" women, 5–6
Thorne, Barrie, 16
Tibet, 32
    descent, 31
    ethnic groups, 9
Tibeto-Burmese
Tietjen, K., 169
Tourist trade, 39
Triangulated research method, 51, 53, 85
Tribhuvan University in Nepal, 57
Tuladhar, Suman K. and Bijaya K. Thapa, 13, 43

U
UN Conference on Poverty, 11
UN Conference on Women, 170
UNDP (United Nationals Development Program), 23, 43, 47
UNESCO (United Nations Educational, Scientific and Cultural Organization), 10–11, 41, 172
UNICEF (United Nations Children's Health Fund), 10–11, 23–24, 30
United Nations World Food Programme 2001, 23
United States, 16
USAID (United States Agency for International Development), 1, 7, 12, 14, 36

W
Water, 94
West, Candace and Don H. Zimmerman, 18, 99
Williams, Christine, 51, 67
Wolfe B. and J. Behrman, 11, 175
Wolf, Diane, 55–56, 148–150, 152, 154, 157, 162
Women
    roles of, 9, 17
    percentage of labor force, 9
World Bank, 1, 17, 29, 35–36, 43
World Education Nepal Organization, 14

Z
Zambia, 17